JOHNNY CIGARINI:

CONFESSIONS OF A
KING'S ROAD
COWBOY

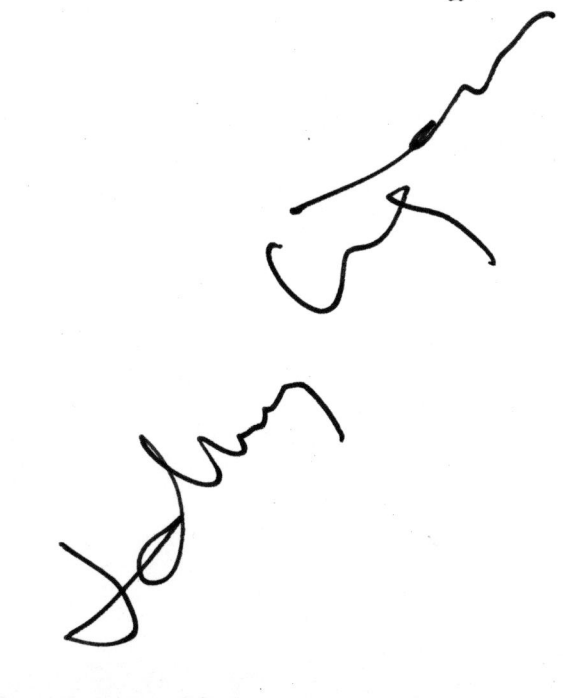

JOHNNY CIGARINI:

CONFESSIONS OF A KING'S ROAD COWBOY

MEMOIRS OF A TERRIBLE NAME-DROPPER

JOHN CIGARINI AND LUKE SHIPMAN

Copyright © 2014 John Cigarini

The moral right of the author has been asserted.

Apart from any fair dealing for the purposes of research or private study, or criticism or review, as permitted under the Copyright, Designs and Patents Act 1988, this publication may only be reproduced, stored or transmitted, in any form or by any means, with the prior permission in writing of the publishers, or in the case of reprographic reproduction in accordance with the terms of licences issued by the Copyright Licensing Agency. Enquiries concerning reproduction outside those terms should be sent to the publishers.

Matador
9 Priory Business Park
Kibworth Beauchamp
Leicestershire LE8 0RX, UK
Tel: (+44) 116 279 2299
Fax: (+44) 116 279 2277
Email: books@troubador.co.uk
Web: www.troubador.co.uk/matador

ISBN 978 1783063 352

British Library Cataloguing in Publication Data.
A catalogue record for this book is available from the British Library.

Typeset in Aldine401 BT Roman by Troubador Publishing Ltd
Printed and bound in the UK by TJ International, Padstow, Cornwall

Matador is an imprint of Troubador Publishing Ltd

MIX
Paper from
responsible sources
FSC
www.fsc.org
FSC® C013056

For me, my friends and you.

*The King's Road in Chelsea
was the epicentre of the swinging sixties
and the seventies London scene...*

This autobiography features the incredibly large number of one hundred and ten people who are no longer with us:

Ruby Cigarini	Cyril Stein
Armando Cigarini	Carl Perkins
Luisa Cigarini	John Belushi
Mabel Davies	James Hunt
Jack Davies	Lewis Morley
Revd Kenneth Senior	David Jacobs
Dr Nora Senior	Steve Marriott
Lord Beaumont	Tony Howard
Bob Brooks	John Bindon
Jim Baker	George Harrison
Len Fulford	Princess Margaret
Allan van Rijn	Keith Moon
Larry Williams	Maureen Tigrett
Ann Pugsley	Peter Cook
Ronnie Holbrook	Jeanne Crain
Robert Mitchum	Christopher Reeve
Vittorio De Sica	Michael Hutchence
Jean Harlow	Paula Yates
Sir Bobby Robson	Dennis Wilson
Tony Curtis	Stevie Ray Vaughan
Herbert Lom	Terence Donovan
Richard Warwick	Marc Bolan
Ayrton Senna	Malcolm McLaren
Elvis Presley	Johnny Chapulis
Marlon Brando	Joseph Cotten
Ossie Clark	Angie Dickinson
Keith Lichtenstein	Bill Graham
Steve O'Rourke	Lesley Sunderland
Alphi O'Leary	Tony Scott

JOHNNY CIGARINI: CONFESSIONS OF A KING'S ROAD COWBOY

Andy Warhol	Tommy Roberts
Buddy Holly	Freddie Hornik
Yogi Bhajan	Victor Mature
Junior Walker	Toni Litri
Jeremy Keegan	Paula Boyd
Gerlinde Kostiff	Peter Grant
Zelda Barron	Michael Kamen
Luciana Martinez	Clement Freud
Michael Powell	Fred Dibnah
Richard Harris	Jack Dellal
Storm Thorgerson	James Brown
Freddy Heineken	Duck Dunn
Sir David Frost	Colonel Tom Parker
Sir John Moores	Krissie Wood
Kirby Brown	John Lee Hooker
Richard Bembenek	Dodi Fayed
John Wayne	Princess Diana
Peter Sellers	Lee Van Cleef
Muriel Belcher	Conor Clapton
Ian Board	Doug Green
Francis Bacon	Baron George-Brown
Frank Zappa	Alvaro Maccioni
Terry Kath	Rodney King
Jimi Hendrix	Allan McKeown
Victor Borge	John Slater
Maria Schneider	Miss Cynderella

Enjoy every day! And stay away from Johnny Cigarini.

Contents

Introduction   xi

Part 1:   1

1.	The War	3
2.	Margate	9
3.	Dean Close	19
4.	Africa	23
5.	Durham University	35
6.	Cinecittà	40

Part 2:   45

7.	Freedom	47
8.	Brooks Baker Fulford	52
9.	King's Road: Part 1	58
10.	Outrageous Sexual Behaviour	63
11.	Patti D'Arbanville	71
12.	Superman	77
13.	Models, Models, Models…	81
14.	Hollywood	84
15.	King's Road: Part 2	88
16.	Eric Clapton and the Chelsea Cruise	93
17.	Bindon	100
18.	BFCS	107
19.	Donatella	111
20.	Stocks House	114

21.	The Hard Rock Story		120
22.	The American Dream		124
23.	Cocaine		131
24.	The East		135
25.	Commercials		142
26.	Breathalysed		145
27.	Saatchi		147
28.	Pink Floyd		153
29.	Italia '90		158
30.	The New Heart Valve and the Farmhouse		164
31.	Apocalypse LA		169
32.	House of Blues		179
33.	Closing BFCS Inc.		184
34.	Travelling		191
35.	Terrible Name-Dropping		206
36.	Curing Tourette's		211

Part 3:   213

37.	Italy, the Return		215
38.	Baja, Master of Two Worlds		222
39.	What's in a Name?		232

Epilogue   *234*
Appendix   *236*

Introduction

It should really be called 'Autobiography of a Nobody'. But who is nobody? Who is somebody?

"This above all; to thine own self be true."
– William Shakespeare

PART 1

CHAPTER 1

The War

He had a beautiful young English wife, three gorgeous daughters and a studio on the Harrington Road. Life must have been sweet for my father in London in the 1930s. It was surely the dream life for any photographer.

That dream came to an end when Italy declared war on Great Britain. It was 1940.

★

Armando Cigarini was born in 1896 to an Italian family in French Tunisia. It had been recently established during the French colonial empire, which was still the second-largest colonial power on the map. When he became an adult, Armando made his way to Paris where he was an apprentice to Marcel, the well-known French photographer, and he saw the First World War – fortunately only as a war photojournalist for a French newspaper, as his heart condition prevented him from being drafted in as any kind of soldier. He was present during the famous retreat from Caporetto in 1917, taking photographs on the Austro-Italian front – as documented by Hemingway in *A Farewell to Arms*. Near the town of Kobarid, Austro-Hungarian forces, reinforced by German units, broke the Italian frontline and overwhelmed the Italian army. It was the war of poison gas, the terrifying stormtroopers, the trenches. Those who read the Hemingway masterpiece would often summarise it with a word: bleak. The backdrop of the First World War, cynical soldiers and the displacement of populations would have been nothing but bleak. It is what my father would have surely seen, like the lines of men, marching in the rain. *A Farewell to Arms* is quite a story of love and pain, of loyalty and abandonment – ironically the exact themes that would encapsulate his own life. But not yet. First he would need to meet her, my beautiful mother.

After the Great War, Armando moved to Berlin where he opened a photographic studio. They must have been fun days during the Golden Twenties in Berlin; a sophisticated culture of architecture, cabaret, literature, painting, film and fashion. Considered decadent by rightists, it was surely fabulous for my father, but he didn't stay long and moved swiftly to London to become a court photographer for the Royal Court, a title of great distinction in those days. He photographed young Princess Elizabeth, now Queen Elizabeth II, and I have a photograph of Sir Arthur Conan Doyle, inscribed 'Portrait by Cigarini'. He was also a society photographer for *Tatler* and *Bystander* out of Fleet Street and for *The Sketch*, the newspaper weekly that cornered high society and the aristocracy. Armando's photographs were hand-coloured, which I believe he did himself and I find that to be quite fabulous. On the internet, I found one he had taken of film actress Eve Gray, and another of Miss Peggy O'Neil, now in the National Portrait Gallery archives.

By the early '30s, Armando had met and married my mother, Ruby Davies, who was a wonderful and beautiful young model. Likely they met on a photo shoot in the studios of Kensington and Knightsbridge, or perhaps even in his own on Harrington Road. They had three daughters: Maria born in 1933, Luisa in '36 and Christina in '38, and they lived in Kenton, North London.

It was 10 June 1940 when Benito Mussolini stepped onto the balcony of the Palazzo Venezia and declared war on France and Britain, bellowing in his uniform to a quarter of a million in the Piazza. "Soldiers, sailors, and aviators… black shirts of the revolution and of the legions… men and women of Italy… of the Empire… and of the kingdom of Albania… pay heed. An hour appointed by destiny has struck in the heavens of our fatherland. The declaration of war has already been delivered…" and the crowd chanted two words back to their Mussolini: "war" and "war".

The reaction from the Allies was swift. In London, all Italians who had lived on British soil less than twenty years and were aged between sixteen and seventy were interned. For the Italians of London, life had changed in a heartbeat. Panic had hit the city streets and what was once a place of opportunity, wonder and excitement had turned overnight into a place where people feared for their lives.

Faced with the certainty of internment, the family packed and moved to Rome. It may have suited my father, who avoided internment, but life was not easy for my mother and the English girls in German-occupied Rome. To begin with, none of them could speak Italian. Only my father could, as he was already well travelled and fluent in Italian, French, Arabic, German and English. Like in all wars, hardship was evident everywhere. The German forces took most of the available food, with bread being rationed to just 100g per person per day. Utilities were cut off, and the family had no electricity, gas or water. Subsequently, my mother had multiple miscarriages during the war due to the hard conditions, until eventually they had their first son, Giusseppe – but he died after just forty days. They had twin daughters, Lilliana and Silvana, but they also died – after just four days. My mother was exhausted, she had no milk in her body, and there was none to buy.

The bombing of Rome took place on several occasions in the early 1940s, most notably in June 1943 when more than 500 Allied planes dropped bombs, causing thousands of civilian deaths, and even the Vatican City was under attack by both British and German forces, despite it maintaining neutrality.

Rome was hit by 60,000 tons of bombs over seventy-eight days before her capture. Yet, quite amazingly, against a backdrop of all of this, in late 1943 my mother fell pregnant… with me. She woke up on 6 June 1944 to a great sound: American tanks on the main street, near home. She left the house, heavily pregnant, and walked up to the American soldiers. Holding me in her tummy, she spoke to them in English, which would have been unusual for the American GIs to hear.

"Which way did the Germans go?" the US Fifth Army asked her as she stood in her long coat. They befriended her and gave her a supply of milk, chocolates and bread. It seemed that day was to mark a turning point in the war in Europe, with Rome being the first of the axis power capitals to fall to the Allies. American troops took control of Rome and the Germans had been ordered to withdraw. Rome was liberated and the people emptied themselves onto the streets in celebration, welcoming the Allies with cheers and applause, hurling bundles of flowers at passing army vehicles. Two days later I was born. It was 8 June 1944. What I've come to realise is that those very provisions the Americans gave my mother enabled me to live. I owe my life to those soldiers on that day. My luck had just begun and I was given the middle name Victor to denote the victory.

★

Being multi-lingual and a wheeler-dealer, my father began to supply the Allied

Forces with dried fruit, which he sourced from North Africa. He became quite rich in the process, but sadly lost most of the money buying a warehouse full of old master paintings, which turned out to be fakes. Quite the businessman, he got involved in an enterprise, which I remember well from my childhood in Rome. He invented a chocolate-banana machine. You put the chocolate and the banana in one end, and the chocolate-covered banana came out the other. The machines were big, about the size of a supermarket freezer. I remember those bananas being quite delicious, but the business didn't take off. I have since only come across chocolate-covered bananas once, in Hawaii.

Likely through his American Army connections, my father was offered the job of running Coca-Cola in Italy but, much to the exasperation of my mother, he turned the offer down. He said he had never worked for anyone else in his life, and he didn't want to start. Whether for that reason or because the war was over, my mother decided she would return to England, which she did in 1949. But before we left, we had a visitor: my maternal grandmother, Mabel, likely giving my mother guiding words from a generation that had seen war before. My mother decided to only take my eldest sister Maria and me, Little Johnny, back to England. By this time, my father was already ill with the heart disease that would eventually kill him. Luisa and Christina, then aged thirteen and eleven, were put in a convent in Rome. The family was beginning to split apart.

Although I was only five, I remember the journey to England. We went for a final pizza before the trip. I went back to the flat sixty years later and after all those years I was still able to walk straight back to our apartment building from the tram. The pizzeria was still there too! I remember my mother wearing her long black coat. I remember us stopping off in Paris. I remember seeing one of my father's brothers there. I remember his family at the station. It was a long time ago; I will be seventy next June. But I remember.

My sister Christina, who stayed behind in Rome, has since told me that my father did not know we were leaving and that he had his first heart attack when he found out. All this because of the war.

When we got to England, my mother left my sister and I with two of her sisters, while she got her life organised. She was looking for a job and somewhere to live and started calling herself Johnson, presumably so my father could not trace her. I still don't know why my mother left him – I guess I'll never know; perhaps I'm not meant to – but it must have been terribly hard for her in Rome during those times. I'm sure she must have missed England dearly.

Maria was nearly sixteen, and was left with Aunty Mabs in Broadstairs, Kent. Mabs was a hairdresser and her husband, Les, a postal worker. I was left in Coventry with Aunty Alice. Her husband Ted worked as a toolmaker at the Standard Motor Company. They had three small children of their own.

That was it, I never saw my mother again. Four months later in London, she was dead. She had started vomiting blood due to a serious liver disease and went into a coma. She died, aged thirty-nine, of haematemesis. The last time I saw my father was when he came over for my mother's funeral in 1950, when I was just five. He gave me a red twelve-inch tin-plate model car with a battery and working headlights. I still have it and it is my most treasured possession, still with the original battery. Armando went back to Rome and died of heart failure in February 1954, aged fifty-seven. My father was dead, my mother was dead, three siblings had died before their first birthday, I had two sisters back in Italy and one I had been separated from in England. I was alone, kind of. Maybe it was the early years that were to shape the rest of me. It would certainly explain a few things.

★

I remember my first few months in Coventry. I don't know whether I spoke any English when I arrived; my first language would have been Italian. Perhaps my mother and sisters had taught me some English when we were in Italy, I don't even know. In Coventry, however, I had no one who spoke Italian, and I lost it, forever. People have always told me that it's in there somewhere, but I can't find it. Even now, after living in Italy for ten years, I still speak Italian badly, like an Englishman.

After the death of my mother, it was decided I should live with my grandmother, Mabel Davies, in Margate, Kent. This reunited me with my eldest sister Maria, who lived nearby in Broadstairs. She was working in my aunt's hairdressing salon and would visit me on Sundays, and we would always make a big meal.

My granny Mabel was a great old bird. She was seventy-six when I went there and eighty-six when I left, at sixteen, just before she died. She brought me up really well, and it must have been difficult for her. She had had no sons but four daughters of her own. Her maiden name was Pearce, and she was from Cornwall. She claimed descent from "Tom Pearce, Tom Pearce, lend me your grey mare", from the folk song 'Widdecombe Fair', and they were also descended from the famous Trethowan family of Cornwall.

In Margate I also had a grandfather, but don't remember much of him. I do remember him chasing me, and him often falling from his bike, but that was it. Jack Davies was around for the first couple of years, but I probably killed him off. He was a stern ex-professional soldier in his eighties and probably didn't much like having a six-year-old running around the house. It is funny thinking back while writing my memoirs, forcing myself to remember; strange, too, the things that come to me, and the parts I have forgotten.

After my father died, my other two sisters came to Margate from Rome. Christina was now sixteen and Luisa eighteen. They were good girls but they were strangers to me, and seemed so much older – more like aunts. Although they had both been born in England, they didn't speak much English. Christina stayed with me at Granny's for a short while, and worked at a deaf-and-dumb school. Luisa studied nursing and lived in the nurses' hostel. Amazingly, she found time to become the Margate Beauty Queen. As I've said, they were more like aunts and women who helped – like my granny. Everyone seemed to be there to help me, or be there to just be there. It was as if they were worried something was going to happen to me as a result of the trauma I had faced in my life so far, but I suppose I was none the wiser. I was happy, in fact, but perhaps the trauma had affected me subconsciously because at about seven years old I began twitching my head. I had fine blonde hair, which Granny thought was the reason (to flick it out of my face), and she put a hairpin on me. I, of course, found it all very embarrassing. No one knew where the twitch came from, what it was or how to get rid of it. Over time, the head twitching turned into eye blinking, and even small sounds came from deep in my throat. "What's happening to him?" I recall them all asking one another, panicked in a frenzy of Italian irrationality. They were only trying to help, I suppose. I would only do one thing at a time, but I had a compulsive need to do something in a repetitive manner. Over time, it settled into the head twitching as being the dominant tic. I tried various cures, including hypnotherapy, but nothing had any effect. For nearly fifty years, it was the bane of my life.

Although I wasn't to know it, the decision for me to move to Margate with Granny would ultimately help shape my entire future. By living in Margate, I would meet someone who would change my life, forever. Oh, he would play with my penis too.

CHAPTER 2

Margate

Margate in the 1950s was the type of town that doesn't really exist in England anymore. There are still popular resorts like Brighton, Blackpool and Skegness, but they have changed. In the 1950s, all the industrial workers went to these towns for their annual two-week summer holiday, often in the rain, as foreign travel was almost unheard of for the working classes back then. Nowadays, with cheap air travel, Brits can take their holidays in the sun, in Spain or in Greece, and that marked the beginning of the demise of those old English seaside towns. They still exist today, but they are poor and rundown. Like Brighton, Margate was infamous for gang violence between mods and rockers in the 1960s, then mods and skinheads in the eighties, but in the fifties, Margate was just perfect... kind of. Well, it managed to change my world.

*

I went to the local primary school, passed my eleven plus exams and got a place at Chatham House Grammar School in Ramsgate, where Edward Heath, later to become British prime minister, once attended. Founded in 1797, dayboys then had to be at school at 5.40am and were not allowed home until 8.20pm after prayers... quite different to today. During the war, the school had entrances to the network of tunnels running under Ramsgate, then used as shelter from the air raids. Most of the entrances have been covered up now, but you can still see a few on the lower playground. It was the 1950s and I would walk twenty minutes each morning to the bus stop and catch a bus the five miles down the Ramsgate Road to get to the school. In those days, eleven-year-olds wandered around on their own; quite a different time indeed.

As I've mentioned, Granny was a great girl and I was now really settled, but she did border on the eccentric at times. She was a spiritualist and the house was filled with photographs of Native American chiefs in magnificent headdresses. My granny thought they were spiritual 'beings' and she would host séances each Monday night in the back extension room (under my room). I would always help her prepare for the séance by putting specially made frames covered in black velvet inside the windows to block out any light. She had a regular group of women who attended, like the doctor's wife. I remember her as the poshest person we knew, and she would bring me comics and chocolate – my weekly treat. I remember being tucked up in bed with chocolate and *The Beano* and *The Dandy* before the séance would begin and the next day, Granny would always say bizarre things to me. "I spoke to your mummy last night" would definitely freak me out. Nothing to do with the séances, but similarly bizarre, she used to tell me that Mother died from eating tomato ketchup.

★

All my life, I have loved rock 'n' roll music. My first musical memory was of Bill Haley & His Comets' 'Rock Around the Clock', which was a hit when I was little. But my favourite was Little Richard and his hits 'Tutti Frutti', 'Long Tall Sally' and 'Lucille'. I remember when I went into the Great Ormond Street Hospital in Carshalton, at the age of twelve, to have my testicles dropped and I sang 'Heartbreak Hotel', Elvis's current hit, in the hospital. At Granny's, we had a Rediffusion radio, whose signal came down a wire. The box looked like a radio, but was in fact empty except for the speaker. I remember I used to go downstairs late in the evening and put cushions around it, lie on the floor so my granny wouldn't hear me, and listen to Radio Luxembourg and my favourite song of all, 'Cathy's Clown', by the Everly Brothers.

With this fascination in music, Granny decided I should learn a musical instrument, and I was given the choice between a piano accordion and a guitar. At that time a guitar was quite an unfamiliar instrument to me, but more to the point, what would an Italian do in England other than play the accordion in Italian restaurants? Needless to say, I did not get to learn the guitar. Keith Richards and Eric Clapton were clearly more switched on than me, and were following Chuck Berry and the blues greats like Muddy Waters and Bo Diddley, but that kind of thing hadn't really made it down to Margate – not to my knowledge anyway. I was soon practising the piano accordion every day for a good hour, and I became quite proficient. Had I done that with a guitar, I may have had a very different life, and my future friends Eric Clapton and Pink Floyd might have been totally different people to me. I'm not saying I would have turned out to be a great guitarist or that I was at all upset with my granny, for the piano accordion was itself a beautiful instrument. I suppose we all have our own journeys in life and mine was destined not to be a rock star, not quite anyway... I played that accordion at hospitals and old people's homes and joined the Margate Children's Piano Accordion Band! My band was even chosen to represent Margate on television in a contest called 'Beat That Town!'. It involved a number of entertainers, like singers, dancers and a Hawaiian guitarist. Going to the TV studios in Manchester was the furthest away I had been from Margate and I really did love that trip. I remember the journey and how shocked I was when one of the dancers went into the toilet on the train with a man she had just met. I didn't know anything about sex in those days – why would I? I was still eleven and living with Granny. For the show, the whole of the accordion band were dressed up as little Dutch boys and girls, with curled-up hats, plaits and clogs. I have a photo of the band taken from a little black and white TV screen, and I'm in the corner grinning from ear to ear – fame!

Television was not something we had at home, on Addiscombe Road, Margate. In fact, there was only one television on the entire street. It belonged to a family with a son who was my age, so every Saturday and Sunday evening I would go there to be with him and we'd plonk ourselves in the front room on the floor and stare at the television in amazement. It was raised on stilts and must have been like one of those old classic images of the kids sitting too close to the screen. The family would give me a Wagon Wheel chocolate biccy and a packet of crisps, things I rarely had in my house. I remember the excitement of *Bonanza* and *Sunday Night at the London Palladium*. Even in black and white, television was thrilling in those early days – totally and utterly thrilling.

Our street also lacked cars in the 1950s, but the family with the telly had a motorcycle and sidecar, and that was all of the available transport on Addiscombe Road. Our house was a basic two-up, two-down terraced house, with a rear extension and an empty field opposite the house where every year a circus would pitch its tent. I remember the knocks at the door from "the man with the bucket" asking for water for his elephants. Eventually, the council built a housing estate on the field and the circus was no more, but the donkeys for the children's rides on the beach would still come and pass our house. My job was to rush out and scoop up their droppings to scatter on the roses.

My sister Maria had Sundays off from the salon and she would visit us for Sunday lunch. My job for the meal was to make the cream and I'd use full fat gold-top milk. Back then, milk came in glass bottles and the different colour top indicated the different type. First I'd boil the milk, let it settle overnight, then the next day skim the top off and compress it through this big old machine of Granny's. It would come out the other end as Cornish clotted cream. Beautiful. I'd help make the mint sauce too, by picking the mint from the back garden. As you can see, life was different in those days, in all the little ways. We had a toilet outdoors, for example, and there was no such thing as Andrex, just a metal hook, and on it, shreds of newspaper – usually the *Daily Mirror*.

In the summer we brought bed-and-breakfast holidaymakers into the house, mainly car workers from the Midlands. We would get the same families every year but, thinking back, I can't imagine now how they'd have all fitted into our small house, with the whole visiting family using just one room. I had another job as well: to take up the jug of hot water for guests to wash in the morning, and then empty the bedpan full of urine. Guests were never allowed to use the house's only bath. It was a zinc tub, which was in a shed out back – that was just for us. I remember Granny and I filling the tub with kettles for our weekly soak, and we would, of course, both use the same water. We were so excited when we got a gas hot-water boiler over the tub. To us, it was the most tremendous and dazzling of modern inventions.

One family of regular holidaymakers had two daughters: one my age, of eleven or twelve, and the other about nineteen. I liked the younger one and she was my friend, but the elder was rather odd to me. She'd tart herself up each night and go out on the town. One Monday, while the séance was happening underneath my room, she came in. I was busy at the time, eating my chocolate and reading my *Beano*. She closed the door behind her and approached me – weirdly she was not too interested in the Bash Street Kids or even Billy Whizz, but rather in something else and she began to touch my penis. I was very naive at the time, and what with my comic book reading to get on top of, the timing was all wrong. I told her if she didn't stop it, I would shout to the séance for help. She left the room in a huff. I continued reading.

*

By now, the town council had appointed a child protection officer to keep an "eye on me". She was a nice lady called June Jolly. When I was twelve, she introduced my family to the chaplain of the public school, St. Lawrence College, in Ramsgate. His name was Revd Kenneth Senior. He was married to a doctor and had a young family. He took an interest in my well-being and paid frequent visits to the house. He taught me how to drive in an empty field and how to swim, but sadly the Revd Kenneth Senior had an ulterior motive. With the approval of Granny, he offered to teach me about the birds and the bees – something Granny considered a man's role, and one less job she had to do. It seems incredible these days, but at that time, and at the age of twelve, I was completely unaware of sex. He explained to me about procreation and taught me how to masturbate. Of course, he taught me by demonstrating it on me. Revd Kenneth Senior was a paedophile, although that was not a term in common use in those days. They were called child molesters or perverts, but whatever they were called, he was one of them.

He never did manage to molest me again, but that was not for want of trying over the years, which is harassment in itself. He would try at the swimming pool and on trips. He begged me to let him have "his fun", like when he took me to Cambridge where we spent the day trainspotting – my passionate hobby in the days of the steam trains. I liked the Stanier and the Fowler, such terrific sounds. When a steam train came in, my entire body would shake. It was to me the most exciting thing in life. Watching old films that capture the deep whistle of the train – the chug chug – it was just as it was. I remember talking to one budding trainspotter there in Cambridge, as we watched one locomotive finish its scheduled turn of work – it was now due its clean-through – and asking him what was happening when the fireman stepped down from the train and entered the shed beside the track. The man had a moustache and a bowler hat, too.

"He's come to report the engine. The reporting clerk will then tell the footplate man where to leave the train in the yard. Its firebox, tubes and boiler will need to be cleaned, or the engine steams poorly and burns more coal than is necessary."

I really did love those steam trains and thinking back now, it was really anything that had an engine. Maybe it was that tin-plate model car with working headlights that my father had given me that had sparked the love – something that I slept next to each night and sometimes even took with me on trips.

When we got to Cambridge, after I had got undressed for bed, Revd Ken Senior tried to molest me again, but I wouldn't allow him. I was resistant and stubborn. I had obviously led him into a false sense of opportunity, what with my fondness for the steam trains and the trip away, but I was only twelve and wasn't to know the mind tricks I was then playing on the man. He became angry and raised his voice, something quite terrifying to me at the time, and all I wanted then was to be back with my granny. "You've had your fun, now let me have mine," he demanded. I must have been a strong-willed young lad to resist the reverend, but resist I did. It was never to happen again.

He even took me on Thames river cruises with what we would now call paedophile rings. Two or three of the cruisers were packed with schoolteachers and young boys, for a week's 'trip' down the Thames. I don't know for sure that the boys were passed around, but I do know that the Revd Ken Senior slept with a small boy in his cabin. I know it for a fact. Meanwhile, as the non-player that I was, I was relegated to the quartermaster's launch, and I remember him sulking all week because he was missing out on the little boy action.

In 1960, the reverend took up a new post at Dean Close School, another public school, in Cheltenham, on the other side of England. My guess is he had been found out at St. Lawrence College and needed to do a runner. In those days, as with priests, schoolmasters were just moved on when their fondness for young boys was exposed. They were rarely prosecuted, mainly just protected. Has much changed?

I was approaching sixteen and my grandmother was eighty-six, nearing the end of her life, so it was decided I should go and be with the Senior family in Cheltenham. They already had three children of their own with another one on the way, but they officially fostered me. I never told my granny about the reverend's advances and it never passed my mind that I should. Not knowing at such a young age what was right or wrong and which way to go in life, I became the Senior family's fostered child and what happened next was quite unusual indeed.

*

The front cover of *The Times* newspaper in 1960 was just classified advertisements. The news started inside, on page two. Revd Ken Senior had put a small ad on the front cover, 'Financial help wanted for bright orphan to pay for school fees'. Perhaps it was then when I realised the power of advertising. He had a reply from someone called the Revd Timothy Beaumont, who paid for all my school fees for three years at Dean Close School. The Revd

Beaumont had one clause: that there should be no contact. I never met him and I was surprised that well into the twenty-first century he was still alive, by then Lord Beaumont of Whitley. When he died a couple of years ago, his obituary explained all. He had been a young Anglican priest and just thirty years old when his mother, a rich American from a shipping family, died, leaving him fifteen million in her will. This was a considerable fortune in the 1950s and he resolved to give it all away in just three years. Reading what Andrew Roth wrote for *The Guardian* in 2008, the man seemed quite interesting to me, and I would have liked to have met him.

> Lord Beaumont, who has died aged 79, never seemed sure of his vocation or political loyalties. He was twice an Anglican vicar, giving up holy orders for 11 years between... The difference between his habitations symbolised the dispersal of the Elm family fortune, which he inherited in 1960. This was generously distributed... Beaumont's volatility derived from the clash between the class and religion into which he was born, and the more radical, liberal ideas he came to hold.
>
> ... in 1960, he returned home, convinced that the Church of England was dominated by worn-out traditions and was failing in its missionary purpose...
>
> ... He was on the executive of the Sexual Law Reform Society; he attracted attention in 1976 with an attack on the Pope as having 'gone right round the bend' for castigating masturbation as a sin, despite the absence, he claimed, of any Bible justification... In the debate on overseas aid, he wanted to reverse the aphorism that 'aid is money taken from the taxation of the poor of the rich world, and given to the rich of the poor world, who then repay it to the rich of the rich world'. He wanted aid to be given directly to the poor of the developing world...

Timothy Wentworth Beaumont, Baron Beaumont of Whitley, clergyman and politician, born 22 November 1928, died 8 April 2008, and I am grateful to him. From what I've read, he seemed to be a great old bloke. As I'm sure you now realise, I was one of the lucky beneficiaries of his inherited fortune. As always in my life, my timing was perfect. I suppose after the lucky birth I had had, this was now the second instance of what would soon become a regular occurrence, and I am talking about landing on my feet. In later life, it was to be known as something more my style: 'Golden Bollocks Cigarini'.

When I was ready to leave Margate to go to the posh Dean Close School, Granny told me to get a haircut. Until that year in 1960, there was a US airbase at nearby Manston Aerodrome, so US-style flat-top crew cuts or ivy leagues were all the rage in Margate. Although according to the local barber, America claiming the origin of the cut was "just unacceptable" and these crew cuts, according to him, were just a variant of the old English brush cut that had been worn since the eighteenth century. "It's sheer nonsense," he declared. Nonetheless, that was the cut I got and it was totally inappropriate for Dean Close School.

When my two sisters came over from Rome, they would date the US airmen. These strapping men would show up at our house in fancy 1950s American convertibles with big fins, and that's probably where I got my love for old American cars. The airmen would be allowed out in Margate, but there was always trouble with the local lads. I remember seeing the military police, with their big batons, strolling up and down the promenade. There were black airmen on the base, but I never saw one in Margate. I was told they were not allowed out into the town, for their own protection.

The family got me away from Margate just in time. I was spending a lot of time hanging out at the Dreamland Amusement Park and becoming quite the yob. Perhaps by then that culture of mod-rocker gang hooliganism was beginning to rub off. Who'd have thought! I recall one attraction called 'The Snail'. Outside, it was like a giant snail, but inside it was pitch black and the corridors had all sorts of obstacles, like soft foam floors, which people would fumble around in. My chums and I would go inside until our eyes got accustomed to the dark, then we would hang around near the entrance waiting for young girls to enter, then grab them and feel them up. I remember the shock I had when I was kissing a young girl and I touched her large breasts. They were just fantastic – trouble is, they were rubber. It's funny now, thinking back over my life and realising how the small, seemingly insignificant events have played a part on the whole. I'm wondering what kind of an effect my chums and I have had on the lives of those girls who went into 'The Snail'!

I was fifteen and working at the Butlins Hotel in Cliftonville, Margate. I fried the eggs for breakfast – about a hundred of them at a time – on a giant flat pan. Late one night, when all the bars and cafés had closed, I was hanging around outside the hotel with a couple of my hotel workmates. Across the road, there was a closed café with the tables and chairs still outside. Three men had appeared and started throwing the chairs around. They were smartly dressed in suits and ties, in the style favoured by London gangsters. For some reason, my two so-called friends shouted "Hard men!" as loud as they could. It was very stupid indeed and they soon realised it. The gangsters dropped the chairs and crossed the road in our direction, then two of them and my two companions started fighting. I was lucky, I got the biggest, but he was also the kindest for some reason. He towered over me, waiting, but he could see that I was only a young whippersnapper and had no inclination to fight.

"You want to start something?" the man asked me.

I knew the answer, of course; it was an easy one. "No sir." I stood there nervously. "To be totally honest with you, I don't know these two men very well and have only just begun working at the hotel. It's where we met."

By this time my colleagues were being picked up by their arms and feet and thrown against a wall. I decided to save myself and darted off in a slalom between the group. Unfortunately, one of the other fighters turned and saw me, and he slammed me in the mouth. I remember at the time seeing my tooth arc through the air as if all time had stopped and only the tooth was moving – in slow motion. It seemed so strange to see my own tooth, in the sky, in the middle of the night, under the stars. It hit the ground and we both looked at one another. I ran like hell. I ran and I ran and they must have chased me for a good two miles. Eventually, I got to the park near where I lived and hid. They gave up the chase and I lived to see another day.

I went home, exhausted, exhilarated, and a tooth short. Granny was, of course, suspicious, what with the reports flying around town of all the thuggery and 'tomfoolery', and I didn't make matters any better by telling her I had walked into some furniture. Even now, approaching seventy, I regret not telling her the truth. It was to be the only time I would ever lie to Granny.

I went back to Cliftonville the next morning and found it. Sound the trumpets! I found my tooth and it was right there, in the gutter. It was a whole tooth and root, and it was all intact, and it was there, and it was mine. It must have been over an inch long and it was simply wonderful to see it. It was as if the bullies were now unable to claim victory, now I had been reunited with my tooth. I later had it filed down and put on a small denture, and my mouth was back to normal.

I don't know whose idea it was – either my granny's or the Revd Senior's – but the decision was made that because I was going to an exclusive school, I should get rid of my Italian name and change it to that of my granny: Davies. England was not as cosmopolitan in those days, and there were not many Italian people around, as the diaspora of Italians had mainly gone to America. I don't remember having much of a say about changing the name. I don't even remember having my opinion sought, but my life was in such turmoil, leaving Granny and going away with my child molester, that I just went along with it.

Sometimes in Margate, it would feel as though T. S. Eliot was right. To quote *The Wasteland*: "On Margate sands I can connect nothing with nothing." Maybe it was all part of growing up. I remember that night running up to my room so I would be with my things and my toy car, the one my father gave me. Sometimes I'd wish he were not dead. Sometimes I would pray for him to return. Her, too.

My name was changed by deed poll to John Victor Davies and it would stay that way for three years at Dean Close School, one year on Voluntary Service Overseas and three years at Durham University, where I was one of five John Davieses. But get this… I found out later that even the Davies name wasn't real! My grandfather's family had in fact been Irish and when they came to England, they changed their name to a Welsh one to avoid being stigmatised for being Irish. People in Durham University were always asking, "John Davies? Which one?" I got fed up with it all and considering it wasn't my real name, or even a real fake name, I changed it back to Cigarini when I graduated and started working in advertising. By then I was pronouncing it the Italian way, with the C like Ch as in 'Chigarini'. Before in Margate, it had always been pronounced with the C like cigar. But right now, I was Davies and I was ready for Dean Close School.

CHAPTER 3

Dean Close

Dean Close was one of the strict Church of England schools in 1960. Pupils had to wear shirts with starched detachable Van Heusen collars in style 11, not 22 (too long) or 33 (too cut away). Jackets had to be done up, but only with the middle button. Hands were not to be put in trouser pockets, and for going into town, pupils wore beige duffle coats and mortarboards. In fact, the students from all three boys' schools in Cheltenham – Cheltenham College, Dean Close School and Cheltenham Grammar School – wore mortarboards in town. This way of life all came as a bit of a shock to me, with my south coast accent (similar to cockney) and my flat-top crew cut. On my first day, the head boy was overheard saying, "I give him a month." I was nicknamed 'Johnny Margate' and the name was to follow me. In the mid-eighties, I was filming on the street outside Sotheby's, Belgravia, when I heard someone shout across the road "Oi! Johnny Margate!" It was one of the old boys. England. Small world.

I was in my first year at Dean Close when some bad news came to me. My granny had died. I immediately went for a walk in the grounds. To this day, I remember the occasion and the feeling of numbness I had. I didn't cry. I just felt... nothing. With both parents having died at an early age, death had already played a big part in my life and I remember even at the time being quite shocked that I didn't feel more remorse over the death of my granny, who I loved. "On Margate sands I can connect nothing with nothing." I walked for hours that day. Hours and hours.

★

In spite of everything, I survived three years at Dean Close School. The first year I was a dayboy, living with the Senior family in a large house near the school. Sadly, there was that same atmosphere of paedophilia in the house, one I had unfortunately come to know about. As well as me, the Seniors had now fostered another boy, Barry, who was a couple of years younger than me. It seemed that Revd Ken Senior had given up on me, and at sixteen, I was probably too old for his taste anyway, but he was happy enough – he had Barry now. The scandal was, as with the priests, that the child molesting was done under the guise of religion. Ken Senior would go into Barry's room at bedtime to do 'Bible reading' and the abuse would occur. I was sure of it, because I would often see him leaving Barry's room with an erection in his trousers. Although I was very aware of it, Ken's wife Nora was either totally innocent and naïve, or she just turned a blind eye to it all – a strange thing to do considering how it was now all happening in her home. Rumour had it that Ken had confessed his weakness to her before they got married, but in my experience, abusers' wives turn the other way, not wanting to suffer the consequences of exposure. It's strange, the secrecy that surrounds child sexual abuse, because it is a secrecy that even carries over to the victims. Barry and I were very good friends for example, but we never discussed it. Never ever.

After a school scandal that was written about in the *Daily Mirror*, Ken Senior left Dean Close School and moved his family to a British Forces school in Wilhelmshaven, Germany, and that was it – they were gone. I had only been fostered for a year, but I was back on my own. Alone. It was strange when they left because I didn't want them to, despite it all. I became a boarder at Dean Close and it remained that way for the next two years.

I enjoyed my time at the school and eventually the other pupils accepted me. Actually, in spite of the twitch, I became quite popular. Also, the school seemed to turn around my descent into Margate uncouthness, taking the edge off my south coast accent. It also taught me how to play sport, namely grass hockey, and I would go for long cycle rides to Cirencester or the Cotswolds, alone of course, turning the wheels of my bicycle softly through the towns, daydreaming, singing sometimes. I loved the light breeze on me that Gloucestershire gave, especially in spring. At times I would visit Cheltenham, which is a beautiful town. Alone, of course.

By 1961, the Senior family were in Germany and my granny was gone forever, so I had nowhere to go in the school holidays. The Rolls Royces and Armstrong Siddeleys would arrive to collect little Henry and his trunk, and I was alone, sitting on my bed, well-behaved like orphans tend to be, and wondered, on many occasion, what to do with myself.

By this time, my eldest sister Maria had moved back to Rome and had married Pietro Rebecchini, the head of operations for Pan American Airways. Pietro came from a well-known Roman family; his uncle had been mayor of Rome for many years. I decided to spend my summer holidays in Rome. My travel lust was beginning to really grow, or maybe the loneliness was too much to bear for one orphan, and I hitchhiked to get there.

I had just turned seventeen. I'd take the evening boat train from Victoria Station to Dover and catch the night ferry to Calais. It would dock around five in the morning and I would usually get my first ride from the ferry. It would take me about three days to get there through France and I would always arrive around the same time, in the middle of the night. My sister Maria eventually got used to being woken up by me, Little Johnny. I would do this journey for the next six years throughout the remainder of my time at Dean Close School and at Durham University.

★

In spite of being a child molester, Ken Senior did very little to harm me, and was, by and large, a benevolent figure in my life – as strange as that may sound. He had two further great influences on me. He encouraged me to apply to university, not something I would have dreamt of doing had I stayed in Margate (more likely I would have become a more professional-type hooligan), and he also suggested I take a gap year and do something called Voluntary Service Overseas. I had never heard of such a thing. Voluntary Service Overseas… what on earth could it be?

At the end of my second year at Dean Close, I took my GCE 'A' (advanced) level exams. My grades were not great – I think a D and an E – but they were still pass grades in the UK and it was decided I should stay on a third year to do them again at 'S' (scholarship) level. In the meantime, Ken Senior had recommended Durham as a fine university. He was certainly right about that.

I went for an interview in Durham Castle, next to the cathedral. I was now in my late teens and very impressed with my accommodation in the keep, and I had an interview with the master, Mr Slater. The interview was rather brief to say the least:

Slater: "When I was at school, Dean Close had a damn fine hockey team" (eyes on his papers).

Me:	"They still do, sir" (wimpy voice, eyes also on his papers).
Him:	"Do you play for the team?"
Me:	(Pause) "Yes sir" (swallows hard). "I do."
Him:	"And if you came here (eyes rising), would you play for us?"
Me:	"Oh… yes sir" (girly voice). "ABSOLUTELY."
Him:	(Eyes back to papers) "We'll let you know."

The next week I got a letter offering me a place, provided I improve my grades one level. I didn't let him down and I became college and university captain of hockey. The grades went up, too. Sports scholarships didn't really exist in England, but I guess that was an early version of one.

CHAPTER 4

Africa

President Kennedy based the Peace Corps on VSO (Voluntary Service Overseas). But the Peace Corps was for youngsters in large groups; VSO was mainly done alone, so it suited me just fine.

The youngsters selected to do the service had to attend an initiation course over Easter weekend at Tonbridge School. There, they were assessed and assigned postings. Ninety-five percent of the jobs were teaching posts, but there were a few plum locations, like the Solomon Islands, that everyone wanted. I must have made a good impression as I was sent to Africa and given a job to work for the Northern Rhodesian Community Development Department, and I took it with a handshake, which is how most things were still being done in those days.

1963 saw the rise of The Beatles, with their debut album *Please Please Me*. Harold Macmillan was our prime minister, but not for long. The Vietnam War was unabating, 70,000 marched in London against nuclear weapons testing, *Lawrence of Arabia* won best picture and the first Bond movie hit the US. In Saigon, a Buddhist monk committed self-immolation and back in London, Christine Keeler was arrested and sentenced for her part in the Profumo Affair. By November, JFK would be dead. It was August. The Beatles had just played their final Cavern Club show, John Surtees won the German Grand Prix, it was the month of the Great Train Robbery in Buckinghamshire, *Cleopatra* was on at the flicks, and *The Great Escape*, too. Martin Luther King had just delivered his 'I Have a Dream' speech on the steps of the Lincoln Memorial. It was August 1963 and I got on a plane and I flew to Africa.

★

Lusaka is a city at 1300 metres, so it's a humid subtropical climate, or, specifically, a tropical savannah. Just the idea of stepping into the landlocked (then a protectorate) Northern Rhodesia was terrifying, but thrilling too. My arrival at Lusaka was ignominious. I was collected at the airport by the head of the Community Development Department and taken to stay overnight in his home. On the drive from the airport, we ran over a dog. It was the first time this had happened to me and I was surprised because it felt really hard, like we had hit a pile of bricks. When we arrived at his garage, he shouted, "There's a rat!" – and he gave me a broom handle to kill it as he flushed it out. The next thing I know, a rat the size of a cat runs out and sends me into the back wall. I was terrified and it escaped. Welcome to Africa! I don't think the boss was very impressed with his new recruit. I couldn't even kill a rat. How was I to survive wild Africa, home of the spotted hyena and the black mamba?

Northern Rhodesian territory was managed by the (British) South Africa Company from 1891, and while I was there, something great was to happen: independence.

I was sent to the North West Province – a large area, approximately five times the size of Wales. Northern Rhodesia was in the last throws of British colonial rule and was soon to become Zambia.

Pre-colonial, it was the African dream of Khoisan hunter-gatherers, migrating Bantu, Tonga people and the Nkoya. More came through the centuries until the nineteenth, when the Europeans eventually added to that influx with Francisco de Lacerda and, of course, David Livingstone, who would name Victoria Falls after his Queen and describe them famously as "scenes so lovely [they] must have been gazed upon by angels in their flight".

Cecil Rhodes then led the British South Africa Company to scout for minerals, which they did find, along with copper metals. The British colony of Northern Rhodesia was established, but by the fifties, after more laws to alter and change the territories, opposition from the people grew and demonstrations rose against any further control by the British. Then the sixties came and Northern Rhodesia was the centre of turmoil, which would characterise the federation in its last years.

Northern Rhodesia became the Republic of Zambia in October 1964, but at independence, despite its mineral wealth, Zambia had problems. The main problem was the "few trained and educated Zambians" available to run the government and the economy was dependent on foreign expertise. Was I part of this foreign expertise invasion? Was I here to save Africa? On that note, the scariest thing you can say to an African is "Hi, I'm white, and I'm here to save you."

It was interesting to see the old colonial ways. I was sent to Kobompo, a small town on the Kobompo River, and it was full of hippos. You could see them clearly and it was all rather scary, as the hippos had a reputation for being quite aggressive, territorial and ill tempered, especially the females, who were protective over their young. The crocs were frequent victims of hippo attacks, but I wondered about humans, as we mainly travelled around in canoes made from dugout trees. I was later to find out that the hippo is considered the most dangerous apex mammal of all Africa. Sometimes, I guess it's not good to read the guidebooks. I was in the boat with my pink skin and straw hat, quite blatantly a guest to them, so perhaps I was just lucky… again.

In fact, there were only five white people in Kobompo: the district commissioner and his wife, a single young district officer – who was partial to the local African girls, the community development officer with whom I was housed, and myself. I really believed the homosexual thing was following me around… D'Arcy Payne, the community development officer, had a young African boy he used to take to his room to 'teach English'. However, he never bothered me. Despite the fact that we were now living and working in a soon-to-be independent Zambia, the district commissioner and the district officer still wore their white uniforms with white-feathered helmets, likely a British pride they cared not to shake off too soon; very colonial rule in image, very proud – and very sick, looking back. We shouldn't, I suppose, have been like that.

I stayed in the North West Province for seven months. D'Arcy had an old 1950s Vauxhall Victor car and we had to push it each morning to get it started. We used to get up at 5am each day to get to the Community Development Hall. It was where all the young African girls were doing their domestic science courses – the ones that I found out, too late, were all being shagged by the district officer. D'Arcy told me one morning when we were pushing his car.

I remember the sunrises; they were just wonderful. I had not been in the tropics before and I had never seen such a huge sun. It was everything I had dreamed of Africa: a giant globe in the landscape that would plunge into the deep each and every nighttime, then return again each day with colours that would dazzle me, delight me, make me want to write home about. But I didn't, because there was no one to tell. Instead, I lived in the now; it was hard not to in Africa.

I did a survey of why the local youths were leaving the villages to go to the Copperbelt towns. This required me to mainly cycle, which I was used to from my time on the bicycle in Gloucestershire, or occasionally drive a jeep into the bush with an interpreter to speak with the villagers. I recall one interesting incident.

My interpreter and I were cycling along a sandy track when we heard the drums a long way from the next village, even from where we were on the track. The drumbeats were so loud it was as if the track itself was shaking, and we could feel the vibrations travel through the bicycle wheels and into our legs. We followed the noise. When we got there, we found a woman on all fours. She was barking like a dog and all of the villagers were sitting in a circle around her, with the men beating their drums as she crawled and barked. She had a spell placed on her by the witchdoctor, a man covered in face paint and the feathers of sky birds. Her crime had been to publicly ask, after a baby had been born, who would want to be born into this world. Because the baby had died, she was blamed. Naturally, the villagers thought the baby had heard the woman, with its baby ears, and had chosen not to live because of her and what she had said. The woman was forced to drink the local honey beer. After barking and hopping around like an animal, in an attempt to exorcise the evil spirit, she would be cast out into the bush where she would not survive. It was an amazing and terrifying scene, but there was nothing I could do to prevent it happening. Nothing at all. I recently watched the magnificent film *Blood Diamond* where the character of Danny Archer manages to summarise the continent with nothing but an acronym. It manages to work, somehow; it was how I felt at the exorcism. T.I.A. was the acronym he used: This. Is. Africa. There is nothing you can do but accept it for what it is. Africa.

All the time I did this survey I was staying in the African villages, sleeping in straw huts and eating the local food. This was mainly cassava, made from a root, which needed to be soaked for days to eliminate the impurities in it and then pounded. Africa was proving to be a magical place for me, and each day would bring with it the suspense and surprise of new adventures, ones I had read about in the big boys' adventure novels. I was living in villages with locals and helping them, if only in a small way. It was ironic that I had Ken Senior to thank for all of this, the man who had molested me. I recall another incident in one village, where all the youths had been locked away to perform their coming-of-age rituals, during which they would be circumcised, likely without anaesthetic, possibly with blades not too sharp, or not too clean. T.I.A.

I managed to buy three leopard skins from the villagers. This wasn't easy because the local people, with their ancestors' history of colonial rule, were all quite suspicious of me with my blonde hair and straw hat, and were reluctant to sell the skins. Mostly, they thought of all white men, even a youngster like me, as figures of authority and didn't want to get into trouble. When I got back to the UK, I sold the skins to a furrier on Regent Street for £150. It was a small fortune for someone on a student grant of £4 a week and I remember how I bought myself a nice blazer with that money. I felt proud to have journeyed to the far corner, to Africa, to sleep in huts and return with those animal skins, to sell them and dress myself in a fine jacket. I remember that night standing in front of my long mirror. I felt like a genuine adventurer and entrepreneur, like a character in a Wilbur Smith book. Perhaps my enterprising father was looking down on me. Perhaps he was watching me. Perhaps.

My next job was to organise a famine relief scheme on the border with the Congo. After the establishment of the First Republic of the Congo, there was a civil war for independence in Katanga, which bordered the North West Province of Northern Rhodesia. The agriculture had collapsed and people were starving. My job was to distribute grain.

While on the border with Katanga, I went hunting with the local Irish missionary where I shot at a herd of gazelles. One of them fell; it fell so hard I could hear its bones rattle and break like dry twigs. The herd cleared and the one lay alone on the hot African earth. I didn't feel sad, but felt connected to it somehow, as if what was happening had pulled me into the hunting world that I was surely part of. It had pulled me into Africa and the pulse of Africa was beating and I could feel it now, in my hand – the one that gripped the trigger I was still squeezing. On closer approach, the animal was twitching, and the closer we got to it, the more it seemed capable of twisting its neck, perhaps managing a ferocious bark. However, the Africans, with the Irishman and I, took no risk. They loved the gazelle and wished it no pain. They pounced on it and clubbed it until it died. Later, when they were skinning it, it emerged that the animal was pregnant and its clinging onto life now became so clear: there was a perfectly formed foetus inside it. All was now obvious to us and it made for an interesting story – even for the hunters. It made me sad but the Africans needed the meat, so I forgave myself again.

On another occasion, I raised my rifle to a magnificent roan antelope – one of the largest species of the savannah. It stood there proud with huge horns, staring me down as if trying to tell me something. I thought of the gazelle and

I wondered if there was an unborn inside this great antelope. I was also intimidated by its thousand-yard stare. My rifle dropped and the power I was feeling in my hands quickly vanished, burying itself in my stomach, and the electricity in my face was gone too. I couldn't shoot and I lowered my gun. I would never hunt again, I told myself. But Africa is a different world, and in different worlds there are different rules.

The Gaboon viper is one of the most beautiful snakes in the world, but also one of the deadliest and people die within minutes of being bitten by one. It is not a very long snake, but wide. We came across one while driving on a remote track. It was sunning itself on the road and was probably asleep. We stopped the jeep and jumped out to look at it. I put my gun above its head and shot it, and I didn't even hesitate. It seemed to represent something very different to the greater mammals of the plains: the gazelle and the Grant's zebra, the elephant or even the spiny mouse. This cunning reptile was sly, knowing and wicked. It was reptilian in all its character. I wanted it dead. I wanted its skin.

Driving around, we would often see snakes on the road. The local technique was always to brake hard and slide over them on the dirt road, so as to kill them, otherwise the tyres could make them flip up into the underside of the car and possibly enter your vehicle. Once I was driving along and a black mamba stretched right across the road. It was so long I couldn't see either end of it. A couple of times I had snakes in my house, usually green mambas, and ants – a big problem too. You could be found standing on an ants' nest and wouldn't feel them until they were all over your legs and body. You would have to take all your clothes off to get rid of them. In Africa, ants can kill a man, and even a horse. They climb all over it, and at a signal that is released throughout the group, probably via the queen, all bite the horse in unison and it dies of a great shock. These ants were fascinating to watch performing their tasks, carrying items ten times their own size. Sometimes there would be an army ant trail a foot wide stretching across the road or in the bush, led by two or three scout ants. The anthills could be as tall as trees, and were quite a different ant breed to the simple ant of the English wood.

While organising the famine relief, I was staying in a remote and empty hunting lodge. It was dusk and a herd of – I counted – thirty elephants lumbered past the lodge, and across the nearby river. There were babies holding the tails of the mothers with their trunks and the first and last elephants made magnificent trumpet calls as they crossed the river. Seeing wildlife for real and not in a game reserve was a thrill – quite different to the donkeys in the Margate field. Everything was different in fact: the animals, the sunsets, the smells, the sounds, the oranges and browns. It was primitive and tribal; it was real and it was something we were trying to change.

My final job in the North West Province was to be an election officer at the first democratic elections for the country to become Zambia. As I drove around, I had got used to the children shaking their palms at me and shouting "Kwacha! Kwacha!" (Freedom! Freedom!), but there was never any feeling of danger or violence. In fact, the only thing I saw in their eyes was light, hope and a zing for life. I wasn't worried at all. The villagers there walked for days to get to the polling stations and they were illiterate, so there were three tins with photographs for them to vote. The one for UNIP, the favourite party of Kenneth Kaunda, had a lion on it. The others were of a corn on the cob and a hoe. Kenneth Kaunda won.

The final five months of my year's VSO were spent at the other end of Zambia, in the Northern Province, on the border with Tanganyika. I worked with an Outward Bound professional called John Pitchford to build and open an Outward Bound school, and John was the warden of the school. Outward Bound schools were a Scottish creation, aiming to train the characters of young men through a month of tough expeditions and physical activity – a bit like being a marine for a month, but in Africa.

The site chosen for the school was near a town then called Abercorn, now called Mbala. It is above Lake Tanganyika, which we used for many of our expeditions, and also near the Kalambo Falls, which at 772 feet of single drop is among the highest of waterfalls in Africa. One of my favourite things to do, on occasion, was to sleep on a flat rock at the edge of the falls. When you sleep in the wild, you must pee walking backwards around your sleeping position before laying down, as they say it keeps the ants out.

Lake Tanganyika is an African Great Lake, 418 miles long and the longest fresh water lake in the world – so massive, in fact, that it touches four countries: Tanzania, the Congo, Burundi and Zambia. It drains through the Congo River system and it moves all the way to the Atlantic Ocean. Part of the East African Rift, it covers a staggering 13,000 square miles with a depth that makes it the second largest rift lake in both Africa and the world. It was the scene of two battles during World War I and Che Guevara used the lake's shores as a training ground for his guerrilla forces in the Congo. He was said to have attempted an overthrow of the government from his camp.

The port near Abercorn was called Mpulungu. It had an old tramp passenger ferry, the SS Liemba, regularly sailing up the lake into Tanganyika and the Congo. German colonialists – when they controlled German East Africa, before World War I – were said to have brought the ship on a train from the Indian Ocean. The lake was 3000 feet below the surrounding escarpment where Abercorn/Mbala was situated, and the Outward Bound students and I used to regularly make the climb.

John Pitchford and I built all the assault courses at the Outward Bound school by hand and then, finally, when we were ready, the new President-elect, Kenneth Kaunda, came to open the school. I have a great picture of me and him standing up one of the rope ladders we had built.

The participants on the courses were mainly African lads who worked for the mining companies on the Copperbelt. They were the first crop of African executives-to-be for the new African nation, and together we would go on long expeditions, some days walking over forty miles through the bush. The boss's wife would make a delicious chocolate cake and thinking about that was often the only thing that kept me going through the heat – that, and a cold Lion lager in a copper mug. It was fun sweating through all of my clothes by the end of each day, feeling fighting fit and strong in my legs. I taught life saving (I had been to a training course in Lusaka) and also rock climbing (I had not been trained, and I was terrified) and one time I climbed up a rock face with the students roped up behind me. I got to a place where I could not go up, back down, or sideways. I was stuck, so someone had to drive for miles to the position above me, then lower me a rope down. I had to hang on for a long time, dealing with all kinds of ugly thoughts with the sun on my back. Once I had the rope on me, I had the courage to continue the climb up and we all completed it. But it was scary; at one point, I thought I was going to die. I didn't like rock climbing at all.

At this point, I had moved and was living in a nice wooden house. It had a wonderful garden full of frangipani, paw-paw (papaya) and guava trees – the perfect place to relax. There, I had a caretaker called Cement and one day he had to leave for the Copperbelt. He left me in the care of his wife, who was beautiful and young and shapely; she was about eighteen. He never returned home in the time I was there. For weeks I was with this exotic African woman, who would stand around in my kitchen, often very provocatively. African women seemed to have a way of tilting their hips naturally, in a very inviting way, and I'd often feel the animal in me return in that kitchen. Looking back I don't know how I resisted. She seemed interested in doing something with me, but in spite of her seductiveness and her African curves, I didn't have the courage to make the first move. There was no communication between us, because she didn't speak any English, which might have made it easier for me had I gone for it. Truth be told, I was totally inexperienced sexually, and later I regretted not being bolder. All these years later, I still think of it and have considered it a missed opportunity in my development as a man. Cigarini... come on!

One incident stands out in my memory of the Outward Bound courses. Three separate patrols of students had to make their way independently across Lake Tanganyika and through the bush to meet me at a beautiful, almost magical secret place that had horseshoe-shaped waterfalls. I arrived but nobody else had, except for hundreds of baboons. Initially it was quite terrifying, but I managed to calm my breathing and then I raised both hands as if to say "I'm here in peace", but they were very curious about me and kept moving closer. I shooed them away but they would not go. I didn't know much at the time, as I looked into all of their faces, about the relationship between baboons and humans, but I did know that there were similarities like in their social orders and tendency towards aggression. Fortunately, they remained calm and I gave up on my shooing. They lost interest and I found a place to rest nearby and stayed the night all on my own, with the baboons.

The next day back at base camp, all came clear: the students told me that "whenever we asked the villagers for directions to the waterfalls, we were told not to go there, because it was a sacred tribal burial ground." It was why there were so many baboons, but no humans. After all the years, the baboons had found peace and a place where they were free of human beings. Perhaps my visit came at the right time. I think they were happy to see me. I certainly enjoyed being with the baboon tribe, if only for a short while. I have since read that baboons are very good at identifying a real menace instead of a pretend one. It seems my pathetic shooing did me a big favour. Baboons make politics, and a hierarchy is established by power, muscle mass and the size of the fangs, but also by the ability to form alliances and to know when to stab an evil one in the back. I don't need to wonder these days if I'm a good person or a bad one. The baboons accepted me so I know I'm good, by default. Oh, on that note, did you know that a large group of baboons is called a congress? It explains a lot, hey?

During a break in the Outward Bound courses, I hitchhiked to Mombasa and Dar es Salaam on the coast of Kenya, which was a doddle in Tanganyika and much easier than through France. There were small bush hotels situated a day's drive from each other, which were the only places to stay, and only about three cars a day would travel in each direction. It was easy to chat someone up over dinner and get a ride – like the Windhams. Sir Ralph was the chief justice of Tanganyika in Mombasa. He and Lady Windham and their twelve-year-old daughter Belinda took me there, and even put me up for a few days.

Near to Abercorn was an outpost of the International Red Locust Control Service. This was a South African-funded eradication programme aiming to control the breeding of locusts, which, if allowed to breed, would swarm all the way into South Africa and devastate their agriculture. The control service would either use amphibious swamp vehicles or small Cessna aircraft, equipped with sprays. The operatives would drink with us in the local bar, and they would tell us all sorts of stories of their adventures. They flew the aircraft very low in order to spot the breeding locusts before giving them a squirt of insecticide. One day a pilot came back with a damaged undercarriage, after a buffalo had stood up underneath him. I flew on one trip with them in the Cessna to the Rukwa Plain. It was hair-raising to fly below the branches of occasional trees, and down narrow gorges, with the cliff faces only feet away from the wings of the plane. The Rukwa Plain was a swampy place where no humans can live, full of abundant game, elephants, giraffes, flamingos, zebras, antelopes, buffalo, and all kinds of wildlife in the hundreds. This was not in a game reserve; it was in the wild.

*

After my VSO time was up, I had a couple of weeks to spare, so I hitchhiked to South Africa. I went to the Victoria Falls, which was a dream for me and the most beautiful place I have ever been in this fine world, before or since: one single mile width of blue water plunging over walls of basalt in a valley bound by hills of sandstone. The spray from the falls can rise to 400 metres and can be seen from far, far away. At full moon, a moonbow is seen in the spray, where normally only a daylight rainbow is evident – except during flood season, when it is clouded in mist. All year, at the cliff edge, spray shoots up fast like rain coming up from the deep ground.

My Outward Bound rock climbing experience came in useful as I climbed along the girders under the bridge across the Zambesi River, which separates Zambia from Rhodesia (Zimbabwe), giving me better angles for my photographs. It was summer when I was there, and the Zambesi was not in full flood, although there was still plenty of water rolling over. I was able to rock-hop across the crest of the falls until I was sitting in the middle. The falls were a mile wide and oh what a thrill to sit in the middle of the river, on the edge of the falls, with the water dropping all around me and the great noise and energy of the thunder. When David Livingstone discovered them in 1855, their African name was Mosi-oa-Tunya, or 'the cloud that thunders'. I think I prefer that name.

They are not the highest falls in the world, but are said to have the biggest volume travelling over, and are twice as high as – and one-and-a-half times the width of, Niagara – In height and width the Victoria Falls can be rivalled only by South America's Iguazu Falls, which you can see in the film *The Mission*. The first gorge the Zambesi falls into in front of the falls is very narrow and there is a footpath across what is known as the Knife-Edge Bridge, where you can stand right in front of the waterfall – probably no more than 30 metres away. The sound is the cloud that thunders and the sight is otherworldly.

I hitched down through Rhodesia to Salisbury (now Harare) and on to Pretoria, South Africa, where I met some young men in what was then the new Mini. It was the first time I had ever been in one. They terrified me the way they flung it around corners on opposite lock, with the tyres squealing. They were hockey players like me, and I stayed with them a few days and we partied hard, but that was it – like it always is when you hit the road. That was the state of mind I was in then: to explore, to learn, to adventure. It's a wonderlust that never died in me and when travelling, I'd often see that same electric travel spirit in the eyes of the other free spirits – ones I'd meet on the side of the road, hitch with, work with. It was the stuff that had always resonated with me; it was life, it was adventure, it was the road. I remember Robert Louis Stevenson telling it once: "For my part, I travel not to go anywhere, but to go. I travel for travel's sake. The great affair is to move." For those who have been bold or lucky enough to move, isn't it just as he wrote it?

After Johannesburg and Bloemfontein, I got a ride in a Ford Anglia right across the Kalahari Desert. The owner and I took it in turns to do the driving. After a few days in Cape Town and visiting the Cape of Good Hope, I hitched up the Garden Route to Port Elizabeth, East London and Durban, before making my way back to Salisbury. From there, I flew back to England.

On the way back I had a day's stopover in Cairo, where I went to see the Pyramids, the Sphinx and the Cairo Museum to see Tutankhamun's treasures. Looking into the shining gem stones, it was as if I was looking back through time. The hands of the pharaohs may certainly have held this gold and these gleaming green emerald rocks and I was looking into them, with my own eyes. Sometimes when I think back to the baboons, the waterfall, the people, the sounds and the smells, tears come. Africa: there is nowhere on earth like it. Everyone should go once.

There was no doubt that VSO definitely made a man of me and I benefited tremendously from the experience when I got to Durham University. Trouble was, I was twenty years old and still a virgin.

CHAPTER 5

Durham University

Most of the other new students were north-country boys who had never before left home. They tended to form large groups, but my friends and I kept it small. There was Rick Napp, an England Schoolboys rugby player, and Mark Allen, who became a rich and successful magazine publisher, and both were to meet their wives at Durham University. We are all still friends. Then there was Howard Davies, my namesake, who became a successful theatre director.

Once in Durham, it didn't take me long to lose my virginity. Wahey! A 'visitor' from the agricultural college, who was not part of the university, took me back to her room. She gave me my first experience of fellatio and I can still remember it, fifty years down the road, as the most fabulous sexual thrill – and I thought you might like to know… I was not able to contain myself for more than a few seconds. Unfortunately, the girl bragged to her college mates that she had a man in her room. We were caught and she was expelled. I never saw her again.

*

For the first Christmas at university, I went to Wilhelmshaven to see the Senior family. I guess I felt obliged to go there and report back to the reverend everything of Africa. I didn't mind, either; we seemed to know where we were 'at' with one another, so to speak. Wilhelmshaven is a coastal town in Lower Saxony, west of the Jade Bight of the North Sea. It was freezing; so cold, in fact, that the open sea was frozen into blocks. You could have walked to an offshore lighthouse if you could climb over the frozen sea squares. It was an interesting place too, where two-thirds of the town's buildings were destroyed during the war, by the Allies of course. Ken Senior was pleased I had done my VSO in Africa and equally pleased I was settled at Durham University. He was pleased with all my news, actually, but of course I didn't tell him I had lost my virginity to a gorgeous girl. I didn't want to open any old wounds with any talk of sex and whatnot. The atmosphere was peculiar. There was a subtext that still remained unspoken, while his wife was in full knowledge (I was sure) of his habits and our history. I never enquired about Barry, but to this day, I wonder what came of him.

As mentioned, I had kept my promise to the dean and was playing hockey for the University First 11 with privileged pre-season bus tours of all the Scottish universities. We would go to Glasgow, Aberdeen, Edinburgh and St. Andrews, where the grass was the best I had ever played on, and hockey was easy work (now I had conquered Africa!). It wasn't just that, but something was clear: Africa had made an imprint, and I didn't realise how much until I had left and returned to England. Everything after Africa was easier, less challenging, and life was much easier to enjoy.

I managed to pass the crucial first year exams, and in the summer I again hitchhiked to Rome.

Back in Durham for my second year, life was much more fun and less academically pressured and I was going out with one of the university beauts, a girl called Lesley Bunce. She was in her final year studying psychology; a clever girl. Drop dead gorgeous, too – a Monica Vitti type with a blonde bob. Although I had lost my virginity during the first year, I was still very inexperienced and Lesley was there to help. She was very sexy indeed, and she taught me everything I'd need to know about sex. Contraception was a new science in 1965 and I don't think the birth control pill even existed, but Lesley was very enlightened. She had been to the Marie Stopes Clinic in London to have a coil fitted and I guarantee she was the only girl in the university who had one. I used to stay in her room at St. Mary's College until three in the morning, fooling around and listening to the sounds of the sixties: Sonny and Cher, The Beatles, The Byrds, The Hollies, The Kinks and Elvis.

It was 1965 and I was in uni and I was in love. It was perfect really; a culture and time that, little did I know, was to become written about and looked back on as something so very special. Years later, I would meet people who would pose the same question: "What was it like… you know… growing up in the sixties?" So many people I met in the nineties wished they had grown up in the sixties and they'd talk about it with such nostalgia, as if the era – my era – was the favourite. Of course, I was in the thick of it and had no idea. I remember

'Good Vibrations' playing by The Beach Boys as I climbed out of her window at 3am, walked across the green, past the rose bushes and the old building and then into my college in the castle. I went back there recently and could not believe the castle wall I used to climb over; it must have been fifteen or twenty feet high. We really did have to do so much climbing in and out of colleges because they were strictly segregated.

Nowadays, there are mixed colleges, but then it was boys or girls, and it was a sending-down offence to be caught after 10pm in the wrong college. That segregation was in direct opposition with the sexual liberation of the time, or, according to the parents of most of my peers, "irresponsible excess and flamboyance". This liberation and feeling of independence wasn't just restricted to Britain and the US; in Africa, thirty-two countries gained independence, of which Zambia was but one. It was something that was happening the world over – like I said, it was a time.

Lesley Bunce left Durham at the end of my second year and I was very sad. The situation I had with Lesley seemed to be quite perfect. With her I had all the benefits of a beautiful and fantastic girl, while at the same time I was (as I had come to like it) alone, but now I was alone without her...

I had to stay in Durham during the summer at the end of my second year, to knuckle down and focus on my dissertation. Durham City itself is a beautiful medieval town, well known for its eleventh-century cathedral and castle that sits on the River Wear. In the 1960s, coal-mining villages surrounded it (most mines are now closed), and because Lesley was so charming and pretty, she and I were the only students allowed into the small pub in the city that was only frequented by miners. There was normally quite a lot of animosity between the miners and the students, but because of her we had special privileges. I had two friends from the pub, both of whom were real hard nuts. One was very tall and the other very short. They would take me out into the miners' villages and would always, always get into fights with the locals – and win, too. It would start with a confrontation, followed by a head-butt, followed by what could only be described as a Fritz the Cat cartoon ball of flying arms and legs, until my two friends would inevitably emerge from the pile, leaving their opponents on the floor battered and bruised – even when outnumbered. I was always lucky to be able to stay out of it, and just perch on a nearby stool with Lesley on my arm.

It got to the stage where we'd enjoy watching, and got really good at scouting out the best place to perch and watch from. On one occasion, I told

Lesley about my flying tooth incident back in Margate, which I realised didn't make me out to look anything but a scaredy cat. That was okay, though; she wasn't after a brawler, she was after me, and I her, and that was what it was back then – a sweet little sixties romance.

After Lesley had left, I was hanging out with John Slater, the son of the master of University College and an undergraduate at Oxford. I took him with my two rough pals to one of these villages one night and he witnessed the violence. I don't think he had ever seen anything like it before. He was petrified and I felt quite smug about that for some reason.

During that same summer, there was a Durham miners' gala, which was the largest trade union gathering in the UK. Over 300,000 people attended, which was then seven times the population of Durham City, and there was a marching parade, with brass bands following behind banners. But more than anything else, there was drinking and there was fighting. I went to the parade, but I was told by my two Geordie friends to keep my mouth shut. Any sign that I came from the south of England and I would be done for. I was even persuaded to learn a phrase of Geordie dialect, which I still remember: "Wai ai, youse mackin gun?" I'm still not quite sure what it means, but I think it's "Are you taking the piss?" – as if I would have ever said that to a drunk Geordie. The pubs in Durham would all run dry of beer and no more drink brought with it bad behaviour, so mostly I stayed at home and kept myself out of danger. I had rented a small flat over the road from the little miners' pub that I'd use, and I remember staying in and listening to the radio and watching telly – and a good job, too. I went to the pub the next day; the walls were splattered with blood and the road outside was covered in broken glass.

At the beginning of my third year, I was chairman of the Fresher's Conference. This was, of course, a dream job and the perfect opportunity to check out the new crop of girls. It was a week-long event, introducing the fresh boys and, more importantly, fresh girls to the university clubs and societies before the rest of the students came back. I was starting to become well known throughout the uni and I had now been playing hockey for the first team since I came to Durham. In my final year, I became captain.

Despite my success in the team, my popularity among my peers and my success with the fresher girls, something was missing and I had begun to think about what line of work I wanted to be in after I graduated. So many undergrads seemed to drift into teaching for want of anything else to do and I knew I didn't want to do that. I stopped asking any of my friends and I began reading books.

I read a new book called *Anatomy of Britain*, by Anthony Sampson, and one about advertising by Vance Packard called *The Hidden Persuaders*. It seemed from Sampson's book that the job of account executive – the person in the advertising agency who looks after the client – consisted mainly of taking the client out for long lunches. Well, that sounded like a great job to me and I applied to J. Walter Thompson, the agency featured in Sampson's book, but they seemed mainly interested in Oxford and Cambridge graduates. So, I applied to the London offices of two other American agencies: Erwin Wasey and Hobson Bates. They both offered me a job – I believe mainly on the strength of my extra-curricular activities, like my time in Africa. Competition for places was fierce and both agencies had over 400 applicants for two or three vacancies. I chose Hobson Bates because there was no stipulation that I had to get a degree. This made my last few months at Durham reasonably stress-free, but I still wanted to graduate, so I had to put my head down and study hard.

I graduated as a Bachelor of Arts with Honours in the summer of '67. It was the Summer of Love and something was about to happen to my world.

CHAPTER 6

Cinecittà

"Which way went he that killed Tybalt?"
– Johnny Cigarini

During my summers in Rome, starting when I was at Dean Close School and throughout university, I worked as a film extra at Cinecittà, the film studios outside Rome. They were the studios used to film *Ben-Hur*, *Cleopatra*, much of the works of the great Fellini and more recently Scorsese's *Gangs of New York*. Mussolini founded the studios for propaganda purposes under the slogan 'Il cinema è l'arma plù forte' (Cinema is the most powerful weapon). I would later come to disagree, of course, and replace 'Il cinema' with 'Il advertising'!

The studios were bombed during the war by the Allies, and following World War II, Cinecittà was used as a displacement persons camp for an estimated 3000 refugees. I was there when all that had come to pass and Cinecittà was on the rise. For me, it was a great job because it gave me some pocket money, but only took up two or three days a week, with the rest of the time to go to the beach. My sister Maria and her husband Peter were members of Gambrinus, an exclusive beach club at Ostia, not far from where they lived at EUR – the beautiful 'fascist architecture' suburb of Rome. Everyone at Gambrinus was shocked that I travelled from England by 'auto-stop' (hitchhiking); it was simply unheard of in Italy. I remember feeling quite proud when they were all so shocked. It even helped me stand out a little.

I wasn't your average common-or-garden film extra; I was what they called a 'figurazione speciale' – a featured extra. Most of the films shot in Cinecittà were now American productions, and the producers didn't want to make it too obvious that they were shooting in Italy, so they employed non-Italians to stand near the main stars. I worked with John Wayne and Kirk Douglas in *Cast a Giant Shadow*, playing one of a group of generals. John Wayne was a friendly man and we would talk often. Kirk, however, always seemed to be in character, and just sat around silently jutting that famous dimpled chin of his. He had a son of around sixteen, who was working as a rather officious assistant director at the time. I met Michael Douglas years later, when we had a stoned evening with Chessy Thyssen, and I asked him if it was he on the set of *Cast a Giant Shadow*. It was.

I worked with a number of other famous stars like Joseph Cotten and Angie Dickinson, but I don't want to over-egg my artistic contribution. I mainly just stood around, rather than acted. It was just a fun job really, giving me that extra pocket money I needed, and it was a great opportunity to see how film sets worked. Sometimes I would just sit on the side for hours and simply watch. I worked with Victor Mature and Peter Sellers on a film called *After the Fox*, directed by Vittorio De Sica. Sellers had recently had a heart attack and had to spend most of the time in his trailer resting, but he was with a new bride – a very pretty woman called Britt Ekland. I saw her and felt rather flabbergasted. I couldn't understand how Mr Sellers managed to gather any rest. Years later, I'd often see Sellers in Tramp and he was still the lucky charmer. He was going out with my friend at the time, a beautiful Swedish Countess named Titi Wachtmeister.

I met an actor from San Francisco called Clint Eastwood, although on this film he was 'the man with no name'. I had heard at the time that he was pretty good, although I had never seen *Rawhide*. I just knocked on his dressing room door with no apprehension at all. He was shooting the spaghetti western *For a Few Dollars More* and was on his break. I asked him if I could work as an extra on his film. I remember he towered over me, his face creased and tensed and his eyes were slit and piercing. "It's not my department," he said to me. Looking back, I had a classic Clint encounter and, at the time, I didn't even know it. He was also a friendly man. So, I was just a kid and I had already met John Wayne, Clint Eastwood and Kirk Douglas. One thing was very clear about these men: they had a sense of confidence, a kind I had never seen before, and I guess I wanted it, too. I also worked with Lee Van Cleef, who was a real hoot. He would punch me in the stomach each morning in the coffee bar, just for laughs. They were good days and the work was exciting – much better than frying eggs in the Margate hotel.

In all my time spent on the different sets, I had only two lines. In these Italian films, the dialogue, especially in the spaghetti westerns, was always dubbed and the recorded dialogue was usually badly translated from Italian. So the exact line I had in *The Tramplers* was, "Up there, it's your son that shot at you!" My grammar teacher would have turned in his grave, but I got the line word-perfect. I was 'working' with Robert Mitchum and his real-life son Jim on the film, and now I had a speaking part, I was definitely part of the gang! I would go out with Jim Mitchum, who was about my age, every night to the Via Veneto, the scene of Fellini's movie *La Dolce Vita*. We would go to Dave's Bar, owned by Dave Crowley, a former lightweight British boxing champion from the 1930s. Jim and I, of course, would be looking for girls and we were 'in the movies', so we found some without much trouble.

In the summer of '67, after my final year at Durham and before I started working in advertising, I had my best film extra job. I was in the Via Veneto one night when I ran into a group of British actors. I met them because I had been to school with one of the actors, Rick Winter, who by then called himself Richard Warwick. Richard was a very sweet man but was not destined to live much longer. He became one of the first victims of AIDS. The rest of the group were: John McEnery, a fine actor; Murray Head, who would become a pop star and have a big hit with 'One Night in Bangkok'; and Bruce Robinson, who later became famous for what is now considered one of the greatest British films of all time, *Withnail and I*. They were all in Rome working on *Romeo and Juliet*, directed by Franco Zeffirelli. I got a job on the film through Richard Warwick and we worked together for a month. The funny thing was, I was an extra in the film for both the Montagues and the Capulets, but mostly I can be seen in the finished film as one of Romeo's gang members.

Director Franco Zeffirelli and his producer Dyson Lovell were seriously gay, and would take young film extras into their trailers whenever there was a break in filming. On my last day, Zeffirelli gave me a line to speak: "Which way went he that killed Tybalt?" It never made it into the finished film, but then neither did most of the parts played by the British actors, and they were professionals who had worked on the film all summer. I, however, was less than an amateur and only on the film a month. I am sure Zeffirelli only gave me the line to soften me up, or should I say harden me up, and I suppose I was grateful to him for it, but there was perhaps yet another ulterior motive. He came into my dressing room just as I was down to my briefs, put two floppy wrists on my shoulders, and said in broken English, "Why you 'ave to leave so soon? I 'aven't seen nearly enuff of you", while staring at my crotch. "Why you no stay in Rome and become actor?"

"I'm going back to London for a job in advertising, because I want to use my brain," I replied, slightly offhandedly. Well, the man went ballistic, defending the acting profession. Perhaps it was a stupid remark, but at least it brought the seduction attempt to an end. I had obviously refined my firewall over the years. The other thing that historic moment did was help me realise how made up my mind was to work in advertising, how determined I now was. Maybe I even had it in me to get good at it? Win some awards? What about even gaining respect? Like some of those movie actors had, or even like my father had gained in his profession.

It was true; the images on the internet I later found, that my father had taken of those movie actresses, was advertising work he was doing. I was following in his footsteps, subconsciously. The war had prevented him from achieving, so perhaps I could continue the things he couldn't – like carrying on a legacy. Maybe even creating one.

PART 2

CHAPTER 7

Freedom

"It's all for nothing if you don't have freedom."
– William Wallace

After my last summer in Rome, and working on *Romeo and Juliet*, I returned to London to start work at Hobson Bates Ltd. I bought myself a cream suit with black pinstripes from Burton the Tailors. It was September 1967, the Mamas & the Papas were top of the charts with 'San Francisco', and *Casino Royale* had just hit the flicks. It was a September I will never forget. I went to work at my first pro job and my salary was £1000 a year, plus luncheon vouchers of course.

I joined on the same day as two other graduates, but when we got to the office, it was all a bit of an anti-climax. To start, no one seemed to be expecting us, or in fact know what to do with us. They all seemed too busy, everything was so frantic – it was the world of advertising. I recall standing at the front of the office, admiring the ringing phones, the papers being thrown, the loudness, the tempers, the red faces. We idled away the morning until someone suggested we go to the pub over the road for lunch. I guess I was nervous and needed to calm the old nerves, so I had a couple of pints that sunny day, but I was not used to drinking at lunchtime. I was also tired from my journey back from Rome. We got back to the office they had allocated for us and there was still nothing to do. I laid myself down on the sofa and went to sleep, but only for a moment. Roy Beaumont, the director in charge of the graduates, came into the office and cried out loud to all who could hear him, "HA... that Cigarini's already ASLEEP!" I suppose it wasn't the best thing I could have done on my first day in the office. An advertising tycoon to be? I wouldn't have put my money on me! But then again, I've never been a betting man...

★

My other sister Christina was by now married to a graphic designer, Gordon Miller. While working at Hobson Bates, I lived with them in their two small attached houses in Colville Place, off Charlotte Street. This made it very convenient to walk to work at Hobson Bates on nearby Gower Street. By 1968, I was living in Chelsea in a flat off the King's Road, with four young chaps. In total, we were paying twenty-five pounds rent a week. In total! Yes, just five pounds each. I was the lucky one (again) because I had my own room, but it was really more like a large cupboard; the bed took up the entire floor and it had no windows. You would simply open the door and fall onto the bed, something that I hear is still quite common for youngsters in London – living on a budget without any money to put down for a deposit on a double room. I think the going rate is a whopping £600 a month these days, just for a room. I don't know how they manage it.

One of my flatmates was Richard Synge, who I had been to school with. He was related to the famous Irish playwright J.M. Synge. Another was a Russian ballet dancer named Micha who was a look-alike for Rudolph Nureyev, and one was Vaughn Ingham, who later became a junkie. John Leaver made up the group. He was into music and introduced me to the sounds of Family, with Roger Chapman, and Sly and the Family Stone. The sixties were almost over and the seventies were coming. I could hear it in the music; there was a change coming, a big change. If the sixties were for me to mark a coming of age, the seventies would be the coming of money. But it wasn't just me, there was a sense of enterprise in people everywhere – they were tired from all the parties and it seemed people were ready to knuckle down and get to work. Or was it just me?

John Leaver sold advertising space for a new gig guide and he thought it was going to hit the big time. I remember when the owners Tony Elliott and his girlfriend had come down early from Keele University to start it. It was a fortnightly publication, and every two weeks they would come over to our flat. We would all sit on the carpet folding the single sheet in two, and addressing envelopes to the subscribers. The later-to-become-legendary DJ from the *Old Grey Whistle Test*, Bob Harris, was co-editor, so he would also come to the flat. The name of the publication was *Time Out* magazine. Tony Elliott bought out his, by then, ex-girlfriend very early, and *Time Out* went global. It is now published in sixty different countries. I still smile when I see a copy. I think back to the gang sat on the floor all those years ago.

In 1969, I bought my own flat. I worked at Hobson Bates with a very nice lady, Carol Adler; she was a copywriter and the daughter of harmonica maestro Larry Adler. She had a small flat at the other end of the King's Road, in a mansion block called Argyll Mansions, just on the corner of Beaufort Street. She was getting married at the time and moving to a bigger flat in Mayfair, so she sold me the fixtures and fittings to her King's Road flat for 500 quid. This is how people got cheap leases, paying what was called 'key money'. Yet again, I got lucky; though on my taxed income there was no way I could ever have afforded £500, my granny had left me that much in her will from the sale of her house. The rent on the flat was cheap, just a tenner a week. Eventually that £500 from Granny escalated on the property ladder to £3 million by 2008. I'm not bragging, I'm just telling you… I'm lucky!

Somehow or other, Carol and I got hot and steamy the night before her wedding. We both managed to resist the temptation to consummate the marriage with the wrong guy, and I think she was always grateful to me for that. I still have strong memories of my first few days in my new flat. It was so exciting for me to have my own place for the very first time, after the years of growing up at Granny's and through uni, and pretty much living out of a suitcase since then. I had very little furniture – just a sofa, which Carol had left me – but that was fine, perfect in fact. The word to describe my life was perfect and I had the most important thing: a stereo system.

Int. King's Road Flat – Night

Johnny lays flat on his back, staring into bliss, his head between speakers. Dylan's 'Lay Lady Lay' seeps out of the speakers and into the room. A smile comes on young Johnny's face. His lips whisper a word. Just one single word.

JOHNNY:
Freedom.

FADE OUT:

As account executive on the Playtex account, I had to attend a sales conference. There were three girls modelling the bras at the conference: two young twins from Malta and an exotic one from British Guiana, Shakira Baksh. She had come third in the Miss World competition in '67 and stayed on in London to do modelling work. As the story goes, Michael Caine saw her on a TV commercial for Maxwell House coffee and thought she was "the most beautiful girl in the world". He became obsessed with finding her, and eventually he did. He tracked her down through his agent and they have now been happily married for over forty years. It's a great story and I was fortunate enough to have dinner with them one night after the premiere of the film *The Mission*. I was taken there by a beautiful Greek-Scottish girl, Stassia Stakis, whose family owned an eponymous chain of hotels. She was a friend of Michael Powell, who was also at our table. Powell, along with his directing partner, Emeric Pressburger, were pioneering film directors from the 1940s. They made award-winning films, the most famous one being *The Red Shoes*. Powell is considered one of the great British film directors of that era – up there even with Hitchcock. He was with his wife Thelma Schoonmaker, who was a film editor, had edited all of Scorsese's films since *Raging Bull*. The food was good, but Michael Caine saying "not a lot of people know that" was even better.

The young twins at the Playtex conference were Mary and Madeleine Collinson. They were seventeen and had just arrived in London, in April 1969. The first Zeppelin album had been released, Nixon had become president, John Lennon married Yoko and I took one of the twins, Madeleine (I think), out for dinner after the sales conference. She came back to my flat and, me being me, I didn't dare make a move. I thought she was just so sweet and innocent. My mistake, she certainly was not. She told me they were living in Connaught Square, with someone called Victor Lownes. The name didn't mean anything to me. I later found out that Victor ran the Playboy Clubs, and had allegedly been sleeping with the twins at that time! The next year they were in *Playboy* magazine, the first identical twin Playmates of the Month. They became B-movie actresses, and made *Groupie Girl*, *Twins of Dracula* and *Some Like It Sexy*.

I stayed two and a half years at Hobson Bates and the client lunches, as promised by Anthony Sampson, did happen, which I took quite a fancy to, but I didn't actually like the work. The problem was that account executives had three or so clients, and you had them for the entire year. This made it quite monotonous, and if you didn't get along with your client, there wasn't a thing you could do. I personally had difficulty finding any chemistry with my accounts. They were tobacco company Gallaher's (I had never had a cigarette in my life), Playtex bras (I didn't wear a bra, and neither did most of the girls I knew) and Reckitt & Colman (I hated Hull in the north of England, where they were based). Also, account executives had to wear suits and ties, and I could see that the creative types were having more fun in the free-and-easy 1960s. I decided to switch tracks; after all, it was 1969 – a year of change.

By that time, my sister Luisa was back in Italy, after a successful career in London as a model. She had been Miss Shell and every Shell petrol station had a life-sized cutout of her on the forecourt. By then, she was working in Milan, as the sales representative for all of David Puttnam's English photographers. David had started out like me as an account executive, but at Collett Dickenson Pearce, and was now a very successful photographer's rep. Later, he would become a top film producer and win a Best Picture Oscar for the great *Chariots of Fire*. He is now Lord Puttnam and I was to see a lot of him when I was a friend of Charles Saatchi – but not yet.

I went to visit Luisa in Milan. I stayed at a hotel called the Arena, but it was known as something quite different – "the Fuck Palace" – and only models were allowed to stay there. Through one of Luisa's photographer friends, I was able to get a room, but I was the only man there (and yes… I did). Outside, there were all the Italians in their Ferraris and Alfa Romeos, waiting for the girls to come out. I met one of my lifelong friends that time in the Arena, Roberta Booth, a photographer and holographer. Roberta was later to introduce me to Baja (pronounced Baha) California, where I was to live in the years to come. Nothing happened between us at the Arena, but we did have a brief fling back in London. She is incredibly beautiful, still a peach and one of my best friends, and I talked through with her how I was considering following in David Puttnam's footsteps to become a photographer's rep. Meanwhile, my sister Christina, her husband Gordon Miller and I had been going out to dinner every Friday – usually to Luba's Bistro off Knightsbridge. They had a lot of creative friends including photographers. Between them and Luisa, I got together four photographers who needed repping. I was all set to go, and just about to resign from Hobson Bates, when one of those fortuitous events that changed everything occurred…

CHAPTER 8

Brooks Baker Fulford

1969 was the year we went to the moon, when Lennon and Yoko did their 'bed-in', *Easy Rider* blew cinema audiences' minds wide open, US troops began withdrawal from Vietnam and The Beatles were photographed on Abbey Road. It was December 1969 and I was at a Christmas party put on by Chappell's, the music publishers. I was standing at a bar talking to a stranger and was telling him my new career plans.

"You should come work for us," he said to me. 'Us' was a new commercials film production company called Brooks Baker Fulford and he was Jim Baker, the producer partner and managing director. The other two names were top stills photographers Bob Brooks and Len Fulford, who had both just started directing commercials. Brooks Baker Fulford was the first of a new wave of production companies that were owned by the directors and not the producers. Colour television had only just happened in 1969 and they were the pioneers in shooting commercials where beauty and lighting were vital, followed shortly afterwards by another visual pioneer, Ridley Scott. We made 'cheers' at the bar and I downed my drink in one. It's funny looking back at where and how the moments came – you know, the big moments, the ones that change it all, like a certain phone call, a ride on the bus, a walk through a park, a drink at a bar at a Christmas party. Jim invited me to meet the directors.

Brooks had a studio in Irongate Wharf, Paddington, and Fulford on Maddox Street, off Bond Street. The production office where Jim and another producer Martin McKeand worked was on Princes Street, off Regent Street in the West End. I was to replace a young man who had just left BBF to become a director at another company, Jenny & Co. His name was Adrian Lyne. It took him two years to be offered his first commercial directing job, but he stuck at it and had the last laugh. He became one of the world's top commercials directors and a magnificent feature film director of blockbusters *Fatal Attraction*, *Flashdance* and *Indecent Proposal*.

Jim Baker invited me to the production office on Princes Street where I met Bob Brooks, Len Fulford and Martin McKeand. They liked me. They offered me the job.

★

Carol Adler, the gal I bought my King's Road flat from, had introduced me to a beauty called Jenny Sieff. Jenny was from the Marks and Spencer family and I met her charming parents. I remember her father telling me "Marks and Spencer doesn't believe in advertising." I smiled about that, years later, when the struggling brand was revived by an ad campaign featuring my mate Twiggy.

Jenny and I went out for such a short time, and such a long time ago, that she will probably be outraged to be featured in my autobiography, but she will be nonetheless. Those months were significant and I shall tell you why. First of all, on a personal level, she was the only girl I have ever lived with, before or since, although only for a few weeks (she complained I didn't talk to her, something I was to hear time and time again). Secondly, and more importantly, she was instrumental to my accepting the Brooks Baker Fulford job. She was a friend of Jenny Armstrong of Jenny & Co. Jenny Sieff and I went to Jenny Armstrong's house in Chelsea for Sunday lunch, and there she invited me to her office to discuss the BBF job offer with Adrian Lyne.

I'll never forget meeting Adrian. He was the first man I had ever seen wearing a wolf-skin overcoat and it just looked fab. Little did I know then that Adrian would go on to be a true superstar director, but looking back, he definitely had a zing. Amazing, looking back… where we all came from, what we're doing now… the journeys, the stories, the lessons learnt. Talking to Adrian persuaded me to accept the job offer at Brooks Baker Fulford. My feelings told me to go for it, so I did and it was the smartest move I ever made. I joined the company in April 1970.

The job marked a big change, leaving behind the sixties for good and beginning a new career. My salary was instantly increased to £1750 per annum. I put away the suit in a bottom drawer and went out and bought a grey leather jacket and some blue jeans – my new work clothes. It certainly was the right decision.

Two months later, we were in Venice at the International Advertising Film Festival. Bob Brooks, Jim Baker and Len Fulford were all sailing enthusiasts, and they had rented a twenty-three-metre racing ketch called Stormvogel for a sailing holiday up the Dalmatian coast, and to provide accommodation while at the Venice Festival. Jim took me for a walk along the quayside and it was there he told me he was leaving the company due to his differences with Bob Brooks. Brooks, a small East Coast American, was famous for having a great temper and would even shout at his clients, sometimes hurling the product at the wall. In 1970, when shooting the famous Cadbury's Smash Martians commercial (voted best commercial of the century in 1999), he even lost his rag with one of the puppets and was ready to throttle the damn thing. I could certainly understand where Jim was coming from. Martin McKeand bought Jim Baker out and became managing director, and within two months of joining the company, I was already the second-in-line producer. The company changed its name to Brooks Fulford and it was decided henceforth to only call itself according to the directors it represented. So in '73 when Ross Cramer joined, it changed name again to Brooks Fulford Cramer. (Ross had been Charles Saatchi's partner in a creative consultancy called Cramer Saatchi, so when Ross left to become a director, and Charles' brother Maurice joined the consultancy, it became Saatchi and Saatchi, and grew to become the biggest advertising agency in the world – Margaret Thatcher's fave!).

Martin McKeand was a nice man to work for. Those were heady days in the advertising business. Selling the directors was an important part of the producer's job and it would usually happen over a lunch. On down days, when we were not filming, we would regularly go for boozy ones with ad agency producers or creative teams to the Trat (Mario and Franco's Trattoria La Terrazza), L'Escargot or other joints in Soho. The clients would invariably offer scripts for a new campaign over the coffee… or the Sambuca.

Martin was a member of the notorious Colony Room Club. This was a members-only afternoon drinking club that managed to serve drinks when all the pubs had to legally shut for the afternoon. It was run by an infamous lesbian called Muriel Belcher, assisted by her equally gay barman Ian Board. It was a typically tiny Soho dive on Dean Street and very popular with artists. Its interior was painted in a vile green or 'Colony Room green', and its staircase stunk so badly, that members even gave going up them a name: "going up the dirty stairs". It was certainly a place for eccentrics, misfits and outsiders, managing to attract both lowlifes and artists. Years later, for the young artists Tracey Emin and Damien Hirst, it was a magnet.

One of the founding members and regulars was the great and famous painter Francis Bacon. I think he was there every time I went in, and we became friends very quickly as we had something in common: the only school he had ever attended was Dean Close School, the place where I had moved to be with Revd Ken Senior and family. We were there in different years though, so we wouldn't have known each other. We'd reminisce about those starched detachable Van Heusen collars in style 11 and how hands were not to be put in trouser pockets for going into town. It was interesting to think back about it all, in the context of having now lived through the sixties.

After a boozy lunch with advertising agency creatives, and then drinking at Muriel's in the afternoon, Martin and I got pretty hammered, but it didn't matter; the producer's work was done for the day if he had scripts for a new campaign in his pocket. Ian Board always called me Big Cock and for years I assumed it had just been his way of coming on to me, but Martin reminded me recently that apparently, in one moment of drunkenness, I had a cock contest with Francis Bacon in the Colony Room Club. For the record, I only have a slim recollection of this, and I guess it's just a pity the winner didn't get a painting. There were all kinds of goings-on in that club. It was, to say the least, bohemian, and later where Kate Moss once worked as a barmaid, Dylan Thomas threw up on the carpet and even Princess Margaret paid a visit.

*

One role of the producer is to find work. This means showing the directors' showreels to the advertising agency producers and creative teams, and trying to get them to give you a job. In America, they have sales reps who work on commission to do that, but that was only just starting to creep into London when I left the business in the mid-1990s. Once the production company has been asked to bid on a job, the producer has to do the budget, which means working out how much the job will cost and how much to charge the client. In my day, this was done very differently – with a calculator and something called a pen and a piece of paper. The production company covers its overheads and makes its profit by what's called a mark-up, on the basic costs of the job. Of course, if it's a fantastic, potentially award-winning idea, then the agencies get production companies to do commercials at cost. Productions are bid competitively, particularly in the US, but in the earlier days in London, they were often just single bids for the director the agency had chosen to shoot the commercial. Before the job is awarded, the agency requires meetings between the director, the producer, the agency producer and the creative team to discuss execution of the script. If it's bid competitively, very often a job is won or lost on the director's interpretation. Once the job has been awarded and signed off by the agency's client (e.g. Coca-Cola), the producer's job is to set up the shoot. This means scheduling it according to the director's availability, organising the casting, finding the locations or briefing the set designer if it's to be shot in a studio, booking the studio, booking the crew, ordering the wardrobe department, and so on – so that on the day of the shoot, everything is ready for the director and film crew to shoot and to run as smooth as silk. Sometimes this can mean protecting the director from the clients, but usually the director will have good communication with the agency creative teams and producers.

Shooting one commercial can usually take between one and three days, depending on the complexity of the production, but if it's part of a campaign of commercials involving a series of films, it takes much longer. It's the producer's job to coordinate everything. Producers and directors usually work as a team and I'm not being falsely modest if I say the director is much more influential and important than the producer. The director is the star, and that's who everyone wants and wants to be. The agency also has a producer, whose job is to liaise with the production company producer. The agency has video playback to see what is being shot and approves it as they go along. BFCS pioneered the use of video playback and was possibly even the first company to use it through Joe Dunton, who developed the system. If anything goes wrong during a shoot, and things often would, the production company producer has to sort it. After the shoot is over, the producer has to coordinate the post-production with the editor, the director and the clients. In the US, this is usually done directly by the agency, and the director has very little say in the editing beyond seeing the final cut. Directors in England, though, would not stand for that.

*

By the late 1980s, I wasn't producing any more. In my capacities as managing director of BFCS Ltd. (the English company) and president of BFCS Inc. (the American one), I was in control of the two companies with the brilliant help of

Linda Maxwell and Gary Feil, the two executive producers in New York and LA. Running a production company is a bit like being the manager of a rock band. You don't get your name on the door, but you have to deal with a bunch of talented stars who earn an obscene amount of money, and with many big egos. There are financial rewards, though; a top commercials director can earn a couple of million dollars a year. Finding and keeping good directors is the hardest role for a company owner, and making them happy and remaining in your company is the name of the game. I have tried hard not to think about any of this for eighteen years; it's big business, big stress, big egos and big parties. It was a heap of fun, though; I'd just never have thought it was all going to move so fast. Had I known, I guess I'd have tried to enjoy the ride even more. Like the great Billy Wilder once said, "Hindsight is always twenty-twenty." But I'm getting ahead of myself. Back to the King's Road.

CHAPTER 9

King's Road: Part 1

The King's Road in Chelsea was the epicentre of the swinging sixties and seventies London scene. Today, although unique places still exist, the global chains have moved in too, and its edge has been lost, its independence. But back then... then it was different, and different to anywhere else in London. It began as a private royal road only for Charles II, but by the mid-nineteenth century, us common folk were allowed down with horse and cart. Some houses date back even to the eighteenth century and the King's Road was where Thomas Arne is said to have composed 'Rule Britannia', nonetheless. The biggest bragging points, however, come from the fact that it's where 007 lived, or at least in a square just off it...

Outside of work my life was mainly rock 'n' roll and not in a clichéd way, in a genuine way. Moving into my new flat on the King's Road, I had stumbled into a hornet's nest of groupies living next door to me in Argyll Mansions. One of them was Dany, a beautiful Swiss-French girl who was friends with a big gang of famous musicians. Next door on the other side was John Morshead, a guitarist in a band called Juicy Lucy. His girlfriend Diane (as gorgeous as they come) worked at *Private Eye*. Dany had a boyfriend, later husband, called Ronnie Holbrook, but for the first few months I was there, I didn't get to meet him – he was "laying low" in Marbella. He had imported marijuana in the panels of his car, a Lancia Flavia Coupé. When he returned to London I bought the car off him, and he always claimed there was still a packet of grass lost in it somewhere. Dany worked in a super-fashionable hairdressing salon in Beauchamp Place, called Sweeney Todd's, where she made the sandwiches. It was where all the rock stars went to get their hair cut, and Dany, being the sexy minx that she was, was friends with all of them. Back in the mansions, with John to my right and Dany to my left, two magnets for famous celebrities, I found myself watching them (the celebs) float in and out of our homes. This included The Faces, Rod Stewart's band – in particular the guitarist Ronnie

Wood and keyboard player Ian McLagan, who were regulars. Ronnie Wood's wife Krissie also used to drop by. Rod Stewart was always up and down the King's Road. It was impossible to miss him, driving his bright red Lamborghini Miura. It was my job to help Rod search in the pubs for Mona Solomons – "the sexiest girl on the King's Road" – who was just one of his army of admirers. Denny Laine, who sang the beautiful vocal on the Moody Blues' first hit 'Go Now', was also Dany's boyfriend while Ronnie was still in Marbella. In fact, Dany moved in with him for eight months, which made Ronnie pretty mad – but he also had a serious girlfriend of his own over in Spain, so what could he say? It was the seventies. Soon after, Denny Laine would become a founder member of Paul McCartney's Wings.

One day, Mick Jagger was in Sweeney's when Dany slipped him a note: "How about giving one to the sandwich girl?" A few hours later, I was trying to watch the footie in her place (I didn't have a telly and it was the 1970 World Cup), but it was really difficult, what with Mick and Dany hot at it behind me. Quite recently, I suggested to David Gilmour of Pink Floyd that I had met him in 1973 at the Hollywood Bowl, but he corrected me: "Actually Cigar, I met you before that, when I was visiting the French girl… next door." Let's just say Dany was a fun girl while Ronnie was away!

Dany had lots of girls staying with her too, mostly ones connected to musicians. I suppose you could describe them as super-groupies, but they were not the kind of groupie to hang out by the stage door. They were a bit, how to say, special. Keith Richards describes them well in his autobiography *Life*, as "friends who looked after us when the band came to town". Dany had three of these girls staying with her, or should I say, staying with us, due to the very 'flexible' sleeping arrangements between our two flats. One of the girls, Donna Curry, moved into my flat permanently, but it became quite the squeeze when Miss Cynderella arrived. She was a member of the first ever groupie band, Frank Zappa's creation, the GTOs (Girls Together Outrageously). Miss Mercy and Miss Lucy were also floating around, like perfect little butterflies. Miss Cynderella eventually married John Cale, the Welsh musical genius from the Velvet Underground. John would come to London and play solo shows at the Hammersmith Odeon. His act would feature live chickens and I thought his music was extremely bizarre. It was only years later that I realised his loud, abrasive and confrontational performances had been the forerunner of the new wave of a music called punk. His marriage to my fling was quite rocky and Cale wrote a song about her, 'Guts', which opens with the epic line, "The bugger in the short sleeves fucked my wife". He was referring to Kevin Ayers and not yours truly (just for the record). They divorced in 1975.

The third of the girls was a redhead, Janet Ferguson, who happened to be Frank Zappa's nanny. One of her friends, Gail, had married Frank, and the Zappas were living in London in a rented house on Ladbroke Grove with their first daughter Moon Unit. They had also just had their son, Dweezil. I went to Frank and Gail's house a few times. Frank was always playing avant-garde music from Eastern Europe, which I also found a bit weird, amongst other things at his place.

Donna Curry was just fab. She came from Chicago and was best friends with the band Chicago. They had just had hits with '25 or 6 to 4' and 'I'm a Man' and it was one of Donna's friends, Pam, who had married Terry Kath, the lead guitarist of the band. He was really quite a genius; a singer and multi-instrumentalist who played lead, rhythm and bass, banjo, accordion and the drums. He died in 1978, playing Russian roulette with a pistol.

Other famous groupies and musicians regularly came to my flat. Cynthia Plaster Caster was a frequent visitor. She had an infamous collection of plaster casts of rock stars' erect penises. She had her own special technique for getting them 'up'. I think it probably involved smudging her lipstick. I asked her if she wanted to do a cast of mine, but she apparently only had enough plaster for one more, and was saving that for David Bowie. I thought that was quite unreasonable myself.

*

I recall a time in 1973 when I was listening to Isaac Hayes in my flat when this scruffy American girl came by. She said she was a musician. In those days, who wasn't? This was well before the punk style was fashionable and I remember thinking, *Honey, you've got no chance, looking like that*. It was Chrissie Hynde, who had just moved to London from Akron, Ohio. She turned out to be a brilliant songwriter and later hit the big time with her band the Pretenders. Oh well, what did I know?

Chicago came to London on their way to the 1970 Isle of Wight Festival. The girls and I took them to the Speakeasy, the musicians' big hangout. Until I discovered Tramp, which was a more upmarket nightclub, I was at the Speak every night. I saw Ozzy and Sharon Osbourne in the Malibu Starbucks sometime in the 1990s, and Ozzy came up to me and said, "Don't I know you from the Speakeasy?"

Chicago hired a bus to get to the Isle of Wight and I was playing tag along. We all piled in and stopped off at Stonehenge en route. With the band was the fiancé of keyboard player Bobby Lamm, and what a beauty she was too. She married Bobby and became Karen Lamm, but later I met her in LA with Dennis Wilson, drummer of The Beach Boys. She had become Karen Lamm-Wilson. Amazingly, she still found time in between them to give me a few flings. I think back to my young days, the time in Margate with the girl who came to my room, in Africa with the exotic maid; times had definitely changed.

At the Isle of Wight Festival, I had two backstage passes from Chicago. I ran into a friend, Daniel Topolski, who used to cruise his Mini-Moke, an open jeep made from the Mini car, around the King's Road. He worked for the BBC and had two media area passes, so between us we had all backstage areas covered. Daniel was the son of well-known artist and illustrator Feliks Topolski, and he lived in a large family house overlooking Regent's Park. Daniel was a rower and he would later become well known for coaching the Oxford crew to about ten consecutive victories against Cambridge.

Chicago played on the Friday night and left, but I was staying on for the main act, Hendrix. I had taken a small tent, and Dan and I slept in that. Due to traffic problems, the show on Saturday ran very late and The Who didn't play until around 3am. They had military searchlights on the stage illuminating the crowd – all 600,000 of us – and by three in the morning, it really was quite a scene. By the time Sly and the Family Stone came on, it was daylight – Sunday morning. The organisers only sold one-day tickets, so when the show ended for the day, even if it was the next morning, everyone was thrown out while people were queuing to get back in for the next. Vendors were selling paper sacks as sleeping bags; the whole thing was just madness. Dan and I, of course, took it upon ourselves to go down the waiting line of people: "Wouldn't you rather sleep in a nice warm tent?" We eventually got a couple of willing girls, and it was hysterically funny having four people in a single tent, with arms and legs sticking out of the sides – very sexy, too, very seventies. Jimi Hendrix came on, opening with 'Foxy Lady', and it was simply incredible. A month later, he was dead.

The Isle of Wight is an island and for many quite an incredible obstacle course to get to. The fact that 600,000 came that year to a place of only 100,000 inhabitants was what made it the great event it has gone down in history to be, and the one that topped Woodstock, in my opinion, thanks to the music of The Doors, The Who, Hendrix, Free, Miles Davis, Supertramp, Procol Harum and the wonderful Joni Mitchell. Something happened on that island and everyone who was there knows what I'm talking about. I was proud to have gone and to have been a part of that great event and to have seen the great Hendrix. They said it was to be the last Isle of Wight Festival, but in thirty-two years that would all change.

CHAPTER 10

Outrageous Sexual Behaviour

There is one interesting sexual anecdote from my time at Hobson Bates and given this is my chance to tell the world of it, I shall. The media director lived in a modern house in the woods near Guildford, where he would have orgies every Sunday. I went for the first time to see with my own eyes that which I had heard of, but only in whispers – like the beds being covered with naked people.

It was the sixties and though this kind of thing happens today, it had not happened before, so when I was there it held something. There was a certain atmosphere where no one knew of the consequences; there was a quality to that, a certain unique kind of a... *je ne sais quoi*. I would go to the parties and I tried it, but to be honest I wasn't really into the group sex thing, or maybe it just didn't come naturally to me. I wanted one-on-one more. There were two parties: a normal one downstairs, where families would sit and drink tea and their children would play and run around (you'd have to see it to believe it), while upstairs, all of the sex action would proceed and certainly not with any caution. There was one gorgeous woman whose face and body I will remember forever, because she was absolutely, totally and utterly mesmerising. A goddess is a word I wouldn't use lightly, but for her I will and I do and I am. She was a goddess. She used to attend the downstairs party each week with her husband. I don't know why, but she wasn't interested in the orgies either. I was really attracted to her and the orgies just seemed to 'lend themselves' to a certain dynamic between the people downstairs – because we all knew what was going on upstairs.

Each week, despite neither of us being interested in the upstairs orgy and despite her being all prim and well-behaved downstairs with her hubby, I would ask her to come upstairs... with me... privately, so to speak. She was reluctant, but I could see she was tempted. Perhaps the orgasmic vibrations of the upstairs had begun to travel down and tempt her even. The dark side was alluring and

I could see it in her eyes, her breath, the way she hung her legs. Her mind was on the smut of the upstairs, the thing that London has had with it since antiquity – mischief and naughtiness – and now it was here for us to use and abuse. Now was the time, for her, for me, but there was a problem: her husband.

After a couple of weeks, she asked him if she could go with me, and perhaps she had been softly easing him in to his decision, as she told me he had given her the okay. I practically came in my pants right there. To me, it was as if God had answered my naughty prayer, or maybe I was just lucky one more time. Her husband had two rules: that she must not get pregnant – well, that seemed fair enough – and we were to use one of the bedrooms where no one else could see. Fine by me too, no arguments there at all.

I put the bedside lamp on the floor and put a sweater over it to soften the lighting. I remember that bit because I burnt a hole in my sweater – but I wasn't too bothered, as she had already begun to give me oral pleasure. It was delightful and I recall how fabulous and erotic she looked while she did it. I don't want to sound obnoxious, but it was as if she had been fantasising about it for some time; the sounds she was making, staring at me with her deep purple eyes and gripping my thighs with her nails, tasting and loving my penis.

Sadly, the fantasy play-out was not to last. Only a few minutes had passed and there was a loud banging on the door. It was her husband, screaming into the room. She leapt off the bed and went out to him. Later, I found out from her that he had gone for a walk into the garden, depressed because she was with me. Unfortunately (for all), while strolling around the garden, he had looked up and seen the shadow of her giving me a blow job on the ceiling of the bedroom. He was furious, because she would not do that to him. She obviously considered it too dirty for her husband, but okay for me. Quite a sweet sentiment, really. Actually I felt sad for him that I had made him depressed, but I probably did him a favour. I bet he got it after that. I hope so anyway; she was to-die-for. I stopped going to the orgies.

*

After I left Hobson Bates, Carol Adler gave me some jobs for Ultrabrite. We were shooting on the Ivory Coast and all staying at a beach club, where a pretty French girl was staying alone. I had enough experience by this stage and knew what my strengths were and how to use them. Let's just say I was a producer from London and Bob Brooks was my director (not a lie in it). She stayed the night with me, exhausted me in fact – I must say, I wasn't expecting to learn anything new from the pretty French girl, but every day's a school day, right? I couldn't keep up with her sexual demands and began joking about it the next day with Peter Biziou, the lighting cameraman, who also fancied her. Peter won the Academy Award for Best Cinematography for *Mississippi Burning*, for which he gave the best Oscar speech I'd ever heard: One word, "Thanks."

"If the pretty French girl is too much for you to handle, could I have a crack?" he asked me in-between takes.

"You can have her tonight," I assured him, "but I want her back tomorrow." However, the handsome devil never returned the goods. In fact, he took her to London and stayed with her for months. Outrageous, the pair of us, but that's how it was in those days – or that's how we were in those days. It was outrageous sexual behaviour. Was this sexual behaviour more commonplace in the sixties and seventies, or were we just young?

I was going out with Suze Randall at the time and she looked a picture with her short blonde hair, swinging about London in her Alfa Romeo 2600 Spider – a very desirable convertible indeed. She had found out that my friend Daniel Topolski was in hospital with hepatitis, having heard of him from the Wet Dream Film Festival. I suggested that she go give him a present. We went in to the hospital to his private room and I introduced them: "Daniel, this is Suze; Suze, this is Daniel." I drew the curtains, and went to stand guard. She gave him a blow job – a true present, and surely better than grapes or chocolates. Later, Suze went to America and became the world's leading female erotic photographer and the first female staff photographer for both *Playboy* and *Hustler*.

The first Wet Dream Film Festival was held in Amsterdam in 1970. Underground pornographic films were considered art in those days. There was not the proliferation that came with videos, adult TV channels and the internet. The first four rows at the cinema were reserved for people who wanted to masturbate, the next four for people who wanted to screw, and so on. Topolski had told me about a 'happening' during the sixties, even before I came to London. It was at the very respectable ICA, near Buckingham Palace. The event was held in a pitch-black room where no one could see anything and everyone inside the dark room was groping everybody else, as they so desired. If nothing else, surely that was the sixties. Doing things without worrying about the consequences, doing things without caring too much about who with, doing the things we always wanted but were never given a stage to play them out on – but there was a darkness to it, what with the underground abortions and so on. It was *A Hard Day's Night* but it was *Alfie* too – not all joy, especially for some of the girls.

I was behaving pretty outrageously myself in those days, but I had my own style with it. It wasn't too smutty and I always tried to remain a gent – 'tried' being the operative word. On a number of occasions, I would take advantage of my third floor balcony that overlooked the King's Road and chat a girl up at the bus stop on the street below. I'd use a corny line, which I'm sure none of them believed, that the buses were on strike and they could "come and wait it out in my flat" – and they would often come up for a tea or a coffee. Dear, oh dear! Many did and many were super cool, but none of them were like Tara...

Tara was from Toronto and we met one night at the Speakeasy. She visited London a few times in the following years and she would always see me. I was her first man, but not the first person she'd slept with. She came from a lesbian home as her mother lived with three other lesbians in her home in Canada. In fact, Tara told me once she had first been seduced by one of her mother's lesbian friends, so she was more experienced than most. Tara was unique in that she had the most seductive chat-up technique I ever saw, and by then I had seen quite a few. She had come to realise that many heterosexual women were curious about a lesbian 'experience' and this was in the seventies, even before being bisexual became a fashionable thing. Tara would always seduce girls for us – it was easy for her, looking like Isabelle Adjani – and it was her who was about to give me one of my most erotic experiences. She brought one girl back to my flat, someone she had picked up that night, and within moments I was lying on my back and the girl (who was very petite) was on her back on top of me, with my cock inside her. Meanwhile, Tara was kneeling on the bed, holding the girl's legs wide open and licking between her legs, and licking me as I went into the young babe. It's a shame things like this don't really happen to me anymore!

Over the years, I have found that many girls like fantasising about being with a woman during a sex session with a man. It seems to really turn them on for some reason. Once I visited Tara in Toronto and I was staying at the Four Seasons Hotel. It had a lively bar scene, one that singles would rely on to hook up. One evening, Tara seduced a woman who was there with her husband (but who was not with her at that specific moment) and she managed, somehow, to get her to come upstairs to my room for a threesome. Without the husband knowing, she had left the bar. It was the woman's first lesbian experience, and she loved it. Tara also stayed one night with me in the hotel. My room was on the fifteenth floor, and it was the only tall building in the area. In the morning, while she was giving me oral sex, a man on a harness suddenly appeared, cleaning the outside of the window. Being on the fifteenth, I hadn't bothered to draw the curtains, and he saw everything. After a few swishes of his wiper and with one flick of his control switch, he disappeared to the floor below. We giggled like a couple of school kids and it was the last time I saw her – Tara, the fantastic lesbian. I still think of her from time to time, like many of the beauts, like the wife who gave me erotic oral sex at the orgy. I make sure I think of them all regularly. I think it keeps me young and what a terrible waste it would be to forget. Don't you think?

It was in the mid-1970s and I went to the South of France, this time producing for director Ross Cramer. We used to shoot the 'Heineken Refreshes the Parts Other Beers Cannot Reach' commercials – a very famous campaign devised by Terry Lovelock at CDP, in which Victor Borge (the famous Danish-American pianist, comedian and raconteur with the laconic voice) did the voice-overs for the whole campaign for many years. In this film, for the only time, he was to appear in person, as the world's richest man (shot of Victor lying on a sunbed by the pool, idly tossing peanuts into the water). He has a beautiful house (shot of a fabulous mansion), beautiful women (shot of half a dozen models), valuable cars (shot of Rolls Royces), private planes and so on, but he is bored and dispirited. So the butler serves him the cold Heineken and it fails to refresh him, proving that it is better to be poor and refreshed, than rich and unrefreshed.

Looking for the location in France, we stayed at the Hotel du Cap, one of the leading hotels in the world. We eventually settled on a magnificent house called the Château de la Garoupe, at the point of the Cap d'Antibes. It had belonged to a British family since 1907 when Sir Charles McLaren bought four acres of the Cap. (According to *The Riviera Times*, it was sold to a nominee company of a London-based Russian oligarch for €22 million.) The chateau is on its own little peninsula on the Cap. You can stand in the main drawing room and look down the steps to the sea, turn 180 degrees and still be looking at the sea. Freddy Heineken, the owner of our client, lived next door. He was a friendly man (I would be too, with a net worth of 9.5 billion guilders) and was one of the richest people in the Netherlands. He came to the shoot with his daughter Charlotte, who is one of the richest women in the world now that Freddy has died. We had a helicopter for aerial footage of the house and the pilot took me up for a spin. It was fascinating seeing all the wonderful homes on the Cap d'Antibes. After that and the shoot, I was feeling good, feeling strong, feeling like a man... feeling like I was ready for more outrageous... sexual... behaviour, so I took one of the models, a great Australian girl called Jill Goodall, to a hotel in Juan-les-Pins for a dirty weekend.

The second Ultrabrite film was set in the Caribbean. As the producer, I decided to take the whole crew on a week's Club Med holiday. It was the most cost-effective method and I chose Martinique where there was a beautiful Club Med beach resort. Location scouts were unheard of in those days, so it was the producer's job to go ahead and find the locations. I booked myself an extra week's holiday at the Club and although I had never been to the Caribbean, I was not getting too excited about it. In fact, I was not feeling very well. I needed to go to my doctor in London about a septic finger, and I explained to him that I was listless, had no *joie de vivre*, and wasn't even looking forward to the trip to Martinique. I had gone from feeling so good after the helicopter, the shoot and the dirty weekend, to feeling so low. What was happening to me? He suggested I return from the Caribbean and go see a psychiatrist.

Going on a Club Med hol was fully inclusive of flights. It required transiting through Paris with an overnight stop and I booked into an old-fashioned Grand Hotel near the Gare du Nord. The only place I knew in Paris was the Café de Flore in St. Germain, a famous writers' hangout. I took a taxi there and a great opportunity presented itself. As I was getting out, a tasty-looking blonde Swedish girl was waiting to get in. I persuaded her to join me for a drink in the café and that quickly started us off on a full evening's crawl of the bars. She showed me St. Germain and we finished up back at my hotel for more dirtiness. There was a wedding reception in the ballroom; we crashed it, joined in the dancing and then went upstairs together.

The next day, I caught my flight to Martinique. On the plane, I threw up after eating my meal. I got to Martinique and settled into the Club Med. I rented a Mini-Moke and drove around looking for the locations and the boat we needed. In those days, I always put olive oil on my skin to suntan, as suntan lotion was unheard of. Driving around in the tropics in the open car, I got severely burnt on my face.

The Club Med had a wonderful breakfast buffet full of every fruit you could imagine, but every day I had to take my plate and sit outside the toilet, so that after eating I could rush in and be sick. I didn't know what was wrong with me. Depressed, vomiting, everything… I thought I'd got a tropical bug, but I had important work to do, so I did what all men are meant to do when they get sick: I ignored it and carried on working.

A couple of days later, I got the drips. The tasty blonde Swedish girl in Paris had given me a venereal disease. All had come clear! I didn't want to go to the doctor at the Club Med as I was too embarrassed, and I didn't want to cause panic in the Club, so I went to a doctor in town. He took one look at me. "Good God man, you're bright yellow!" With the burnt skin, I hadn't noticed that what I thought was a suntan was actually hepatitis. A day or so later, my eyes went yellow and my hepatitis blood test results were so bad that I was ordered off the island. My preparation week was nearly up, so I telephoned London and told Bob to bring another producer for the shoot. His first remark was not too sympathetic: "Did you find the boat?"

I met Bob and the film crew at the tiny airport and according to Bob, "I saw this yellow apparition approaching me, with its face hanging off."

I left the next day, but as I was waiting for my flight, I thought I would have one final swim. I trod on a sea urchin and could barely walk to the plane. When I got back to London, I had to go back to the doctor to have him pull the needles out of my foot. An infected finger, the clap, hepatitis, severe sunburn, and a sea urchin stuck in my foot. I was off work for three months.

★

Bob Brooks directed and I produced some wonderful shoots for Benson & Hedges, thanks to Lindsey Dale, the creative director on the account at Collett Dickenson Pearce. They were usually third-world spy or espionage stories, and were sixty seconds – twice as long as a standard TV commercial. They were for the cinema, as TV advertising for cigarettes was banned by then. This was in the mid-1970s.

The first one was set in the souk in Istanbul. It featured George Cole as a hapless spy trying to pass a military secret, disguised as a cigarette, to a Peter

Lorre-type character. Benson & Hedges 'Istanbul' won every award going, including a Gold Lion at the Cannes Advertising Festival, and that festival's first ever Classic Commercial Award.

The second B&H film was set in a rundown Middle Eastern port. For this shoot, the recce was the fun part. Bob, Lindsey Dale and I went to the Lebanon, Israel, Cyprus and Greece, and Hvar, Dubrovnik and Korcula in Yugoslavia, to look for a suitable port. We settled on the beautiful Venetian town of Hvar, now in Croatia and full of oligarchs' super-yachts, but in the seventies it was different – communist and quite rundown. We cleared the whole quay of boats and imported an old tramp steamer from Albania. The scene was a customs post on the quayside, manned by a customs official played by Herbert Lom (Police Commissioner Dreyfus with the twitchy eye in the *Pink Panther* films).

One evening there in Hvar, I met a pretty girl from Denmark. She looked young – I thought eighteen or nineteen – but I was still pretty young myself so I didn't mind. Like I said, she was pretty! We stayed together a few wee hours, making love and chatting about this and that in my room. I remember her well; she was the first girl I had ever met who smoked a pipe. In the small hours, I was walking her back to her hotel and ran into a very angry man. It was her teacher. It seemed she was on a school trip and hadn't told me.

The schoolgirl from Denmark, the Swedish girl, Jill, the pretty French girl, the erotic beauty at the orgy, they have all played their little roles in what has become my life – like I, I'm sure (I hope), have in theirs. Outrageous sexual behaviour would become a renowned reflection of the sixties and seventies that I lived through, but fortunately it didn't end there. A romance was about to begin.

CHAPTER 11

Patti D'Arbanville

During my convalescence from hepatitis in the King's Road, I was hanging out in a restaurant called the Casserole owned by Keith Lichtenstein, just over the road from my flat. It was the trendiest spot in town, featuring all the heroes of the swinging sixties, like David Bailey, Manolo Blahnik, Ossie Clark and Bryan Ferry. Keith was wealthy and owned an ex-artist's studio around the corner in the Vale in Chelsea, and a lovely Manor House in Sussex, which Bryan Ferry later bought from him. Keith had a fantastic collection of art deco furniture, until he tired of it and Elton helicoptered in and bought the lot.

Two of the regulars at the Casserole were Jose Fonseca and Amanda Lear. Jose owned Models One, the best model agency in town, and later married Dickie Kries, another of the old school swinging sixties mob who ran the Casserole. With huge eyes, long dark hair and inherited Portuguese genes, Jose was beautiful and herself a former model. Amanda Lear was tall and blonde, also drop-dead gorgeous, and very funny with it. She was even rumoured at one time to be transgender and she certainly had the humour of a seaman, which is what she was reputed to have been. I stayed a few days with them one Christmas at Keith's mansion. I hadn't been invited, but I was in the neighbourhood checking on a car restoration, so I dropped in to say hello and finished up staying a few days. When Christmas arrived, I had to vacate my room because they were expecting Susan Hampshire, the film actress. Amanda offered to share her room, but I was feeling a tad shy – after all, I hadn't really been invited, so I declined. I have always regretted that decision, not spending some time with Amanda and checking her out for myself. But they say everything happens for a reason and tracing back my steps, it was declining that invite that led me back home, to the Casserole and the place where I would meet her: Patti D'Arbanville, the woman I was about to fall in love with.

Patti was one of – if not *the* – great loves of my life. She was tiny, very cute, sexy as hell, but most of all she was a heap of fun. To put it simply, I adored her. She was, at that point, already a model. Andy Warhol had discovered her during a gig as a club DJ and cast her in his film *Flesh*, when she was just sixteen. It was after that she was discovered and began working as a model. When we met, she had just split up with Cat Stevens, who had written the song 'Lady D'Arbanville' about her and she was also the inspiration for his hit 'Wild World'. In fact, Steve (as we called him) seemed to be having difficulty letting go (and I was about to learn all about that). He would often accompany Patti and myself on our first few dates, usually to Parsons on the Fulham Road.

Patti lived in a basement flat in Draycott Place, off the King's Road. We would mainly go to hers to hang out because I had all sorts of people living at my place. She had a flatmate, Annie Hanson, who was another model and Casserole regular. Annie had a boyfriend too, who, interestingly, in spite of being very prim and proper himself, was in fact a cat burglar of country mansions – and every weekend he would come back with jewellery and other fine valuables. By this time, I had bought Ronnie Holbrook's Lancia Flavia Coupé. It had been styled by Pininfarina, and as Ronnie said, "If you squint, it looks like a Ferrari." It had reclining seats, and Patti loved nothing more than screwing in it on Park Lane, with all the traffic rushing past us. She also wanted to do it on the window ledge of a room at the nearby Hilton, and I had to book a room high up so she could show off to all of London.

There was a heatwave the summer we were going out. It was so hot, in fact, that I had taken to wearing a kaftan. I wore it when we went to Primrose Hill, one of my favourite parks in London, boasting a view of the entire city. There, we made love on the grass. We were aware of prying eyes behind every tree. I think it may have even been a gay cruising spot. What we were doing may not have been their cup of tea, but I think we gave them a good show nonetheless.

As I mentioned, due to the chaos of random people moving in and out of my place, we'd mostly go to Patti's. It was the spring of 1971, and in the middle of one night, in climbed a long-haired man through the wide-open window, maybe hoping to get lucky with my girlfriend. He was out of luck that time, but he stayed the night on the sofa and in the morning we became friends. Little did I know, this was the beginning of a wonderful friendship. His name was Isaac Tigrett and he was from Tennessee. Both his parents, who were divorced, were very wealthy. His mother Frances's family had built the railway into Jackson, Tennessee, and she still had a lot of real estate in the centre of town.

His father, John Burton Tigrett, was a financier who, among many things, was the backer of Jimmy Goldsmith's company, Cavenham Foods. Isaac had been sent over to the UK (I think to get him out of trouble) to work at Carr's Biscuits in Carlisle. He began exporting Rolls Royces and Bentleys to New York. He made a small fortune and teamed up with another rich-boy American, Peter Morton from Chicago, whose father was Chief Financial Officer for the Playboy organisation. Through that connection, Peter had got backing from the UK-based boss of the Playboy Clubs, Victor Lownes, to open London's first genuine US-style hamburger restaurant. It was called the Great American Disaster, and it was on the Fulham Road, near where I lived. Peter and Victor had an agreement that if they wanted to buy each other out, they would put sealed bids in an envelope. The higher bid would get it. Somewhere amongst it all, Isaac met Patti, and now he had climbed through her window and had met me. It is amazing to look back and remember where I first met my lifelong chums.

Isaac had an idea to open a rock 'n' roll-styled restaurant, and he had found an old car showroom in Piccadilly. Morton had the restaurant expertise and contacts, so it was a perfect team. After Isaac had climbed through the window, he was still a month or two away from opening. Patti, Isaac and I all hung out a lot during that time, and finally, on 14 June 1971, the first Hard Rock Café was born, and Patti and I went to the opening party.

I love Isaac; he's got a great sense of humour and will even make the cops laugh. He used to drive around London in a black 1950s pickup truck. On one occasion, the police stopped him, leglessly drunk, for driving the wrong way down a one-way street. "Didn't you see the arrows?" the officer asked him. "Offisher, I didn't even see the Indians," Isaac replied.

A short while after the Hard Rock opened, sons of some London gangsters tried putting the muscle on Isaac. It was probably the Kray or Richardson families. As the Hard Rock was a young people's hangout, I guess the younger generation of gangsters thought they could make a name for themselves that way, or maybe they were getting pushed by elders to muscle in and teach us youngsters a lesson. Isaac refused their demands for protection money. I was there the night the gangsters struck. It was a concert by the band Kokomo. There isn't really a stage at the Hard Rock, so the band were squeezed in on the raised platform near to the booths. It was a large band and the area was packed, and I stood there watching the jostling for quite a while before the fight started. Then all hell broke loose. It was like another scene from a Peckinpah movie and just like being back in Durham again. I saw one thug smash a full bottle of wine over a musician's head from behind and the wine spray through the air in slow motion. Then the musicians began breaking their guitars on the gangsters' backs. Chairs were being thrown… it was chaos, and I was outside by then. The gangsters had a Bentley and they opened the boot to show Isaac that they had sawn-off shotguns inside it, but he wasn't phased. I'll never forget the sight of my mate Isaac holding the leg of a broken chair, shouting at the gangsters, "Come and get some, motherfuckers!" He was very brave and never gave in to their demands.

★

By this time, Donna Curry – my lodger and friend to the band Chicago – had gone back to the US and a likeable young man I had met in the Casserole, John Stephen, took her place on my sofa. He moved in for the weekend and stayed eighteen months. He was very popular with the Holbrooks, who were, at this point in the story, 'official' and in the flat next door. Dany had Ronnie back in town and they had got married. We all called John Stephen 'Butch' because of the way he would crash through cinema doors. In fact, Butch, Ronnie and I had another nickname on the King's Road: because we were all very thin, with matching long blonde hair and identical outfits of tight jeans and faded denim jackets, we were The Beverly Sisters – a well-known, but corny, English female singing group from the fifties!

My new lodger Butch and another guy Bo Meftah had made some money making American football-style T-shirts, with 88 printed on them. Everybody on the King's Road was wearing them. Eventually he got a job as a barman in a King's Road bar, then as manager for Peter Langan's Odin's restaurant. He was much liked by John and Jan Gold from Tramp, so they sent him over to LA to be manager of the Tramp over there. He came back to London and was founder and chairman of Chinawhite.

Butch and I practically lived in the Hard Rock the first month, playing pinball – we just loved the place. We were living the *American Graffiti* dream. After about a month, Peter Morton said to us in his Chicago drawl, "Hey, you guys. I'm only going to say this to you once, but I really appreciate you coming here for the past month. Without you, we would have been empty."

Patti D'Arbanville was partly instrumental in picking up the business too, although it would inevitably have happened in a matter of time. She was a friend of the Andy Warhol crowd and there was an Andy Warhol production of a show called *Pork* at the Roundhouse in Chalk Farm. Each night, Patti and I would take the cast of *Pork* to the Hard Rock after the show. Most of them were outrageous New York queens, and this was pre-gay lib. At that time, London had never seen anything like them. They were dancing on the tables, with the jukebox turned up high. Pretty soon after it, the place was packed, night in and night out. Carole King even wrote a song about it, 'At the Hard Rock Café'. Queues started forming around the block. There are now 175 Hard Rock Café locations in fifty-three countries. Those days, I was more in love with Patti than ever.

★

Patti liked to swing both ways. She had a particular friendship with a French actress called Maria Schneider, who had just made a film with Marlon Brando called *Last Tango in Paris*. As I mentioned, Patti was great fun, and she and I would fantasise for weeks about what we were going to do to Maria when she got to town. When the film arrived, Patti asked me if I wanted to go to Tramp. Maria wasn't yet in town and I was shooting a commercial early the next morning, so I declined, but I stayed the night in Patti's flat anyway. The next morning, when I was leaving at the crack of dawn for location, Patti arrived home. She'd run into Marlon at Tramp and been up all night with him doing who knows what – I didn't even want to think about it. We had a row on her doorstep. The next day, Schneider arrived with an entourage that included a good-looking gypsy. He took Patti's fancy, and that was the end of me. I went to Marbella alone, where every bar was playing Cat Stevens' songs, most notably 'Lady D'Arbanville'. I was heartbroken.

Later, Patti had a long relationship with *Miami Vice* actor Don Johnson and they had a son. She appeared in many movies including *Rancho Deluxe*, *Wiseguy*, and another Warhol film, *L'Amour*, before making her name in the TV series *New York Undercover*.

The last time I saw Patti, she was filming in the Hollywood Centre Studios, where BFCS Inc. had its office, but it wasn't at the most appropriate of times. She was walking between the studios in hair curlers. She was delighted to see me, just a bit embarrassed to be caught mid-costume change.

I did finally meet Maria Schneider some time later, when I visited her in Blake's Hotel. She was snogging my friend Kellyann Page, who was a Patti D'Arbanville look-alike. I left before I got in the way. I don't think Maria was into men or me, or maybe I never did fit into that bunch after all. I still think back to those days in a depressed kind of a way. I was in love with Patti and she threw me aside for some gypsy that Maria had brought into town. I'm sure it wasn't that black and white, though. I'm sure after all it was never meant to be, and deep down I am happy for the life that she's had and the man she fell in love with – but I still can't listen to that song. Anyway, there were plenty more fish out there and I was about to catch one.

CHAPTER 12

Superman

It didn't take me long to fall in love again.

After my split with Patti, Jose Fonseca, the owner of Models One, played matchmaker and introduced me to her friend Jenny Marriott. Jenny was a beautiful lady who had just separated from her husband Steve Marriott, formerly lead singer of the Small Faces and part of the super-group Humble Pie. Like Cat Stevens, he was also upset about the break-up and would call in the middle of the night. Sometimes it would be me who answered the phone when he called. I guess I didn't want to be like one of those people who cling on, and although it had been hard not to contact Patti, I let life move me on. Otherwise, what was I going to do? Be depressed and listen to Cat Stevens for the rest of my life? Gimme a break! Steve died a few years later in a house fire – something very likely caused by drunkenly falling asleep in bed with a lighted cigarette, but we'll never know.

Jenny and I had fun while it lasted with one very romantic weekend in Paris. She was an antique dealer and had a commission to buy Daum and Galle lamps. She was obviously used to having a lot of money – the cash was literally falling out of her shoulder bag – and although I had been around a lot of money people, I had never seen anything quite like this before. In Paris, we stayed at a country house that belonged to friends of hers. We went to the Marché aux Puces and other antique markets which she scanned for fine rarities, and she could sure spot them. Jenny had a terrific eye and could pick out a beautiful piece inside a crowded and bustling stall, when to me it all just looked a shambles.

Back in London, she took me to my first Alternative Miss World – an annual event devised and hosted by Andrew Logan, the artist. The entrants were mostly gay, presided over by Andrew who sat on his throne in a half-man, half-woman costume.

Although paintings and artworks seemed to appeal to me, the story of my father's past was still haunting me slightly and I'd often think of how he had lost his gathered fortune to old paintings when staring into the deep oil colours of the great works that would often totally engross me. Later, in the eighties, I did become a big collector of Logan's artworks. Jenny also took me to the Ossie Clark show. She had known Ossie since art college in Manchester. He was a legendary sixties dress designer, using fabrics created by his partner Celia Birtwell. Having influenced Yves Saint Laurent and Anna Sui, Ossie has now gone down in history as one of the main swinging sixties fashion gurus. There is a famous David Hockney of Ossie and Celia, known as 'Mr and Mrs Clark and Percy'. It now hangs at the Tate and is one of the most visited paintings in Britain. Ossie also became a good friend of mine, right up to his premature death, when he was in a bad way due to alcohol and drug dependency – but that's not what killed him. In 1996, fifty-four-year-old Ossie was stabbed to death in his flat in Kensington by his then twenty-eight-year-old former lover. An Old Bailey jury was told that Italian-born Diego Cogolato stabbed him to death in a frenzied knife attack because he believed Ossie was the devil. It was tragic. Jenny still has a wonderful collection of his dresses; they are collectors' items now.

I also got reacquainted with David Gilmour of Pink Floyd when Jenny and I went to a Guy Fawkes party at his Essex country home. She was also great friends with an underground filmmaker, Michael Kostiff, and his wife Gerlinde. They were collectors of art deco and art nouveau, and I bought some nice pieces from them. Later, in the eighties, they opened a very happening club in Soho called Kinky Gerlinky – famous for its outrageous fashion and drag.

Sadly, and although I really liked Jenny, it was not to last. She met and married James Dearden, the writer of *Fatal Attraction*. I was again heartbroken, and then I kind of gave up on love and just spent my time dating models. I would meet them through work, at Tramp or at the model agency Christmas parties. I was a friend of the owners of all the top model agencies at this point, like Gillian Bobroff and Laraine Ashton of Bobtons. I would often stay for weekends at Gillian's country home that she shared with her boyfriend, David Charkham. Her business partner, Laraine Ashton, was also a good friend of mine. She would later open an eponymous model agency under Mark McCormack's IMG umbrella of sports management agencies. Laraine used to go out with the great war photographer Don McCullin.

One day, I was in their flat and opening a bottle of champagne when Don started freaking out. "Don't let it pop," he pleaded. Due to his traumatic war experiences, he had become highly sensitive to any small bang. Laraine later met, and I believe is still with, Terry O'Neill, Britain's best-known celebrity photographer, who had previously been married to Faye Dunaway. Everyone was getting married to everyone else, but I wasn't. Was I destined to walk this world alone and forever? Perhaps go back to Africa or even Margate and live the solitary life of a recluse? Give up on the world and just go and write books? I suppose I was beginning not to mind the idea of being on my own. Maybe being with one person forever and ever just wasn't my cup of chai.

It was from the Laraine Ashton agency that I got to know Gae Exton. I seem to remember that she was a booker at the agency, but she may have been a model. She was a stunning woman herself, and I knew her when she first got married to the rich industrialist David Iveson. He was a very nice man indeed, and I used to weekend at their country estate. In the late 1970s, after she had split from Iveson, Gae met an unknown American actor who was shooting a movie in England. His name was Christopher Reeve and the film was *Superman*.

Chris and Gae stayed together for many years and had two wonderful children. I would see them regularly, either at their house on Hollywood Road, Chelsea, or I would see Chris in New York, where he lived on the Upper West Side. I really did love New York and was often there in the eighties. I loved Chris too and he was a good friend to me. He took me bowling for the first time; I remember it well because I knocked down all the pins with my first ever throw. He was impressed, but it was beginner's luck. "I've been lucky my entire life," I explained, although I've stopped telling anyone that these days – I guess they don't want to hear it. Sometimes I'd wonder if it were really true anyway, that I was genuinely lucky, or perhaps it was just my outlook. I think I'll leave that one up to you. Chris and I talked about that a little and other things too, like flying. We'd hang out in places like Studio 54, which was the hot place then. We went in the VIP room and, I'll never forget it, a dealer came to us with a doctor's bag full of cocaine. I had never seen so much.

Christopher Reeve was passionate about gliding and flying. He used to fly a small plane back to New York from the UK. This meant going mainly overland, so that he could refuel on the Scotland, Greenland and Newfoundland route. One time he came back from a trip and told me he had had a complete electrical failure in the dark, as he was coming in to land. The wheels would not go down and he'd had to glide the plane to a crash landing without power or wheels.

Everyone assumes that Christopher Reeve was made a paraplegic by being violently thrown from his horse. It is a tragedy that it was much more gentle than that. His horse pulled up at a fence and Chris slowly slid down the horse's neck. He landed on top of his head and broke his spine. He was my friend and I miss him.

After Chris died, I couldn't watch *Superman* for a long time, but since I began writing this book, I decided to give it another go and it's been great to see him again. I guess through his films he lives on forever. After watching the film, I ran a search online to see what Christopher Reeve things I could find and one fan had made a list of the top ten Christopher Reeve quotes. I read them and didn't feel sad as I expected. Instead, I felt empowered. One read, "You play the hand you're dealt. I think the game's worthwhile" and I find that to be quite correct. Christopher Reeve – he really was a superman.

CHAPTER 13

Models, Models, Models...

It was the mid-seventies and I was so disillusioned with love that I was only going out with foreign chicks – foreign models in fact – because they would always move on, doing the international modelling circuit of London, New York, Paris and Milan. It meant they would only stay in London about a month and then leave, so I had no danger of emotional attachment. They were mainly Swedish and American girls, so gorgeous and über gorgeous – they were beautiful and they were all of the time. Jose Fonseca once rang up: "Darling, I have 'Miss Young Germany' coming over next week... and she doesn't know anyone. Could you show her around?" "Sure thing, Jo!"

I went out with one buxom gal from Chicago; she had been a *Playboy* centrefold. Her name was Cindy Russell, and she was as sexy as Jane Russell. Eventually she went to live with the infamous Peter Grant, the manager of Led Zeppelin. At the time, I had a 1956 Ford F100 pickup. I painted flames down the side of it and Cindy just loved that. I think it took her back to America. We went to the British Grand Prix at Silverstone in it.

I also had a girlfriend from Peru, Maria Badeaux, who would visit London frequently. She was a superstar model in New York and would do all her magazine cover shoots when she came here. One thing about Maria: she always had a gay entourage with her. It was all a bit of a cliché I suppose, but at the time it was just fab! I would sleep with her every time she came to London.

I had another American girlfriend who was often in London, Connie Stumen. I would date her whenever she was in town. She had done many *Vogue* covers; she was rich and she was successful. She bred horses back in the US and drove an E-Type Jag. In London, she always stayed in a basement flat in Chelsea and had a half-Hawaiian model roommate, who didn't seem to know anyone in London. However, that would all change when she modelled for, and married, David Bailey. Her name was Marie Helvin, and keeping in the vein of the book and terrible name-dropping, she's now a big celebrity, and I'm very likely the person she has known longest in London.

In 1972, I had an affair with Carroll Baker, the star of the 1956 hit Hollywood movies *Baby Doll* and *Giant*. Jan Gold, the wife of Johnny Gold, one of the owners of Tramp, introduced us in the club. I used to go to Carroll's home in England's Lane, off Haverstock Hill, Hampstead. She was a very nice, beautiful and sexy lady, but it was a new experience for me to have an older girlfriend. I was twenty-eight and she was forty. All her friends were producer types who were even older and I didn't feel comfortable being a toy boy, so I ended it. It seemed to be the pattern of my relationships. I was definitely afraid of commitment. I would dump fabulous girl after fabulous girl after a month or so, and for no good reason. For me, being in love was being in pain.

One night, Butch and I were at a concert at the Royal Festival Hall. Standing outside afterwards we met someone. She wore a fringed chamois-leather mini-dress. She was very statuesque indeed and looked like Hiawatha. It was my first meeting with Siobhan Barron, who was to become one of my best lifelong friends. She told us she had been modelling for Anthony Price, the clothes designer who styled the Roxy Music album covers (it was what introduced Jerry Hall to London society. In fact, Jerry initially went out with Bryan Ferry, the lead singer of Roxy Music, until Jagger stole her off him). That night, Butch and I took Siobhan to the Hard Rock Café and in the weeks that followed she was always in my flat on the King's Road. By this time, I was sleeping with her.

She met some American musicians living in the next-door building and kept telling me I should meet them and that they were nice guys. I never bothered. I think I was a bit jealous or something, or the idea of them chatting her up while I was there wasn't something I wanted to hear. They were the Eagles and they were recording their first album in London with the legendary English record producer Glyn Johns. His wife Glynis would later produce commercials with me. They are now good friends of mine, but I didn't know him in those days. The King's Road was proving to be the nexus in London for anyone that wanted to make money, meet celebrities or become one.

Before you could say "Bob's your uncle", I was in the Brompton Hospital in Chelsea, visiting Siobhan and her mother. Siobhan was having an abortion with my child. It seemed she was younger than she had let on and may have only been sixteen, but she was extremely well developed and she looked more mature than that – well, I thought so anyway. Her mother, Zelda Barron, was very nice about it, and I think she appreciated that I went to the hospital. I became good friends with her, which I suppose, looking back and considering the circumstances, was a little strange. She was a well-known figure in the film industry, a writer/producer and a collaborator with Warren Beatty on *Reds*, and she was often in Los Angeles when I lived there.

This is how Siobhan remembers it, in an email to me, after starting to read a draft of these memoirs. In Siobhan's words:

OK, I am up 2 the brooks fullford days. its giving me the creeps and reminding me of bob Brooke's making me cry when i was doing wardrobe. Also Mum use 2 work with him. it also brought back the memory of how she new you . i remember her sitting by my bed while i was having that barbaric force labour abortion. u popped in with your squash bag for 30sec's to . you and her were all chatty work stuff while i layed there having an induce labour and then the fetus came out and was getting cold between my legs. i didn't know what to do or say as no one had explained anything 2 me so i just laid there looking and you and mum chatting and laughing, and then you left. X

Gulp! Powerful and heartbreaking stuff. It makes me feel quite ashamed. It was like Alfie in *Alfie*. Did Alfie get his comeuppance? It was the dark side of the sixties and, sadly, I was one of many men who were making it so.

In the 1980s, Siobhan became the doyen of the music video business. She ran a successful company called Limelight with her brother Steve Barron, a director, and they shot Michael Jackson's 'Billie Jean' video, as well as innovative videos for Dire Straits' 'Money For Nothing' and A-ha's 'Take On Me'. Steve also directed *Teenage Mutant Ninja Turtles*, which was the highest-ever grossing independent film at that time, and *Coneheads*, which starred my mate Dan Aykroyd, so I was able to go on location. Steve has also directed many mini-series including *Merlin*, *Arabian Nights* and *Dreamkeeper*.

When Siobhan and I lived as neighbours in Malibu during the 1990s, she would delight in introducing me to people as "my first abortion". I was only twenty-eight; I can't be blamed for being young and naive, can I? I mean, I hadn't even experienced Hollywood… yet.

CHAPTER 14

Hollywood

"Hollywood is a cross between a health farm, a recreation center and an insane asylum. It's a company town, and I happen to like the company!"
– Michael Caine

It was the early seventies and on every break I would head to the hills. Hollywood Hills. LA to me was magnetic, simply being there in the heat, next to the beaches, the babes, the creativity, the craziness, the chaos. It was to me everything I had ever read about the town, multiplied by about a trillion, and I revelled in it, ya know, just for a bit of fun. On one occasion, I went to the commercials production companies to look for a job. I wanted to move there; I wanted to be a part of the Hollywood conveyer belt… did I know that within twenty years I would have my own American production company? I suppose slightly, maybe, in my arrogance… yes!

I always stayed at the Chateau Marmont on Sunset, the famous 1930s hotel that looks rather like a French chateau. It's now been restored and is trendy, but in those days it was a bit rundown – better actually, more real. I once had Jean Harlow's honeymoon suite. I lay there where she would have, naked, surrounded by pink walls and chuckled slightly. I remember the occasion. It was that sense of being on holiday in a fun place, being naughty when no one else was looking. It had a large veranda overlooking the Sunset Strip and the back of the iconic billboard of the Marlboro man. One time when I stayed there, my great friend and fellow Chelsea supporter Tony Howard was also in the hotel, and he was managing Marc Bolan at the time. We hung out a lot together, including a great evening watching the fabulous Al Green in concert. Coincidentally, there was a restaurant right over the road called Oscars, which was run by a girl called Michele. She used to work in the Casserole on the King's Road, so it was all very much a blast from the past for me. It's where I ran into Karen Lamm and her new husband, Beach Boy Dennis Wilson. A short while later, on 21 July 1975, The Beach Boys played at Wembley Stadium, with the Eagles, Joe Walsh and the headline act Elton John. I was there, of course! The Beach Boys were on next to last, before Elton. I still remember that sun. It was setting and it glistened off the Lurex worn by the band, as they sang all those surfer classics like 'Fun, Fun, Fun' and 'California Girls'.

Karen asked me if I would book a table for ten people at Tramp after the show. I did and I was sitting at the table all night, waiting for her and The Beach Boys to come – all on my own at an empty table for ten, imagine it. They never did come. Karen and Dennis had had a row.

★

In LA, I would hang out at the Rainbow Bar and Grill, which had just been opened by Lou Adler and some other music business moguls. One night I met a girl there, a portrait artist. I asked her if I could go back to her house for her to draw a portrait of me. Truth be told, I had been tipped off that she was a bit 'kinky' and I was curious, so to speak. On the drive home, she kept saying things like, "While I am drawing, you have to sit very still", and "I am a very strict mistress" and that was just the start. When we got to her house in Santa Monica, she left me in the sitting room as she went "to change into something more comfortable". A few minutes later, the door flew open and she charged in, wearing a baby-doll outfit, stockings and suspender belts. She carried a cat o'nine tails whip in each hand, which she was cracking through the air. With the lighting and all, it was like a scene from a fantasy porno, but the best thing about it was – I was in it! I thought that we'd all got it out of our systems in the sixties, what with the orgies and all, but in fact we hadn't. It, whatever it was and is, was not something we had got out of our systems – it was something we had developed. Before I knew what was happening, I was chained and handcuffed to the bed, and she was whipping me and sitting in split-crotch panties – all over my face. Wahoo! Was it wrong to have got very excited by the experience? The following year, when I was visiting LA again, I went back to her house… for more. It wasn't as good the second time, and that was my last experience of S&M. We were awoken early the next morning by a medical team who had come to take her to rehab. She had become a junkie.

I had another experience with a junkie back in London, at around the same time. I went to the Speakeasy to see Leon Russell and his band The Shelter People. I was familiar with, but had never met, the two back-up singers, Claudia Lennear and Kathi McDonald. They had both been Ikettes in the Ike and Tina Turner Revue, which I had seen many times. I got off with Kathi and we went back to her hotel room. After making love, she asked me to hold her tourniquet while she shot up. I had never seen anything like it before. If the sixties sex perversions were about liberation and expression, the seventies were depression and, I suppose, self-harm. Heroin: I have never and will never touch the stuff. I'm currently reading the book *Shantaram*, in which heroin is referred to as "the everything-and-nothing drug: it takes everything and gives you nothing in return". Kathi was sharing a room with Claudia Lennear. By then, Claudia had returned to the room and Kathi had passed out. Claudia was lying down and I was trying to persuade her to allow me to cross the room to her bed. Unfortunately, she was waiting for a phone call from the drummer, the legendary Jim Keltner, who was down in the bar. She had the hots for him, and not for me. It seemed to be a recurring story – not being unlucky, of course, but being shunned for someone who could play a cool instrument… as opposed to the piano accordion.

*

In 1973, I met Pink Floyd at the Rainbow Bar and Grill. They were there every night after rehearsals and their shows at the Hollywood Bowl, for their *Dark Side of the Moon* tour. I had already met David Gilmour, the lead guitarist and singer, through my neighbour Dany, as he'd later remind me! I had never seen the band before, but let me tell you, for all the youngsters out there, Pink Floyd really were *that* good, and still are. The concert at the Hollywood Bowl truly was sensational. Embarrassingly, I didn't have any of their records, but even still, the concert took my breath away. They were one of a kind and, the truth is, there won't be anyone like them again – and I happened to be mates with them… me, a nobody from Margate, or was it Italy?

On top of everything, I was stoned. It wasn't something I did very often because I can't smoke – not for medical reasons, I'm just shit at it. I don't know how to do it, with my fingers and everything. I didn't need to, though – there was some hash cake being passed around! The Hollywood Bowl was swathed in pink light. There were five searchlights behind the dome pointing up into the sky. The stage was in the dome, and I had one of the open boxes in the front, which I had got from the band. I had never seen a show like it. When the stage exploded at the end, I was at my highest and wasn't expecting it at all. In my paranoia, I thought it was a tragic accident and not part of the show. I didn't know too much about Pink Floyd at the time, but they basically started the use of solid-state lasers and huge inflatable puppets – techniques now copied by all the big stadium bands. The band employed pioneering lighting and production designers Arthur Max and Marc Brickman. I knew them both. Arthur used to go out with Joanna Jacobs in the 1970s. He is now an Oscar-nominated production designer on the Ridley Scott movies, and when he started as a set designer, I got him a job on a commercial I was producing with Bob Brooks. Arthur walked off the shoot when Bob shouted at him. I knew Marc Brickman from Malibu, where he lived with Gaby, a friend of mine and the former wife of another friend, Aubrey 'Po' Powell, who, with his partner Storm Thorgerson, had a design company called Hipgnosis, which designed all the Pink Floyd album covers. Have I name-dropped enough yet? My relationship with the great Pink Floyd had only just begun, but I think my relationship with fantasy submission porn was kind of over – but never say never, right?

CHAPTER 15

King's Road: Part 2

During the sixties, seventies and eighties, the fashionistas would walk the King's Road on Saturday afternoon. It was quite a scene, full of the beautiful people. In fact, I stopped playing hockey at Richmond in 1969 when I discovered the delights of the King's Road on a Saturday. My friends and I would usually have lunch in the Aretusa, a cool hangout owned by Alvaro Maccioni, who later owned the famous La Famiglia restaurant at World's End. The Aretusa was one of the first restaurants that had a sliding roof, so in the summer it was open to the sky, and every Saturday it was packed with all the Chelsea trendsetters. The King's Road was a great hunting ground for girls. I would regularly meet a particular girl who would always come back to my flat to give me oral sex. She was very kind to me; I did very little in return.

★

I always wore my Granny Takes a Trip finest outfit. Granny's was a store on the King's Road at World's End, where all the sixties and seventies rock stars used to buy their tight satin trousers and velvet or taffeta silk jackets, and I had the lot. The shop had the front end of a 1940s Dodge sticking out of the window, an idea later stolen by all the Hard Rock Cafés in America. Granny's was part-owned and run by two New Yorkers. Gene Krell, now a big fish for Vogue Japan, who couldn't have looked the part more with hair down to his hips, and his good looking partner, Marty Breslau, who was dating one of the GTOs. They had an English partner, Freddie Hornik, who wasn't often in the shop, and when Granny's opened up on Doheny Drive in LA, I used to stay with Freddie and his girlfriend Jenny Dugan-Chapman in Laurel Canyon. I had known Jenny for years, since she worked at Mr Freedom further down the King's Road. She came from the wealthy Zilkha family, who owned the Mothercare stores, and she had the best legs in town, which would be shown off in very short hot pants. They seemed to make up the culture that was the King's Road: the bright colours, the sounds. Looking back now, it was like we lived on a seventies film set and everything was perfect.

430 King's Road, where Mr Freedom was situated from 1968-70, has had quite the illustrious history indeed. The place was as relevant to the time as anywhere I could have shopped and hung out. Earlier in the 60s it had been the home of Hung On You, the happening boutique operated by the legendary Michael Rainey. Tommy Roberts, the owner of Mr Freedom, was a swinging sixties clothing pioneer. His bright-coloured clothes were part of the pop art fashion. His featured styles of broad-brimmed hats, close-fitting maxi dresses, silk-screened cartoon character images on jersey tops and winged shoes made quite the imprint on the movement. His shop attracted people like Mick Jagger and model Jean Shrimpton, as well as the rising star Elton John, who had adopted the Mr Freedom winged boots and jumpsuits as his stage wear.

When Tommy Roberts moved to Kensington Church Street in 1970, his partner in Mr Freedom, Trevor Myles, took over the shop and called it Paradise Garage. He was also a pioneer. He sold Osh Kosh B'Gosh dungarees, which were all the rage on the King's Road, and antique Hawaiian shirts. He was the first person to sell second-hand faded denim jeans and jackets. I see them everywhere these days, but he was certainly the first. I've recently walked down the King's Road, but too much has changed and I can't help but miss what it was. In a way, it seemed to bring so much more then – things that stood for change. I feel like it has now gone the wrong way, but it might change for the better again one day, and I'd like to see that – but if they do, this time I'll just be a bystander.

The Jean Machine, owned by Jay Scott, further down the King's Road, followed suit. Jay, who was a good friend of Ronnie Holbrook's and mine, used to buy shipping containers full of old denim from America. The King's Road and California basically started the denim craze that swept the world. Trevor Myles was also noteworthy because he drove a fastback Ford Mustang, flocked like a tiger. I found a double-page spread of it from the *Sunday Times* colour magazine a few years ago and gave it to him. We were overjoyed to hold it and look at it together, and a smile came on both our faces. He is still around on the King's Road and sometimes in the Chelsea Arts Club. Others were at it too, like Jay Scott, who teamed up with Tony Lonsdale who owned a shop called the Pant House on Hornton Street. They started manufacturing their own jeans in Hong Kong and opened up a Jean Machine store on every high street; they had five stores on Oxford Street alone. People were hitting it with the right products in the right location and at the right time. Tony Lonsdale had an Australian girl too, to top it all off, called Checkie Maskell, who worked in the Pant House. He finished up marrying her, the lucky bugger. He also bought my Mercedes 280 SE 3.5 Cabriolet – even luckier.

Malcolm McLaren had a small stall in the back of Paradise Garage, selling his collection of 1950s memorabilia and vinyl records, and he later took over the premises when Trevor Myles closed the boutique. He and his schoolteacher girlfriend Vivienne Westwood first sold Teddy Boy outfits, and the shop was called Let It Rock. I lived a hundred yards down the King's Road at that time and I was always in there, and became very friendly with Malcolm. I remember groups of Japanese Teddy Boys, dressed in perfect English Ted outfits, posing for photos by the jukebox. After a while, Malcolm and Vivienne changed the name of the shop to Too Fast To Live, Too Young To Die, selling Marlon Brando-inspired motorcycle rocker clothes, because they got fed up with the Teddy Boys hanging around the shop. I still have an old torn black leather jacket that I bought from the shop with an 'M' badge on the sleeve (for Matchless, a 1950s brand of British motorcycle); I just can't get into it anymore. The big change came in 1974, when they flipped the name again to SEX and started selling everything punk. Vivienne Westwood defined the look of the movement, pioneering the use of bondage clothing for fashion, and torn clothes and safety pins. Fashionable Chelsea artist Duggie Fields also painted people wearing safety pins, but I don't know who did it first. It probably came from the street. Chrissie Hynde worked in SEX as a shop assistant before she got the Pretenders moving.

There was always this group of young lads hanging around SEX and in the Roebuck, the pub opposite my flat. They were around for months. One night, I saw them at a party given by artist Andrew Logan, of Alternative Miss World fame. He lived in a huge loft in Butler's Wharf, next to the River Thames. He was either a squatter or a sitting tenant. The owner eventually set fire to the building to get Andrew and the other occupiers out, and they all had to flee the flames.

In 1976, Malcolm McLaren and Vivienne Westwood staged the notorious Valentine's Ball in Andrew's loft, which I attended. The gang of loitering kids from the store had formed a band, and they played at the party. I think it was their first gig. I clearly remember thinking they were just the worst thing I had ever seen. I thought they were just a bunch of kids from the pub. I had never heard the Ramones, the New York Dolls or punk music. The kids called themselves the Sex Pistols and within months were a media sensation, under the shrewd management of Malcolm McLaren.

By the way, 430 King's Road, the famous shop, is still operated by Vivienne Westwood, who of course is a superstar designer and now a dame. She first called it Seditionaries, selling military-style clothing, and now calls it World's End. It resembles an eighteenth-century galleon, has a sloping floor, and a large clock on the outside, which spins backwards.

My corner of the King's Road and Beaufort Street was to become the centre of the universe for punks in '76, in particular the Roebuck pub, the Water Rat and the Man in the Moon pubs further down the block. In addition to the Sex Pistols, the Clash, the Damned, the Stranglers, Adam Ant, Siouxsie and the Banshees, Poly Styrene and her band X-Ray Spex, and Jordan with her famous beehive hairstyle were all regulars in the pubs. Jordan worked at SEX. Every Saturday there were crowds of punks in fantastic outfits and hairstyles outside my flat, waiting to be photographed by tourists (for cash). I practically lived in the Roebuck in those days, hanging out with my pals Nigel Brickell and Little James, who had a punk shop, Smutz, in the Beaufort Market. There were always a lot of young girls in the pub. Paula Yates was one of them, later to marry Bob Geldof.

Although I had just turned thirty myself, I liked to hang out with young street kids; they were fun to be with. I had seven youngsters in the Sting Ray on one day, driving down the King's Road – although it was only a two-seater coupé. We had a party in my flat every night when the pub shut at 11pm. I probably had one of the first video players on the King's Road – the Philips model that only played one-hour tapes – and I had bootleg videos of all the latest movies, including *Saturday Night Fever*. It's different nowadays, where it's all available on tap through the internet, but back then bootlegging a movie was quite an achievement.

★

At around this time, I had a one-night stand with Christine Keeler, who lived off the King's Road. This was a big thrill for me, because she had been a big masturbatory fantasy of mine in 1963 when I was at school and she was at the centre of the Profumo Affair – a scandal in 1963 involving the British Minister of Defence John Profumo and a sexy girl, Christine Keeler, who was a former model and showgirl. The main problem was she was also having an affair with a Russian spy. It resulted in the resignation of the minister, after he lied to Parliament. I had a clear recollection of the sexy image of her naked, straddling an Arne Jacobsen chair, in the famous Lewis Morley photograph, and I thought of that while I was doing it.

★

In 1977, I had to produce a commercial with a cameo appearance of a punk. I told Annie Fielding, the casting director, that I knew all the real ones and I could get one. She said they would not be reliable and may not show up, and she knew a person who we could make up to look like one of them. This young man came in to do the job, and looked pretty realistic by the time wardrobe and hair had finished with him. He was a personable chap from Newcastle, near to where I had lived at Durham University. He told me he wasn't really an actor and he was getting a band together. Once again, like with Chrissie Hynde, I remember thinking, *Yeah, yeah, I've heard it all before*. My cynicism was ill founded. He was Gordon Sumner, also known as… Sting.

CHAPTER 16

Eric Clapton and the Chelsea Cruise

Nigel Carroll is my great lifelong friend and we were introduced through our cars. Mine was a green '58 Corvette and his a regal red '56 Cadillac convertible. We met in '72 at the Chelsea Potter on the King's Road. People with cars like that always talk to each other, not in a snobby way as if people without them aren't worthy. No, it's just that cars connect people with other car people. I'd like to think I hadn't turned elitist, that was for sure. We were, however, the only ones with fancy cars – and would both be parked right next to the pub. We started hanging out as friends, and every Saturday night we went to the Potter. Soon, a friend of Nigel's, Lev, began to join us. He had a '61 red Corvette, and then came two others who also had Corvette Sting Rays. It had become a Corvette club, but not for long.

Word was spreading and, little by little, different cars came. They came in abundance and the King's Road was their new camp. By the following summer, both sides of the road near the Chelsea Potter were lined with old motors – mainly American ones, from the 1940s through to the sixties. There were no parking restrictions on the road in those days and that gave rise to the now legendary Chelsea Cruise. *Custom Car* was a new mag we all read, and they took it over, promoting it for the last Saturday of every month. It wasn't too long at all before hundreds of cars began to show up. My friends and I had started something we could not control... by accident.

Within one or two summers, crowds of locals and tourists were lining the King's Road to watch the cars drive by. It became a real event for us, but eventually, beer glasses would end up in the road and traffic couldn't get through. The police got involved and the King's Road at Sloane Square became closed to any vehicle other than a bus – except me. Because I had a driving licence with a King's Road address, the police couldn't stop me entering the street, and, I will say, I took great delight in being the only vehicle that could drive past the crowds in my Corvette. In the end, the police, with the cooperation of *Custom Car* mag, transferred the whole event to Battersea Park. It turned into something huge in Battersea, and Nigel and I had started it from the pub entirely by mistake!

★

Nigel was working for the property developer Peter Beale, who had a deal with Frank Dale and Stepsons, the Rolls Royce dealer in Fulham. He could buy a used car and get his money back when he returned the car a year later. In the early seventies, there was a rising market in Rolls Royces, so Peter had two Silver Clouds, the last of the great rollers – one for him and one for Nigel. In property, Peter bought the short leasehold of a huge house in Hans Place, Knightsbridge, just behind Harrods. His modus operandi was to buy a three- or four-year lease, which was too short for anyone else, fix the place up, negotiate a longer lease from the Cadogan Estates, and then sell the building on. This house in Hans Place had seven floors with huge rooms, one of which Nigel was living in. He bought a job heap of large old gilt picture frames at an auction at Bonham's. Tony Litri was a friend of his, and he could do perfect copies of old master paintings. They installed Tony in the top floor attic, which was rather similar to a Parisian artist's atelier, and gave him an electric fire. Nigel would hold a frame up to a wall in a room and say, "Tony, this feels like a Matisse" and Tony would get to work. He would age the paintings in front of the electric fire and, in no time, the whole house was filled with old masters. There was no attempt to deceive and it was only ever done for effect. Each painting had the word FAKE written across the back. Of course, for the Arab punters who came to buy the house, the paintings were included, and they never looked at the backs of them.

Apart from the house, I spent a lot of time with Nigel in the garage in Claborn Mews. It was Nigel, myself, the two Rolls Royces, a 1950s American pickup truck and the mean-looking black '69 Stingray. We simply loved our cars. Once, I went to buy a 1966 427 Corvette Sting Ray convertible. I only wanted it because it had rare knock-off wheels and I wanted to put them on my '63 Sting Ray. I swapped the wheels and sold the new car, which was a big mistake – they're now worth a fortune. As you can see, the car thing was beginning to get addictive and I'm not sure where it came from – maybe from Margate when the American boys came to take my sisters away in their classic motors. Nigel came with me to buy the Sting Ray because I needed someone to drive it back. On getting back to London, we went to Kensington High Street, where the second McDonalds had just opened. We sat eating in the car and I told him: "Happiness is a Big Mac and a new Corvette." Smug as hell, I know, but I guess I couldn't resist.

At the time, Nigel was going out with Paula Boyd. She was the youngest sister of the infamous Boyd girls. Pattie Boyd had been married to George Harrison since the height of The Beatles fame, but she was now living with Eric Clapton and would later marry him. Her sister Jenny Boyd was married to Mick Fleetwood of Fleetwood Mac. Nigel became great friends with Eric Clapton and, before long, started working for him. He still does, in fact, do the merchandising and looking after of Eric's hot rods. To begin with, as far as I could see, Nigel was employed to be a 'buddy' to Eric. He used to drive Eric to see his beloved West Bromwich Albion football team in the Midlands, and he would go on tour with him. However, as Nigel once told me, although they were friends, "Make no mistake, if Eric wants a pack of cigarettes at three in the morning, I'd be the one to go out and buy them."

Through Nigel, I met Eric on many occasions. We often hung out, just the three of us. At the heart of it, we were boys; boys like Ferraris and Eric had a big collection of them, so we'd go to car meetings and Ferrari gatherings. We went to the Hard Rock Café, both in London and New York, and Isaac Tigrett had seen me with Eric. He was always trying to get me to get a guitar for the café, but there was no way I was going to ask him – or even Nigel – if I could nab one of his guitars for my mate. In the end, and with nothing to do with me, Clapton gave the Hard Rock a guitar to hang over his favourite seat. Pete Townshend of The Who heard about it and gave one of his, and then it all began spreading like wildfire – the Hard Rock became the biggest collectors of rock 'n' roll memorabilia in the world.

My production company was a member of the Glyndebourne Opera. One time I took Eric and Pattie, and Nigel's new girlfriend Jaki, who would later become his wife. We were all dolled up in black ties and evening dresses and had a picnic on the lawns. A picnic on 'the lawns' with Eric Clapton in black tie; had I made it? Was I in? Was I happy? I was beginning to see in so many of the people who had 'made it' just how unhappy they could be at times. It was as if they were like normal people all along, with downs as well as ups. Unfortunately, I hadn't been given very good seats – in the front row, right underneath the stage – but Eric seemed to enjoy the opera and was nodding his head to keep time all the way through. I just wanted everyone to be happy and not sad like I had been when I was on my own, in Dean Close. Like I said, he seemed to be having a good time. That was the most important thing… I guess.

One particularly memorable trip for me was when I went on the road with Eric's band in America. They were going from New York to Philadelphia for a show in an all-silver aluminium Viscount turbo propeller aircraft. Touring bands regularly used it and inside were armchairs and sofas and coffee tables, and no aircraft seats at all. The most impressive thing for me was when we landed. I was used to flying internationally, when you have to go through security and customs. On this occasion, on either side of the aircraft as we taxied down the runway, lines of stretched limos ran alongside us. We got off the plane, climbed into the limos and, with a police motorcycle escort, sped through the traffic with sirens wailing. We then moved down the ramp and were in the stadium. Rock 'n' roll!

Nigel and I had dinner with Roger Forrester, then Clapton's manager, behind the Four Seasons Hotel in LA. Eric's *Unplugged* album had just hit the charts at number one and his security man, a gentle giant called Alphi O'Leary, was also there. He told us an interesting story: as they were leaving the recent Chicago Blues Festival, he had climbed into a helicopter but couldn't do up the safety belts because he was too big. He got out and blues legend Stevie Ray Vaughan stepped in. That night, the helicopter crashed in the fog after hitting the top one foot of an artificial ski slope. Everyone on board perished, including Stevie.

I went to Eric's Italianate home outside Ewehurst, Surrey, many times with Nigel. On one occasion, like a pair of kids, we went just to see his Ferraris, and another time for a small party for the legendary Carl Perkins. We also went a few times to Eric's Christmas show at Guildford Town Hall, and then back to his home. His granny and other members of the family were always there. I always felt an affinity with Eric because he, like me, was brought up by his granny. I always noticed that he would walk around the house holding a guitar, doing finger exercises on it. He wasn't actually playing – no sound ever came out – but I realised it's why he's so good: he practises all day. Maybe if I played the piano accordion… oh, never mind.

Nigel and Jaki got married and had their wedding reception at Knebworth House. Clapton was Nigel's best man and his band played. I think I must have been nervous, because I got trolleyed when I arrived. A psychiatrist would probably put it down to losing my best pal and playmate, but I don't know about that – maybe I just felt like getting pissed. A friend of mine told me later I downed seven pints of lager in about as many minutes. He also told me I was breakdancing, spinning on my back with my legs in the air. I was also stoned and I had started on cocaine by then. As Eric was playing, I kept drunkenly shouting out the name of one of his best-known songs, 'Cocaine' (apparently). Later, Clapton told me he thought it was a request, not an offer, and at one point Nigel came outside and caught me taking off Jaki's bridal garter with my teeth. Oops.

Since I now live in very isolated places, I rarely see famous people like Eric Clapton and I miss seeing him. The last time I saw him I was walking down the King's Road and he was driving past in his new Ferrari. He slammed on the brakes, jumped out and gave me a big hug before inviting me to his house for a cuppa. There I met his new girlfriend, now the mother of his daughters. That was the last time I saw him. Fortunately, I still see Nigel and Jaki. She still looks as beautiful as the day Nigel married her.

*

Hanging out with Clapton was great – hanging out with rock stars in general is great – but in the mid-seventies, I had a different experience altogether. Yes, it involved another rock 'n' roll superstar, but the biggest of all time. I was staying in LA at the Chateau Marmont Hotel. I liked to go to a café called the Old World, just over the road from Tower Records on the Sunset Strip. I would sit there and have a beer and watch the cars go by. It was often quite a sight on the strip. You could really soak up LA – its size mostly and how big everything was. The cars were big, the roads were big, the people, their pets… Mostly, it was a freak show – and I loved it. One day I saw a VW Beetle that had long hair like an Afghan hound and another car with grass growing all over it.

Another day, I was sitting there on the raised terrace and just below me was a man hitchhiking, but he was no ordinary man. First of all, he was wearing a white matador's shirt with billowing sleeves. Secondly, he wasn't just hitchhiking, he was doing an Elvis impersonation and hitchhiking – I think to that old sixties dance, the Hitchhike. He was waving his left thumb, shaking his knees and singing, "Uh-uh-uh, uh-uh-uh, yeah yeah, I'm all shook up!" At the end of the hitchhike arc, his left fist slammed into his right arm and he shouted, "Fuck you, asshole!" to the car that had just passed him by, which I thought was pretty interesting. He did this for a while, much to my amusement. I decided to talk to him; apparently, he was once invited to sing in Vegas. Then, suddenly, just as he was doing the hitchhike dance and shaking his knees to more of 'All Shook Up', he casually says "Hi El." My head turned and I looked up, and there he was: the real Elvis, driving slowly down the other side of the road, and he was as cool as a cucumber. He was in his famous black Stutz Bearcat, a very rare car that I later saw at Graceland. I couldn't believe my eyes: a mad Elvis impersonator hitchhiking and the real Elvis driving past! That evening, I said to the girl I was seeing, "You'll never guess who I saw today. Elvis!" Her family owned Schwab's, the drugstore on Sunset Boulevard. She told me he went there at the same time every day to collect his meds. Not so long afterwards, he was dead.

When I went to my goddaughter Augusta Tigrett's christening in Memphis, Tennessee, we had a tour of Elvis's Graceland mansion. There were thirty-three godparents and some of them, like Dan Aykroyd, were celebs, so we had a private tour of the house. The guide was more indiscrete with us than she usually was with the general public. She told us that Elvis used to have TVs in every room, hallway and corridor, showing the same show, so that he could watch it while he was walking around the house. I thought he was into fried peanut butter and banana sandwiches, but according to the guide, he only ate bacon – about half a pound a day – and he died sitting on the toilet. Anyone who has done the Atkin's Diet will know that only eating protein will make you constipated, and being constipated puts a lot of strain on the heart. That's what probably happened to Elvis – you read it here first!

*

In 1991, I saw Eric at Ronnie Wood's birthday lunch in London. I asked him if he wanted to come down to Wiltshire to do some fly fishing. Eric is passionate about fishing and the Nadder, my local river, is particularly good for trout. He told me he couldn't because he was flying to New York the next day to see his four-and-a-half-year-old son Conor. A couple of days later, after Eric had got to New York, Conor tragically died falling from a fifty-third floor window. Unbelievably, the windows of this skyscraper could be raised from the floor. The maid had opened the window; Conor was running from room to room playing aeroplanes and fallen right out of the opening. Eric ran ten blocks through the streets of Manhattan from his hotel to the apartment building when Lori del Santo, Conor's mother, called him, but there was, of course, nothing he could do. He managed to channel his considerable grief into one of his most beautiful songs ever, 'Tears in Heaven'.

★

The Chelsea Cruise faded away some years ago, but underwent a grassroots revival in 2004 by some nostalgic car enthusiasts. To this day it takes place on the King's Road on the last Saturday of the month.

CHAPTER 17

Bindon

Ronnie Holbrook had come back from Spain and I met him for the first time at the Isle of Wight Festival. At first, he was a bit suspicious of me. I guess he thought I'd been banging his missus, and I suppose he had every right to be wary, but as neighbours we soon became good mates. He picked up a marginally more legal trade too, and had become an antiques dealer with a stall in Antiquarius on the King's Road.

Ronnie knew a lot of the Chelsea villains and it was through him that I got to know a man named Johnny Bindon. 'Biffo' Bindon was the son of a merchant seaman and he was a notorious villain. Ken Loach first approached him in a pub and gave him his role in the film *Poor Cow*. His next break came with a role in *Performance* next to Mick Jagger, where he played a violent mobster, and then a crime boss in *Get Carter*. His roles earned him critical praise and typecast him for future parts, but I knew the man and he was no actor. The man was a thug and everyone knew it. He loved beating people up, and wherever he went, a fight ensued. He did have qualities though and nobody could deny it. He was a very funny raconteur because of his confidence, and he did have good stories. Whenever he was in the pub, you'd find his circle of sycophants hanging on his every word. It was quite sick if I'm honest and, in my experience, it was all done out of intimidation. He was a gangster, he was dangerous and he was frightening – although, not according to author Philip Hoare, who called him "an all-round 'good geezer'". I can't say I agree with Hoare. I got to know him quite closely; the man was a bully.

More than his acting and his thuggery, though, Bindon was famous for the size of his cock, and he would love showing it off to everyone. He could grasp it with two large hands and still have plenty left over to swing in a circle. Dany called it, in a French accent, "le pink élicoptère". It was like a hose. His party trick in pubs was to put empty pint glasses on it, and put his penis through the handles. I believe he could do ten at one time, or something ridiculous. I was having lunch with him in the Great American Disaster one day, when the waitress came to take our order. Without lifting his haunches, he draped his cock across the table, stuck a fork in it and said, "Can I have this lightly grilled, darling?" Yes, that was John Bindon, the thug with the giant one.

It was a bright and glorious summer day. We were outside the Chelsea Potter on the King's Road. There was currently a government survey into the UK sex trade, being led by a very upright and proper English aristocrat named Lord Longford. Bindon saw Longford approaching on the pavement, so he whipped out his cock and started swirling it. "How would you like to put this in your report, Lord Longford?" he shouted down the King's Road.

★

There had been a property boom in Chelsea and Fulham in 1970 and '71, but I had only just started earning decent money, so missed out. Terry Donovan, the brilliant photographer and director of the pioneering Robert Palmer videos 'Addicted to Love' and 'Simply Irresistible', was a good friend of my sister Luisa, from her modelling and photographic repping days. Along with fellow photographers David Bailey and Brian Duffy, Terry helped create the Swinging London of the 1960s, with the high fashion and the celebrity chic. They were the first celebrity photographers, the kind of photographers, particularly Bailey, who were the inspiration for the Antonioni movie *Blow-Up*. Terry told me the next place where houses would go up in value would be Peckham, South London. It was true that there were some rather nice houses down there, going for £12,000 instead of £25,000 in Fulham and £40,000 in Chelsea, so I bought a house there in 1973, to get on the ladder. It needed renovating, and when the builders moved out, the squatters moved in. Conveniently, though, I knew Bindon.

At that time, the law was very sympathetic to squatters. All they had to do was change the lock and the house was legally theirs. You couldn't force them out and they never left the property vacant. They were often very streetwise and had done their homework on the law, so they always had at least two people in the house, to have a witness of any forced attempts to get them out. I made a decision to gather a bunch of big, rugby-playing types to try to persuade the squatters out, but my solicitor Stephen Wegg-Prosser, an old university friend, told me I must not, "absolutely must not", touch them – not even a push, in fact. I had arranged to meet a bunch of mates in the Roebuck over the road from my flat and Bindon happened to be there. It was just too good an opportunity to pass and conveniently he had with him one of his lieutenants. Hard cases from the country would often do jobs for him that he couldn't handle on his own and this particular character was quite something, as his numerous facial scars attested. Word spread fast about what we were up to and Bindon insisted on coming with us. I remember how I had to beg him not to get violent because I had notified the police and they were going to be standing outside the house. Had it turned nasty, I might have ended up behind bars – and I was bringing Bindon, so I was quite aware that anything could happen.

We got to the house in Peckham, and without wasting any time, Bindon crashed through the front door as soon as it was opened, throwing the kid who answered it into the side wall. Before I even stepped into my living room, Bindon had the two squatters up against the back wall, which they seemed to press themselves back into. He really did put on a terrific performance. I watched as the squatters were pinned to the wall by Bindon's wrath and I saw it in their eyes: they were shitting it. Amazingly, though, they were incredibly plucky and would not budge. I suppose I respected them for that. Even though they were in my house, they were standing up for what they believed in and that was surely a good thing.

Bindon stormed off in a terrible huff then and went rushing around the house until he found what he was looking for. He reappeared, holding a bag of grass held tight in his fingers, his face grinning in triumph. "Okay boys, the game's up. Do you want me to take this outside to the coppers, or will one of you go and find your friends?" Bindon was referring to the other squat around the corner. The bag of grass was the smoking gun and it was great to watch, as now they were left without a card to play. One of them left to go to the other squat while the remaining squatter was left without a witness, so Bindon took him and threw him outside.

I had thought ahead and had a locksmith standing by. He quickly got to work while I emptied the house of all the squatters' possessions, before they repossessed it. As we were piling all their stuff into the gardens, the policemen came over. The squatter had returned with some mates, but they were outside the house. Was the power struggle going to shift again? Was I in a world of it? The bobby stood there with the squatters lined next to him. Bindon and his lieutenant were there too and I was bricking it. The squatters were protesting that what we were doing was illegal. I didn't want to go to jail and the kid was right – it was illegal. However, then something wonderful happened, the power of my golden bollocks returned.

"We don't like your sort around here. If I were you, I would get a van and get your stuff out of this nice gentleman's garden – because we're leaving now, and when we've gone, I think these two could make mincemeat out of you," the copper said, looking at Bindon and his mate. I later found out that the 'lieutenant' personality with the muscles and the scars was one of the most hunted men in England, and was wanted for shooting a policeman.

★

In 1977, Peter Grant, the manager of Led Zeppelin, gave his approval for Richard Cole, the band's tour manager, to hire John Bindon as a security man on their US tour. Bindon and Cole were friends from the King's Road, and I was also a friend of Cole and his wife Marilyn. Towards the end of the tour there occurred what has become known in rock 'n' roll history as The Oakland Incident. Bindon had a fight with promoter Bill Graham's security chief and knocked him unconscious. This then escalated into an all-out brawl between the two sets of security men. The band was performing and unaware of the incident. Zeppelin then said they would only perform the second Oakland concert the next night after Bill Graham had signed a letter of indemnification, absolving the band of any responsibility for the incident. After the second concert was over, Graham changed his mind and sued the band for $2 million. After months of legal wrangling, the case was settled. Peter Grant later said that hiring John Bindon was the biggest mistake of his management career.

Bindon was also a friend of Steve O'Rourke, the manager of Pink Floyd. He sometimes did security work for the Floyd and Steve, Bindon and I went out on the town one night, just the three of us. We were driving around in Steve's Mercedes 280 SE Cabriolet. It was a lovely summer night and he had the convertible top down. We went to a few pubs and then hit Tramp. After being there a while, Steve suddenly cried out in terrible panic. He rushed out of the club, but returned minutes later: "That was lucky. I left my briefcase on the back seat. I'm going to the States tomorrow… I've got my ticket, passport and £4000 in cash in it." We left Tramp and hit the Speakeasy, but I noticed that as soon as we got there, Bindon was on the public phone in the lobby. A while later, Steve was told that someone had smashed open the boot of his car and the briefcase was gone. We were discussing the incident at the bar with a member of the American band playing that night, and the musician said, "I saw who did it."

"Oh yeah? Who?" Bindon asked him, but from the tone of his questioning it was clear who it was.

"It was you", the musician said, and Bindon knocked him out cold. It seemed he had telephoned a friend to pass the briefcase on to him, then went out and stole it and returned to the club to join Steve and I. He would do that, even to Steve O'Rourke, a friend and employer. That was the kind of man that he was.

Bindon had an aristocratic girlfriend, Vicky Hodge, the daughter of a baronet. A classic case of a posh lady liking a bit of rough. I knew her around Chelsea and through that connection, Bindon was invited to Mustique – an exclusive private island in the Caribbean Sea – on a number of occasions. There, he met the late Princess Margaret, the Queen's sister. She denied it, but I know there exists a photograph of them together. The story goes that she had heard about the size of his penis and they went for a walk down the beach so that he could show it to her. Bindon claimed that when they returned to London, the princess would frequently send a car for him to visit her in Kensington Palace.

One of Bindon's pals was blues and jazz singer Dana Gillespie, who was – and still is – a regular in Mustique. She is also aristocratic and was friends with Vicky Hodge, so that may have been the reason Bindon and Vicky went there. Dana was going out with my friend Leslie Spitz at the time, and I often saw them in London. I also spent some time with them in LA in '72, during the David Bowie tour for *The Rise and Fall of Ziggy Stardust and the Spiders from Mars* album. Dana was a best friend of David's wife Angie Bowie, about whom Mick Jagger wrote the song 'Angie'. We all hung out at the Beverly Wilshire Hotel – note, scene of the Richard Gere and Julia Roberts hit movie *Pretty Woman*. Bowie didn't hang out with us; he was at the other end of the hotel, being looked after by his bodyguard. Nevertheless, Angie had access to all the trappings of a superstar existence – with a phone call she could summon a stretched limo for us when our stomachs rumbled and we needed a restaurant. I remember we always had that great Stevie Wonder track 'Superstition' on the limo radio. It was a fun few days for me, living the Hollywood dream.

One day, back in London, I was with Leslie and Dana, and Angie and a male friend. We were driving back into London from the country and were stuck in traffic on the Cromwell Road. Stuck in the traffic alongside us were the Russian Ambassador and his wife. At least, I presumed that's who they were because they were in the back of a chauffeur-driven Zil limousine – a heavily armoured Russian car used only for soviet leaders and the Russian government. They were high above us and looking straight into our car. I think, from the looks on their faces, they were rather shocked – one of the girls was giving a blow job to one of the men in the back of my car.

Bindon was a good friend of Leslie Spitz and Tony Howard, and they were always at Tony's house in Chelsea. Just to show what a sadistic bully Bindon was, one night he beat Leslie up, for no good reason, outside Tony's house. Leslie is a tiny man, not over 5'6" tall, and he was Bindon's friend. Other news was spreading too, and word on the street now had Bindon connected with the Kray twins and the Richardson Gang.

Johnny Bindon lived in a Belgravia mews house next door to my friends Bill and Hazel Collins. Bill, the younger brother of Joan and Jackie Collins, is another Ferraristo. Jackie always used to be in Tramp during the seventies, and her now-deceased husband, Oscar Lerman, was one of the owners of the club at that time. Later, she moved to Los Angeles. Bill would often be the DJ at Tramp, which is how I got to know him – that and the fact that his Jamaican wife Hazel is one of the most gorgeous girls in London. I had a falling out with Jackie one night. We had all been to the premiere of *Saturday Night Fever* and Jackie said to me later in Tramp, "Don't you know a commercials director who could make a film of my book *The Stud*?" I think it was the first book she had written. I'd had a couple of drinks and I made an obnoxious remark, which I immediately regretted, something to the effect that "New directors want to do something more worthy for their first film." It was a stupid thing to say, for apart from being very rude, I hadn't even read the damn book. Jackie eventually got the film made and it became the biggest selling video at that time. So much for my opinion!

In 1978, John Bindon killed another villain, Johnny Darke, in an afternoon drinking club in Putney. They had a fight, and Darke, who must have been very tough to do so, was straddling Bindon on the floor, while repeatedly stabbing him in his chest. Bindon managed to get his knife out of his boot, and he thrust it up into Darke's heart. Seriously injured, and wrapped in a blood-soaked blanket, Bindon managed to make it by train and ferry to Ireland, where he went into hiding in a monastery. He eventually offered a deal to the police, that he would return to face justice if he could plead self-defence, to which the police agreed. Bob Hoskins was a character witness for the defence and Bindon was tried and acquitted. He got away with a lot with the police and there were rumours why: either he was an informer or he had secretly taken compromising photographs with Princess Margaret, which protected him. This story is featured, although Bindon is not mentioned, in the 2008 film *The Bank Job*, written by my mate Ian La Frenais and Dick Clement, about the 1971 Lloyds Bank robbery and the attempt by the secret service agency MI5 to get some 'photographs' stored in the bank safety deposit.

Johnny 'Biffo' Bindon died of an AIDS-related illness in 1993.

CHAPTER 18

BFCS

Work was non-stop. I was producing commercials for our top directors Bob Brooks and Ross Cramer. Len Fulford was also one of our stars, but I rarely worked with him. He made award-winning ads for Guinness and Courage Best Bitter. He had worked on the stills and commercials for the 'Go to Work on an Egg' campaign and once told John Lennon, "I am the egg man". He liked to think that was where Lennon picked up the line. Len became known for shooting food commercials. Delia Smith worked as the home economist with him and Bob Brooks, before making her own programmes and hitting the big time. I was working with the people at the top of their game. Good quality work brought with it good quality parties and that moved everything on at lightning speed. The years had felt like they had just vanished.

By 1977, I had been there for seven years, and Martin McKeand resigned as managing director of Brooks Fulford Cramer. He had ambitions in TV production and possibly could take no more of Bob Brooks' fiery outbursts, but I was luckier and worked closely with Bob as his producer. I liked him and he liked me, and his temper didn't bother me. Even when we were equal partners in the company, I always knew who was boss, because Bob was a brilliant director and he was the star. I had come to realise I didn't want to be the star, I didn't want to be famous. I remember my time in Rome, at the Cinecittà studios, when Clint and John Wayne and Robert Mitchum and Kirk were the stars, and in my later years when it was Eric Clapton or Bob. I, though, was never in the centre and I was happy about that. I had it in me, I think, to be smarter than to want that and to know that that wasn't really me anyway. Bob was Bob, I was Johnny Cigarini, and that was that. Bob and I would certainly have disagreements, but generally speaking, we did accept the other for who they were. So, I stepped in and bought a third of the company. Thus, I became managing director. Golden Bollocks Cigarini... managing fucking director. I guess he was still watching me from up there. Mum, too.

My first idea was to suggest to Brooks and Fulford that we take on Michael Seresin as a fourth director, although he probably doesn't know that. They agreed, and the company was then known as Brooks Fulford Cramer Seresin. Shortly after, we took on another director with an S initial, Richard Sloggett, and Ross Cramer left. As I was a company partner with a C initial, it was decided to call the company BFCS Ltd. and leave it at that. That was the end of the name changes and my initial was in there, kind of.

Michael Seresin is a brilliant cinematographer. He had lit many of Bob's commercials and had been director of photography on the great Alan Parker feature films *Bugsy Malone* and *Midnight Express* before joining BFCS, and afterwards *Fame*, *Shoot the Moon*, *Angel Heart* and *Angela's Ashes* – and as well as being a talented fucker, he was a handsome bastard. It is well known in feature film folklore that the director of photography (DP) often gets the lead girl. If I was a cynic, which of course I'm not, I would suggest those were attempts by the ladies to get photographed in the most beautiful of film lights, but I think it's more likely that the babes are drawn to the genius behind the camera without the ego, like the bass player in the band – the man of rhythm, of intelligence, of experience in the game. Michael had that going for him, but he also had another advantage: he was devastatingly good looking and a charmer.

On *Angel Heart* in New Orleans, he was great friends with the beautiful Charlotte Rampling and with the hot and exotic young American Lisa Bonet. I think the directors would often get jealous that Michael was getting all the female attention. And it wasn't just Michael Seresin. Hugh Johnson, another handsome cameraman, worked on Tony Scott's debut feature *The Hunger*, and went off to live in Paris with the leading lady, the iconic Catherine Deneuve. It was times like these when I would often wonder, *Why didn't Granny give me a camera instead of the piano accordion?*

Michael had been directing commercials with his friend Souter Harris before joining us. He became a star commercials director with BFCS and won many awards for films for the VW Golf, Stella Artois, Renault (the Papa and Nicole campaign) and Citroën. He had illustrious producers like Glynis Sanders, before she went off and started her own company with Richard Sloggett and another of BFCS' producers, Jenny Huie, in the late eighties. While she was working at BFCS, Glynis married Tony Scott, Ridley Scott's younger brother and director of *Top Gun*.

I knew Tony in the early days; we used to meet up at Tramp. She had a very unhappy experience during the marriage. While Tony was shooting *Beverly Hills Cop 2*, he had an affair with the leading lady, Brigitte Nielsen, who was married to Sylvester Stallone. It was all over the newspapers and was very humiliating for Glynis. She had met Stallone and he would ring her house. That was the end of her marriage to Tony. Last time I saw Tony Scott, he was very friendly to me and invited me over to the splendid new RSA offices in Beverly Hills. His brother, Ridley, always greets me in the same endearing way, on the occasions we meet in restaurants or in the Sunset Marquis Hotel: "Hello, Wanker!" would be considered quite normal.

Angie O'Rourke, wife of Steve, the manager of Pink Floyd, also produced for Michael Seresin. Earlier in her career, she had been Alan Parker's PA, so she and Michael knew each other well. Another person to produce for Seresin was Michael Hayes, who had formerly been married to Jenny Armstrong of Jenny & Co, both of whom I had first met with Jenny Sieff before I first joined Brooks Baker Fulford. Hayes was later to marry Annie Pugsley, Len Fulford's producer, who took over from me as managing director of the UK company when I moved to LA. Ronnie Holbrook also produced for Seresin – yes, that Ronnie from the King's Road. After a stint as an antiques dealer, he started working as a freelance assistant director on commercials. Due to his considerable charisma, we offered him a staff job at BFCS as a producer.

Michael Seresin would still go off once a year to light Alan Parker's films. He was so busy and profitable shooting commercials the rest of the time, the other partners didn't mind him taking the time off. One time, Michael had just finished a film with Alan and was asked by Sidney Pollack to do *Out of Africa*. In effect, Michael wanted to go off and do two consecutive features, which was quite unheard of. He told me, "If ever there is one film I want to do in my life, it is this one." I told him that if it was that important, he should take the job, but they couldn't agree on the fee and the job went to David 'Wendy' Watkin.

I guess in life some things are meant to be, as Watkin won the Academy Award for Cinematography. Michael was also unlucky not to shoot *Mississippi Burning*, which also won the Oscar for Cinematography. He had been DP on all of Alan Parker's films, but missed out on that one because he was busy directing *Homeboy*, a feature film of his own. Peter Biziou, a contemporary of Michael's in London, did a great job on *Mississippi Burning* and won the Oscar. The point here is thus: if ever there is a cinematographer who deserves the Oscar, it is Michael Seresin. Alan Parker told me in Cannes one year that

Michael and Vittorio Storaro were the two greatest cinematographers in the world, quite a statement coming from one of Britain's finest directors.

In 1995, after I had left BFCS Ltd. in the UK, the partnership fell apart. People had been telling me for years that would happen. Seresin contentiously bought out Bob Brooks and Len Fulford, and he went into a new partnership with Derek Coutts, director of all the Nescafé Gold Blend commercials, featuring my friend Sharon Maughan – the wife of my other friend, Trevor Eve. I was out and it was continuing, but BFCS Ltd. finally closed in 2001, after thirty-five years of existence – a long, long time in the commercials production business.

Michael still works as a director of photography on movies. His time is also taken up with a very successful vineyard he has in his homeland, New Zealand. He probably won't remember this – but it is true – he was going to call the wine by the name of the place it comes from, but I told him he was mad and that he should call it Seresin. He did.

Tony Scott died jumping off a bridge in Long Beach, California in 2012. The news was devastating.

CHAPTER 19

Donatella

Love came, again. I'm old now, but I think it was the summer of '77 and I was in Ibiza visiting – maybe even staying with – my friend Peter Adler, at his finca. Peter is the brother of Carol Adler, who I worked with at Hobson Bates and whose flat I'd taken over on the King's Road. Also staying with Peter were two beautiful young girls who had just left Cheltenham Ladies College, quite possibly the poshest girls' school in England. Their names were Serena Scott Thomas and Donatella Moores, and they were both exquisitely beautiful.

Off the coast of Valencia, Ibiza is one of the Pine Islands and shouldn't be known only for its tourism. In fact, at Peter's farmhouse cottage, we were hidden, engulfed in the warmth and the sweet smells of the Med, which only the Balearics could ever muster. You would never have imagined a few miles away that hundreds were getting trolleyed on coke and ketamine. We were in heaven.

I would drive my little Fiat 600, looking at Serena and Donatella sat there in the back through my rearview, often causing me to nearly drive it off the road. Serena was particularly impressive; she used to read Dostoyevsky on the beach, in Russian! She became an actress; her sister Kristin Scott Thomas is better known, but was not famous when I knew Serena.

Donatella was an equally gorgeous, slight wisp of a gal, with a mane of naturally curly hair. Her family was the Littlewoods family of football pools, high street stores and mail order catalogues. They were always featured in the Top 10 in the *Sunday Times Rich List*. From what I could gather, Peter didn't seem to be dating either of them, and we all had a very nice platonic holiday. It was a breath of fresh air actually.

After returning to London, I was driving my classic '59 red Corvette through Eaton Square when I saw Donatella waiting for a taxi. You could spot her mane of hair a hundred yards away. I pulled over, offered her a ride and she jumped in. One thing led to another and we began dating. I went out with her for four years, and it was my longest romance ever – before or after.

She lived with her parents in a sensational penthouse apartment that stretched across four large Eaton Square houses. Her father left home around the time I started going out with Donatella and I never met him. I spent a lot of time in the penthouse and I saw a lot of her mother, who was Italian – hence the Donatella name. She, the mother, seemed permanently depressed, which was not surprising considering her husband had just left the family home. She was a nice lady and was very generous to me, but she was not a great physical beauty like her daughter. I wondered where Donatella got that from, until I met her grandmother who was visiting from Naples. She was an incredible looking older woman, fit and well spirited too. Donatella's mother didn't seem to mind the age difference between us, although I was quite aware of it. When we began going out, I was thirty-four and Donatella was just eighteen.

The Moores family, or it may have been Donatella herself, owned an estate of four or five Oliver Messel-designed houses on the beach in St. James, Barbados, right next to the Sandy Lane Hotel. Not bad for an eighteen-year-old, eh? We went there for Christmas every year I went out with her, but Donatella and I never lived together. Eventually she moved out of the family home and got her own flat in Chelsea, but by then I had moved to my own penthouse that stretched over four houses in Notting Hill. I was obviously trying to emulate the Moores' residence in Eaton Square… or just generally show off.

One evening, I was having dinner with Donatella. Elton John had just bought Watford Football Club and it came up in conversation. "My Grandfather, Sir John Moores, owns Everton," Donatella said. I was genuinely shocked; Everton was one of the biggest clubs in England. I found out years later that the other side of the family – presumably descended from Sir John Moores' brother Cecil Moores, the pools side of the family businesses – also owned Liverpool Football Club, Everton's great city rivals. Littlewoods Football Pools originated in Liverpool and when David Moores, who must be Donatella's cousin, sold Liverpool FC to some American businessmen, his family had owned the club for over sixty years. The Moores family sold Littlewoods for £750 million in 2002. The point is: she was great, she was fun, she was beautiful, she was successful and she came from a history of money – but it wasn't to last.

Donatella Moores and I split up late in 1982 after four years together. I had had heart surgery in September of that year and I think she put it off for a while until I recovered from that. Over the last few months, she had seemed rather depressed and she eventually told me it was over – because I didn't talk to her (again!) and she didn't think I was capable of giving love. I was devastated, but I think I agreed with her about not being able to give love. I didn't fight it, I didn't plead with her or even discuss it. I just froze.

I have never been in a romantic relationship since. Thirty years have passed now and I definitely have issues with women. When I am in a relationship, I self-destruct. I am so frightened that the relationship is going to end, my fear overwhelms me and I ruin everything. As my friend Sid Roberson used to say: "Bringing about that most feared, by the means taken to avoid it." Also, I was very self-conscious about my twitch and I couldn't understand why any girl would want to be with someone who kept flicking his head.

Fifteen years later, when I was in LA having psychiatric counselling to help me give up work, I discussed with the therapist my inability to have relationships. It emerged that I had abandonment issues, going back to being left by my mother with her sister at age five and my mother's subsequent death. It seemed it had hurt me harder than I realised. I still blame the war – my not being able to love Donatella was a direct result – and all that the war produced, what with my family's split, the inertia between my parents and being sent to Margate. I don't think that five-year-olds can really grasp the concept of death, so they see it as abandonment, and the scars run deep. Deep. That's why I dumped so many beautiful women, to get in first before they dumped me. It was as if I was trying to take revenge on the female race, apparently! But really, it was a defence mechanism, the irony of course being that it wasn't and it was destructive. So destructive in fact that I cannot love, and what is more destructive than that? I decided after Donatella to withdraw from romantic involvement, and to be honest, I have been happier since.

My being alone seems stranger to my friends than to me, although I don't think any of them see me as a sad and lonely man. Maybe this chapter will explain it. I have felt alone my entire life and that's how I am comfortable. I have never had a stable family life, so I do not feel the urge to find that stability, to have children and a family of my own. I am happy with my situation of just me – because it's all I've ever had. Although I have sisters, they are always far away, just as they have always been. I am, and always will be, an orphan. Meanwhile, I don't actually 'suffer' from loneliness and being single has made me much more gregarious, and that has contributed to my interesting life. It has contributed to me having more time to develop my interests and just focus on me – I suppose – 'cause nobody else did, apart from the reverend.

CHAPTER 20

Stocks House

Back on the King's Road, Butch, one of the three matching thin blonde Beverly Sister men, had moved out to marry a Brazilian babe, Christina Viera. Christina and her sister Andrea (Rio) had taken London by storm when they arrived in the seventies. Andrea married Guy Dellal and had a daughter, Alice, who is now a big-time model and punk musician. Guy was the only son and heir to 'Black' Jack Dellal, a rich financier and property developer. Jack's most famous deal was when he 'flipped' Bush House, the BBC building on Aldwich. He bought it for £55 million and sold it to Japanese investors for £135 million. He made a profit of £80 million without setting foot in the place. Jack also had some well-known-about-town daughters: Lorraine Dellal, who is married to Simon Kirke, drummer and owner of the band Bad Company, and Gaby, who was married to Eric Fellner, of Working Title Films.

EMI had sacked the Sex Pistols, Jimmy Carter succeeded Gerald Ford, Fleetwood Mac released *Rumours*, and *Star Wars* opened in cinemas. It was 1977 and I had two Brazilian girls living in my flat on the King's Road. Fifi was very pretty and very sweet; Lara was very very pretty and very sweet. Usually when I came home from work, they would be cavorting on the carpet, making out with one another. I had seen worse things in my life, and few better.

One day I got back and there was a great big bunch of flowers, addressed to me, from Ladbrokes Casino. I thought it a bit strange, as I had no interest in gambling, but I didn't think much about it. I telephoned the person on the visiting card and thanked her, and asked what it was all about. She suggested that perhaps I would like to go to the Ladbrokes Casino, but I wasn't interested, so I put the phone down and continued watching the Brazilians kiss and fondle one another. There was something iffy in the air. Before long, I had received a call from a financial journalist. It seemed that the Ladbrokes approach was highly illegal, and the Gaming Act had banned any advertising or promotions on behalf of the casinos. An article appeared in *Private Eye* magazine about me, and I was interviewed for a TV financial programme. Ladbrokes' madcap scheme was called Unit Six and was run by the Danish head of marketing, Andreas Christensen.

It transpired that someone had taken down car registration numbers outside the famous Clermont Casino in Berkeley Square. My car at that time was a silver 1963 Corvette Sting Ray (which looked a bit like a spaceship). It may have been parked outside the Clermont, but I had never been in the gambling club. More likely I was in Morton's, which was in the same square. It turns out that a corrupt policeman had accessed the Police National Computer in Nottingham and found out my address. I twiddled my thumbs and rubbed my chin... the Brazilians twiddled their nipples and rubbed their... well, ya know.

Morton's was a sophisticated restaurant and bar, set up by Peter Morton after the success of the Hard Rock Café. I went there after work on most evenings for a couple of years. I once took Jerry Bruckheimer, when he was setting up a movie and wanted recommendations for British cinematographers. I knew Jerry from earlier in the decade in LA, through Joe Boyd and John Head, who were friends of Dany Holbrook. Jerry Bruckheimer is now the biggest film and television producer on earth. One of my regular drinking buddies in Morton's was Mike King. Mike had had his moment of fame as part of a singing group, The King Brothers. They had a number of English hits in the fifties and early sixties with covers, but their career peaked when they were bumped off the Ed Sullivan show for a new, unknown band called The Beatles. Mike had been married to Carol White, the sexy star of sixties films *Cathy Come Home* and *Poor Cow*. They had had two sons, but by then were divorced. I told him about the incident with the flowers and the financial journalist, and this marked the beginning of my next adventure... into the world of the Playboy Bunny. Mike was a weekend regular at the UK Playboy mansion, Stocks House, and he mentioned the incident to Victor Lownes, boss of all the Playboy clubs and casinos worldwide. He was based in London and I received an invitation to Stocks House... it was meant to be just for the one weekend.

★

Victor, or rather Victor Aubrey Lownes III, had had an interesting life. As the story goes, his father gave him a cigar to smoke at age twelve, which he did and then requested another. Sadly, at around the same time, he had accidentally shot and killed his best friend. As a result, he was sent to the military and he went through university in Chicago. By eighteen, he was married with children – but he hated his life, and felt trapped. He abandoned everything and he moved to Chicago; there, he met Hugh Hefner with a girlfriend, who suggested Hefner dress the hostesses in the image of a tuxedoed Playboy Bunny. Hefner agreed and then Victor moved to London and grew the empire. When I met Victor, he was most certainly an anglophile and London was, for him and all of us, the most exciting place in the world. Victor loved English country pursuits like riding point-to-point, so he had bought an old girls' school in Hertfordshire, about an hour's drive outside London, in beautiful countryside. During the week it was used as a Bunny Girl and croupier training centre; at weekends, it was Victor's private home and used for… well… parties.

Mike King was one of a very small group of male guests at Stocks House, known as Stocks regulars. He took me to meet Victor one weekend, and together, he and I discussed the Ladbrokes case. He was a nice man and we liked each other. Victor took up the complaint against Ladbrokes and weeks later I would discover, through Victor, that Cyril Stein, the boss of Ladbrokes, had warned him that if Playboy were going to fling mud, he (Stein) would fling some back. I asked Victor if he was worried about that happening and he said there was no mud to fling at Playboy. "We are whiter than white," I remember him telling me. Unfortunately for Victor, though, coincidentally or not, four years later someone falsely claimed to have dealt cocaine at the Playboy Club and they lost their gaming licence, and Hefner sacked Victor. I felt responsible because my bunch of flowers had started it all, or rather, that place I parked!

Meanwhile, while all of this drama was continuing, the Brazilians were at mine, making out and fondling each other in the nirvana of love and leisure. Life could be so simple for some people, I remember thinking as I stood in the middle of what was basically a scandal. Was money, high society, membership of elite clubs and long expensive dinners with celebrities really all it was cracked up to be? It was hard, but whenever I doubted my movements, I thought back to my time in the hotel in Margate and the eggs I'd have to stand there and fry. Perhaps there was a sweet spot in between it all? I was also trying to be careful. I didn't want to complain about anything. After all, things could have been worse – like for the men my father photographed, in the rain, in Caporetto in 1917. It could have been worse. Like Hemingway wrote, it could have been bleak. I didn't want to complain. The Brazilian girls continued on.

My father with gunners during the First World War

My father with the colonel during the retreat from Caparetto in 1917

My mother, portrait by my father

Sir Arthur Conan Doyle, portrait by Cigarini

Pond's advertisement, portrait by Cigarini

Me, a small boy in Rome

The Cigarini family, all still together in Rome in the 1940s. I am the baby

Early days with Granny

Inscription:
To my little Johnny, his Dad,
Rome 1950

*The model car my father gave me when I was 5,
on the last occasion I saw him*

Me with Granny and my accordion

Fame! Photo of a TV, of the Margate Childrens' Piano Accordion Band, with smiling Johnny on the right.

Reunited with my sisters in 1958, aged 14

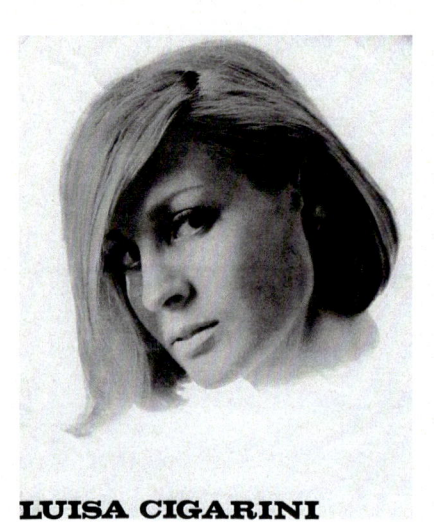

LUISA CIGARINI
My sister Luisa's modelling headsheet.

My photo of Jimi Hendrix at the Isle of Wight Festival in 1970

With Zambia's first President-elect, Dr. Kenneth Kaunda, at the opening of the Outward Bound School in 1964.

My shot of Sly and the Family Stone, from the stage at dawn, at the Isle of Wight Festival in 1970

Frank Zappa and Dany

The 70s look. Me in 1972 aged 28

Patti D'Arbanville

*Me with then girlfriend Jaleh at the 1975 Models Ball.
Photo Gloria Lorandos*

Trevor Myles on his tiger skin Ford Mustang, outside Paradise Garage. Photo Tim Street-Porter.

Bob Brook and George Cole in Istanbul, filming for Benson and Hedges

Not a bad evening's haul of Clios in New York

Me and Donatella Moores

Isaac Tigrett delivering the Hard Rock Café lunch to my hospital room

Victor and Marilyn Lownes

VW racing a falling chimney

Volkswagen Golf "Dropping Car"

Me with Tara (L) and a girlfriend

Receiving the Palme d'Or from the Mayor of Cannes, one of 6 times

The famous BFCS T-shirt.

The two young ladies I stayed with in Bangkok

Chessy Thyssen, with Gianni Agnelli, owner of Fiat and Ferrari

Bryan Ferry at my 40th birthday party

Me in 1982, aged 38, after chopping off my long hair

Me and Michael Seresin with Muhammad Ali

Me and Trevor Eve in the 80s

Jacuzzi time! Me and Victor Lownes and some of the Stocks House regulars.

Charles and Kay Saatchi on their wedding day

Doing my Elvis Presley act at the Saatchi wedding, showing the Nazi graffiti

Lorraine and Simon Kirke, and Jo and Ronnie Wood, at Ridge Farmhouse

Maureen Starkey with my Andrew Logan Tiger

Me and Charles Saatchi at the Amanpuri Hotel in Thailand

Me with Jerry Hall and some other lovely ladies, at Mick Jagger's house in Mustique

Mick Jagger at his Mustique home

Tony Curtis with my sister Christina at one of my parties

My penthouse in Notting Hill

Peter Cook dancing, and Trevor Myles, at one of my parties

L-R, David Puttnam, Kay Saatchi, Michael Buckley, Charles Saatchi, Richard Branson, in Thailand

Christmas with Pattie Boyd and Jose Fonseca

Nigel Carroll and Eric Clapton with his Ferrari 275 GTB/4.

Me with Eric and Pattie Clapton in my Corvette after a party at the Hard Rock Cafe. Photo Alan Davidson

Eric Idle and Kay Saatchi on board the motor yacht Havre de Grace

Me, Mike Powell, and Prince Albert of Monaco

Maureen and Isaac Tigrett getting married in the South of France.

Pink Floyd in Venice, the crowd gathering for the evening show.

Pink Floyd manager Steve O'Rourke with wife Angie, at the Le Mans 24-hour race.

*Danny Mindel, me and
Keith Richards,
in Antigua*

*With Ian McShane
at one of my parties
in the penthouse.*

*House of Blues Brothers,
me with Dan Aykroyd.*

Michael Hutchence's birthday, with Stephen Dorff, Helena Christensen, and Christy Turlington

Ridge Farmhouse in Wiltshire

Partying with the England football team after they had been knocked out of the 1990 World Cup

Skinny-dipping at dawn with Gazza and Barnesie, after the all-night party with the England World Cup football team

The photo of me and Princess Diana in the News of the World

Roger Waters, at my pool in Beverly Hills.

The 90s Malibu look

Glyn Johns and friend in the burnt-out Malibu landscape

Keith Richards cooking the barbeque lunch in Antigua.

*Jeff Lynne,
Ian La Frenais,
Michael Vartan,
his mother Doris
La Frenais, and
Johnny Gaydon*

*Me on right with my 3
nephews after I had
retired in 1996, aged 52*

*The usual
morning's catch for
Jeff and the boys.
Photo Gun Bush*

*Cinema in the Sand
Photo Gun Bush*

*The Vermilion Sea,
from my house*

*My Baja
California home*

Baja California friends

*Twiggy and
Leigh Lawson*

*A typical
Umbrian
expat lunch*

*My house in
Tuscany*

*Me in Tuscany in 2011, aged 67
Photo Gun Bush*

*Me in Baja January 2013, aged 68
Photo Gun Bush*

THE CAR GALLERY

1958 Corvette, famous on the King's Road in the 1970s

1963 Corvette Sting Ray and 1954 Jaguar XK 120

Alfa Romeos, Giulietta Sprint and SZ

Aston Martin DB4 Mark IV

1955 Ford F100

Ferrari BB512 Boxer on a wall

Ferrari F40

Ford Mustang GT350

Jaguar XK 120

Little Red Corvette

E-Type Jaguar

Maserati Ghibli spider.

Mercedes 280 SE convertible
R.I.P. John Lewis

The Corvettes, my 3 on the left and Nigel's on the right

Hollywood car. Cadillac Eldorado convertible

Ladbrokes lost their gambling licence, due to the Unit Six operation, and it was estimated that the closure of their casinos cost the company £100 million. All because of my parking. Oops!

★

The London Playboy Club and Casino was the most profitable part of the whole Playboy group. This was in the days of the rich Arabs coming to gamble in London. Playboy made $31 million profit in 1981, the year before they lost their licence, and lost more than $51 million the following year.

In the meantime, I had become good friends with Victor and was a regular at Stocks. I still see him from time to time, for lunch and whatnot. He is still with his lovely and tremendously supportive wife Marilyn (former *Playboy* model Marilyn Cole, who was the magazine's first full-frontal nude centerfold).

I went to Stocks every weekend for four years and Victor was incredibly generous to me there. It was rumoured to cost £500,000 a year to run the house, which was a huge amount in the 1980s. Stocks House had had an interesting history. To begin, it was inherited by the First Viscount of Falloden, Sir Edward Grey, from his grandfather, but he flogged it to Mary Augusta Ward, the novelist, who hosted gatherings and dinners for leading intellectuals – like her Fabian nephews Aldous and Julian Huxley, and even George Orwell. From Ward, it got passed to her son, a member of parliament, then the girls' school came of it, where they were taught the art of the deep curtsey as well as the philosophy of the Enlightenment. The house, though, did eventually come to Victor and by then had seen quite a few parties – nothing though, I'm sure, like what happened through the seventies and eighties.

Not surprisingly, there were very few male guests. The regulars were my friend Mike King, whose job it was to project the film after dinner on Saturday nights, singer and comedian Kenny Lynch, comedian Peter Cook, Viktor Melik (the famous French crooner Claude Franck) and Stash de Rola, son of Balthus, the painter. John Cleese also became a regular, as did Allan McKeown and Ian La Frenais.

There were also many visitors who were not regulars. Due to his riding activities (Playboy sponsored the local point-to-point meetings), Victor often had members of the local gentry to dine. Visiting Hollywood celebs would appear if they were filming in London, like Tony Curtis, who stayed for weeks, but kept mainly to his room with a very buxom girlfriend indeed. She offered to come to London to "tit-whip" me. The mind boggles! It never happened... sadly. Tony did, however, get out of the house to come to my party in London. He was wearing a Stetson hat on that night – a class act all the way.

There were a lot of girls at Stocks. The dining room had a huge table. One weekend at dinner, I counted twenty-five girls and six men. Fantastic! Victor would have formal dinners every evening, served by waitresses. Dress was informal-smart, but woe betide anyone if they were late; they would get Victor's wrath and I saw it occasionally – more terrifying than Johnny Bindon! Many of the girls were regulars, too – friends, ex-Playboy employees and sometimes former girlfriends of Victor's. Many had worked as Bunnies, but there were very few girls who were currently Bunnies. I don't think Victor encouraged that, but the girls were all young and attractive. I wanted them all! Not all the girls had Playboy connections, though. One such and a very nice regular was Tessa Dahl, daughter of Roald Dahl, and the American film actress Patricia Neal. Tessa was always there with her young daughter Sophie, who must have been about ten or eleven. Sophie's father was Julian Holloway, son of actor Stanley Holloway, but she took the name Dahl and would later become the world-famous model, Sophie Dahl.

Victor had a pet monkey that used to jump out at the end of dinner. It didn't seem to like women and would bite at them from time to time. Maybe it just sensed their fears, but the girls tended to sit away from him at dinner. "It's because they sense your fear," I'd tell them, "... trust me, I've slept with African baboons!"

It wasn't one giant orgy at Stocks and most of the pairing-off was done quite discreetly, but due to the imbalance in numbers, it was not uncommon to have 'interesting' combinations. I sometimes took two women to bed and the facilities, let us just say, 'lent themselves' to trysts between the guests. There was a huge tropical jacuzzi room, with accommodation for about twenty. There was a disco and a games room with all the pinball machines. Outdoors in the summer, there was a large pool with underwater music, a tennis court where Peter Cook, Mike King, Kenny Lynch and I played each weekend, and there was a squash court and riding stables. Every activity was covered. There was even a clay pigeon shoot, but I was useless – so bad in fact that Victor made some plastic badges just for me that read 'Save the Clays!'.

As I said, Victor Lownes was a tremendously kind and generous man. When

I had heart surgery, he visited me in the Princess Grace Hospital and when he heard I was worried about going home alone, he invited me to stay for a couple of weeks at Stocks. I accepted his kind invite and the staff all looked after me like I was family.

I sometimes took Donatella Moores, and although she 'quite' enjoyed the glamour, not surprisingly she didn't love it. She did, though, come to the now famous twenty-five-hour Playboy 25th Anniversary party in '78, where we were buzzed by two helicopters – one piloted by wine merchant Ronnie Sichel – going around and around while we were up to no good... near the woods to top it all off. Al fresco?!

The end of Stocks was dramatic. Victor had fallen off his horse on an icy road and had fractured his skull. I visited him in the John Radcliffe Hospital in Oxford. Whether coincidentally or deliberately, the whole business of the irregularities at the Playboy Club came out too – just as Victor was out of action. The licence was at risk, and Hugh Hefner panicked and relieved Victor of his duties. He sent over two executives from the Playboy organisation in the US, both of whom had Italian names. It was the worst thing Hefner could have done. The British Gaming Board knew and trusted Victor, but they were paranoid about mafia infiltration into the British gaming industry, and had already refused the Hollywood actor George Raft a licence due to alleged mafia connections. Eventually, Playboy wised up and appointed a British establishment figurehead, Sir John Treasure, an ex-Admiral of the Fleet but it was too late and Playboy lost its licence.

I was at Stocks House the weekend Victor lost his job. The whole Stocks dream was over. Victor wouldn't leave his room. There was even talk of him having a gun in there.

CHAPTER 21

The Hard Rock Story

I had been diagnosed with a heart murmur back in the early 1970s. It was kept under observation until it was decided in the summer of 1982 to do an aortic valve transplant. *Chariots of Fire* won best picture, Villa won the European Cup, Spurs the FA Cup, Men At Work hit the charts with 'Down Under', the Falklands War began and I was having a pig valve stuck into my heart. I checked into the Princess Grace Hospital the afternoon before the operation. The surgeon, Mr John Wright, came into my room in the evening. I had only met him briefly a month earlier in his Harley Street office. I was very nervous and trying to lighten the situation.

"Where's the pig?" I asked.

"What do you mean?" he said.

"Well, I was expecting two beds, one for me, and one for the pig."

"This is not a laughing matter," he said and stormed out of my room. I lay there grinning. What else to do but try and make it funny? I was having pig put in me for goodness' sake.

I smuggled a Polaroid camera into the operating theatre, and before it all began, I asked one of the intensive care nurses to take snaps of me after it was done. She did an excellent job and I have a full set of pictures of me lying unconscious, with tubes sticking out of everything – yes, including my penis.

Every day I was in hospital recuperating from the surgery, I would get a call from Isaac Tigrett at the Hard Rock Café. "Hey, Johnny-Boy! What do you want for lunch?" I fancied testing the calibre of the pig valve they had fitted, so I chose the half-pound burger with cheese and fries, and Isaac would come to the room every day with the Hard Rock signature blue-and-white-checked gingham tablecloth, the Heinz ketchup and American mustard, and serve up, right there in my room. What a mate!

Every day he would tell me the inside story of the business. Right now, he was in litigation with Peter Morton. Apparently, the old car showroom they had found on Piccadilly back in '71 only had eighteen months before it was due to be demolished. The idea was that Tigrett and Morton would put up twenty-five grand each, make a quick killing, and get out in eighteen months, but the plot thickened. Squatters next door at 144 Piccadilly had moved in, in high numbers, but this time for the better; them being there consequently saved the Hard Rock from being broken down. 144 was a big building, and there were now hundreds of squatters. The law was still biased in favour of them, and it took a long time to get them out, so the developers were not able to tear down the terrace of buildings. In the meantime, Parliament had become concerned about the number of fine old buildings that were being torn away to build hotels in that part of Mayfair. The Hilton and the Intercontinental had already been built, but they passed a Preservation Act protecting, from now on, many old buildings, including the one housing the Hard Rock. The building was saved, the café was able to negotiate a new twenty-year lease and I had just finished my burger.

They started making lots of money and Isaac went to India to be with his guru, Sai Baba, while Peter was left concentrating on his clubs Morton's and Maunkberry's. While the Falklands drew to an end, the squatters grew in number and Thatcher's Britain saw unemployment rise to a record high, my friends and I were making money, but they were also falling out and Isaac bought Peter out for one million pounds. Peter moved to LA and opened a Hard Rock Café there, and he put it on the map fast, as it was the hangout of the Brat Pack, teen idol movie stars Sean Penn, Emilio Estevez, Judd Nelson and Rob Lowe. Isaac was a little shocked: "But I've bought you out!" Morton retorted, "You only bought me out in London", and the litigation continued. Eventually, it was settled that Isaac got the whole world except the US west of the Mississippi River, which was Peter's territory along with Hawaii and Australia.

I went to the opening parties of a couple of the Hard Rocks that Isaac opened, in New York and Dallas. Andy Warhol was at the New York opening, but I couldn't talk to him; it would only bring up the memory of Patti. I still thought of her – I think of her even today. The Dallas Hard Rock building was a classic style, with columns and a portico on the front, and Dan Aykroyd christened it 'The Supreme Court of Rock and Roll'. By then, the Hard Rock corporation had a serious collection of rock 'n' roll memorabilia and the Dallas café even had Buddy Holly's trademark spectacles, pulled from the wreckage of the plane crash that killed him. They still belonged to the Holly family, but were on loan to the Hard Rock. Isaac always had interesting pieces like that. In his house, he had a collection of broken drumsticks that had been destroyed by Keith Moon of The Who. They had been astutely saved by the group's roadie and were worth a small fortune. I met Keith on many occasions. He was always in Tramp, and what a party animal!

Isaac went public with his half of the business and I was there in the New York Stock Exchange when the stock was listed. The Blues Brothers Band played at 8am on the floor of the Exchange. The band featured Dan Aykroyd and Dave Moore (of Sam & Dave fame) as singers, Dave Moore taking the John Belushi role, as John was already dead. He died in my old stomping ground, the Chateau Marmont Hotel on Sunset Bvd. The band also included the famous Memphis Group of Steve Cropper on guitar and Duck Dunn on bass. The Memphis Group had been the Stax Records house band on great tracks by Wilson Pickett, Carla Thomas and Otis Redding. They also had a wonderful hit album of their own, *Green Onions*, under their name Booker T and the MGs. I already knew Duck because he had been in Eric Clapton's band.

Watching The Blues Brothers Band on the floor of the Stock Exchange was remarkable, but even that didn't boost the stock; the Hard Rock Café stock price didn't do very well. The problem was that Isaac was very meticulous about the cafés, and was consequently slow at opening them. Peter Morton, backed by Steven Marks, who had gone public with the French Connection clothing stores (from whom I had got my penthouse in Notting Hill), was opening cafés like gangbusters and that was the way to do it. It seemed to be a result of Isaac's personality; he was too punctilious and the business didn't need that. It needed to be pushed, but that's not to say Isaac was at fault. If anything, it was meant to be, as the following story should illustrate.

Eventually Isaac's share went private again, when bought by the British company Grand Metropolitan. Isaac made about a hundred million dollars, of which he spent half building a hospital for Sai Baba that parallels a giant Taj Mahal. Grand Met eventually bought out Peter Morton's half, comprising many more cafés, for $450 million, and Morton kept the Las Vegas Hard Rock Hotel and Casino. I had lunch with him last year in LA, and I asked him whether he still had the hotel. He said he had sold it, "very well", to an Indian tribe. I went back to my hotel and Googled it. It turns out he had sold it "very well" for something like $750 million. Very well indeed! For an initial investment of twenty-five grand, Peter Morton came out of it with over a billion. The Seminole Indian tribe also bought out the Grand Met share, so now own all 175 Hard Rock Cafés. I thought the Indian people weren't meant to embrace the free market? Hey ho, I guess it grabs a hold of us all eventually, even Sai Baba it would seem.

CHAPTER 22

The American Dream

The company was in its heyday, winning more awards than we had time to receive, and it was time to expand and open in America – the land of opportunity that has always attracted me. America to me was the most liberated and free nation of the modern world and I adored the constitution, just less the power establishment intent on rewriting it. I travelled there with a feeling of adventure, in search of the American dream. On the back of our great successes in Europe, in 1982 I got on a plane and went to open an office in New York.

In the late seventies and early eighties, we had won the Palme d'Or at the Cannes International Advertising Festival six times. This is the award for the best overall production company in the festival, judged not on one film or the ideas of the commercials, but on the production values. It is the final award of the festival, donated by the Ville de Cannes and presented by the mayor. I collected it personally on four occasions on behalf of the company. I had a flashback as I stood receiving one award. Shaking the hand of the mayor, I looked at the audience; I heard the sounds of their hands clapping and I seemed to stand for longer than was appropriate, but I did not feel uncomfortable. I was thinking of my life, all of it, from the deaths of my parents, leaving Italy, to Margate and Durham, Africa and my beloved London. I didn't need to force a smile out, it came onto my face and it didn't leave me for the rest of the ceremony. I stood with my smile and our award, and I watched the people. Were they really happy for me? Did they really care? Did I? Yes. I thought of the reverend; had he helped me or ruined me? I thought of Granny, Maria, Patti, my mother.

★

It is true that BFCS was the most successful production company in the world in the first half of the eighties, judged on awards. In addition to the six Palmes d'Or, altogether BFCS won over 100 Cannes and Venice Lions, and over forty US Clio Awards, including eight in one year at the 25th Anniversary Awards held at Radio City Music Hall in '84.

The International Advertising Film Festival in '83 was held in Venice, and the Palme d'Or equivalent, the Coppa di Venezia, was won by another London company, Park Village Productions. The location used to alternate between Cannes and Venice, but in the seventies the organisers got fed up that the hotel workers would always go on strike in Venice during the festival. After a break of a few years, they thought they would give Venice another try in 1983. Björn Borg retired from tennis after winning Wimbledon five times, *Return of the Jedi* opened in theatres and customs officers in Italy confiscated all the worldwide film entries to the competition until a bribe was paid to release them. SAWA, the organisers, did not go back to Venice again.

*

It's amazing how perceptive the human mind becomes after sixteen hours of anaesthetic, but as I lay in a hospital bed after my heart surgery, with nothing but yellow walls and the buzz of machines, I knew that my partners were screwing me over.

Bob Brooks had left the company in 1980 to direct *Tattoo*, a feature film starring Bruce Dern and Maude Adams. He told me he never wanted to shoot another commercial. It was something true filmmakers would often say: commercials were, to the older generation of film directors, jobs and nothing more. It was the nature of the beast, the great leviathan that is the most unnatural beast of all, the king of the jungle, the matrix itself – the economic machine. Great filmmakers would often find themselves in the black hole of making ads instead of movies, as they paid better and were less risky. However, many of the new generation of filmmakers were coming from commercials. It took courage to step out and go for it in film, and I had nothing but respect when storytellers like Ridley Scott and Alan Parker did eventually embrace movie making – but sometimes it would grab hold of a man and not let him go.

It was different for me. I wasn't creative like Adrian Lyne, and I didn't seem to have that inner calling to get behind a camera and tell stories to the world through films, but I would often stand aside and watch how it owned the storytellers. I had come to respect that about humanity; how, as a species, we are great storytellers and souls brave enough to let go of the security of salary and contracts and step into the unknown of the storyteller – just because we know that that is what we are on earth to do – is really quite incredible to me. I applaud it, but it wasn't me. I was part of the machine that would help those storytellers rise; I was the man behind it all; I was the producer, the architect, the one who gives and takes all of the world's shit. It was no problem for me.

Bob Brooks sold his shares to Michael Seresin and began down the risky road of the feature film. Sadly, though, the experience was not good for Bob and ironically this was due to his producer, Joe Levine, who was a very difficult man. Bob was used to getting his own way making ads, and it was different with Levine. Bob decided he wanted back into BFCS. He gave film a go, but he wanted back in. Brooks was always my big supporter, but without him I had no protection while the others were wheelin' and dealin'. Fulford and Seresin decided (when I was in hospital) that they didn't want to give up their shares, and that they and Brooks should each have thirty percent, and I should have the remaining ten. So, they would drop from thirty-three-and-a-third percent to thirty and I should go down to just ten. I had made the mistake of inviting them to a party at my penthouse and, due to its opulence, they obviously thought I was making too much money as a producer – maybe they were right.

A couple of years later, Brooks could see that I was miserable – mostly due to the cocaine I was taking, although he did not know about that. In fact, I was thinking of setting up another company with Richard Sloggett, who by then had won the D&AD (Design and Art Directors) Gold Award (now the Black Pencil), but Bob persuaded the others to reinstate my equal shareholding. I accepted on condition that I could bring in Sloggett as a partner, to which they agreed. So we became five partners, each with twenty percent of the company. It was a better arrangement, and that way, eighty percent of the company was owned by income-generating partners. Sloggett eventually left to set up his own company, in partnership with two other BFCS producers – Glynis Sanders and Jenny Huie.

By the mid-eighties, I was spending a lot of time in New York and loving America. Meanwhile, the exchange rate was favourable for the Yanks to shoot in London and it almost reached parity of one dollar to the pound. This made UK productions back home very cheap for them and not only for the productions. I remember one shoot when the clients went to Harrods; they bought trunks and filled them with everything but the kitchen sink to ship back to New York. Bob did some multi-million dollar productions for Dr Pepper, Schweppes and Cadbury, and Michael Seresin spent a month shooting for BMW USA at the factory near Munich.

I produced another job, with Bob Brooks directing, for an American cigarette client, for overseas use. It was shot in New Orleans and Venice – and this would be the right time in my memoirs to tell you that I have always been a bit of a man for a girl in a uniform. Before you tell me I like to be dominated and go quoting Freud or some other dead guy, I'd like to see you turn it down. Once, in Durham, I made love to a policewoman and got taken home afterwards by one of her colleagues in a police car. Sadly, the woman wasn't wearing her uniform, but I enjoyed the post-coital ride home in the 'naughty' car. I suppose this is why: I had always been amused by the 'I'm Jo. Fly Me' and 'I'm Cheryl. Fly Me' posters for National Airlines, which inspired the 10cc song 'I'm Mandy Fly Me'. I always thought they had a sexual connotation, which I'm sure was deliberate, having worked in advertising for a million years.

Encouraged by that campaign, during the flight from LA to New Orleans for the cigarette shoot, I got cute with one of the Delta stewardesses, with quite a degree of success. We were kissing and cuddling in the back row of the plane, and for a lot of the journey too. I was enjoying having my hands all over her and inside her uniform, and I got a special kick when the other flight attendants stopped by and complained that she wasn't doing any work, but she was cool and didn't give a damn. Bob and the film crew were on the flight and they knew what the heck I was doing. When we landed, they couldn't wait to hear about it. It was like we were kids again and I was the lucky one. We disembarked in New Orleans and she had to continue working to Tampa, before returning for an overnight stopover back in New Orleans. She promised she would come to my hotel. I waited all evening, but she never came. It was definitely like being back in school. Man oh man, girls knew how to drive me cuckoo.

When I first opened the US company, I was flying standby economy because we weren't yet making any money, but, within a few years, we were all going over regularly on Concorde. I must have flown on that wonderful aircraft ten times. On one occasion, I checked in beside an American in a baseball cap. I always liked that classic American look; there was something very cool about it, and the man. It was Steven Spielberg and we had a brief chat about the previous evening's Super Bowl. On another occasion, I sat next to Harvey Weinstein and I even had the stewardess stop the pompous Robert Maxwell from smoking a cigar, which was banned (but cigarettes were allowed). Concorde's most frequent passenger was David Frost; for a while, he travelled on it every week. I sat next to him once and encouraged him to sign up for an air miles scheme – he had never heard of them.

Once, Bob flew to New York for a pre-production meeting at JFK and flew back on the same aircraft. He had breakfast in London, lunch in New York, and was back home in London in time for supper with his wife Suan. We were high flyers on Concorde, going with awards and respect, talking to the biggest names in the business on planes and in taxis. It was fun, but it was sick at times. It was the eighties and it, whatever it was, was all starting to change. The politics was changing, the way films were being made were changing too, the album charts were filled with people like Van Halen and Judas Priest and the drugs were changing. Organic, naturally growing psychedelics to open the mind were ending and the faster, more quick-fix vibes that people craved were being met with a return to the West of a crystal that came from the coca plant. For thousands of years, indigenous tribes have chewed the leaf of the coca plant and, like all things in this world, it was another thing that would come and go and come back again. It was on its way back; it was cocaine and I was about to become an addict.

★

During the eighties, I fancied myself as a bit of a star maker in London. Some of my contemporaries will probably laugh at that and find it boastful, but other people told me it on a number of occasions. I would bring in new unknown directors like Richard Sloggett, Bryan Loftus and Allan van Rijn and get them good scripts, which helped them become top directors. It was difficult to get a new director going, but I had good friends in the advertising agencies. One of them, Alfredo Marcantonio, would always give my new directors a break because my track record was starting to speak for itself and he trusted my judgment. We were like Italian brothers. He and I were practically the only two people in the London advertising business with Italian names and he was one of the few who managed to consistently pronounce Cigarini 'Chigarini'. I guess as an orphan, a brother was a nice idea.

In New York, almost every agency had a partner with an Italian heritage, such as the gang at Ammirati & Puris – probably our most loyal agency after Collett Dickenson Pearce in London. Ozzie Spenningsby and Susan Shipman were great clients too – friends as well – and they gave all our directors, especially Bob Brooks and Michael Seresin, many campaigns. Their agency was the only one in New York that matched the creativity of a top English advertising agency and that was a great triumph.

Both Bryan Loftus and Richard Sloggett won the D&AD Gold Award, which was pretty much a guarantee of a long and successful career. Bryan won his for a K Shoes spot, where a man gets a plate of spaghetti put on his head by an angry girlfriend. It was the first TV commercial to use titling across the screen during the spot, which is now a very common technique, but unheard of then. The agency was Bartle Bogle Hegarty, and their creative director John Hegarty (now Sir John) was a good friend of mine, but he would never work with Bob Brooks because Bob did what he always did: he shouted.

Richard won his D&AD Gold Award with a campaign for Holsten Pils, featuring Griff Rhys Jones. The ad agency was Gold Greenlees Trott. Dave Trott, their creative director, was a friend of Bob Brooks, and apart from being friends, they both had lovely Asian wives, Cathy Trott and Suan Brooks. One Sunday they went to the movies to see Steve Martin in *Dead Men Don't Wear Plaid,* and after it, Bob told Dave it would be a great idea for a campaign. Dave agreed, and entrusted the work to a young creative team, Steve Henry and Axel Chaldecott. They came up with the Pils campaign, inter-cutting an actor with old Hollywood movie footage of stars like George Raft, Cary Grant and James Cagney – the same technique Hollywood used in *Dead Men Don't Wear Plaid*.

Unfortunately for Bob, I had already worked with Henry and Chaldecott with our new director Richard Sloggett. We had done a production in Fort Lauderdale, Florida, which was notable for being two feet under flood water, and also for the fact that the camera crew spent their whole week's per diem allowance on the first evening in a lap-dancing club over the road from the hotel. They were really suckered in by the girls, who told the film crew that they would come to their rooms when they finished work. Of course, none of them did, meanwhile relieving them of their cash. Henry and Chaldecott were a new creative team, and they didn't want to give the Pils job to an established director like Bob – they wanted their own man. Richard Sloggett and I had got on very well with them on the shoot in Florida, so they chose Richard to direct the campaign and me to produce it.

Griff Rhys Jones wasn't Richard's first choice for the role; he wanted Robbie Coltrane, but was prevented by the Holsten client, who thought Robbie was too big to advertise a beer. Consequently, Bob missed out on a fistful of awards won by the Holsten Pils campaign, but he was happy the job went to one of BFCS' new directors. Mainly on the strength of that campaign, Steve Henry and Axel Chaldecott opened their own agency, HHCL, which was voted Agency of the Decade by *Campaign* magazine in 2000 – and mostly because of the success of his Holsten Pils work, Richard later opened his own production company.

From the mid-1980s, BFCS also had a fifty-one percent share in an Italian production company based in Milan, BFCS srl, in partnership with English director David Deveson and producers Fred Turchetti and Piero Cozzi. They were all jolly nice, but Brooks, Fulford and Seresin closed the Italian company in '93 after they bought me out of the UK company. It had not weathered the recession of the early 1990s well.

Where was I? Ah, yes. Cocaine.

CHAPTER 23

Cocaine

If the seventies were my decade for sex and romance, the eighties were the dark ages. After breaking up with Donatella Moores in '82, I wanted nothing more to do with love. Love to me was dead.

I started seeing a girl I knew from the King's Road before going out with Donatella. We didn't go out, actually; we stayed in, and we did cocaine. We did lots of it. Her name was Henrietta, but no one will recognise her; she didn't meet any of my friends. I didn't take her anywhere, not to the cinema, not to restaurants. She just came to my flat each and every weekend and we did coke. This happened for ten years and it was my big secret. I would usually see her on a Friday to give me maximum time to recover for work on the following Monday. We would stay up all night doing two or three grams and engage in all manner of deviant, stoned, sexual practices. I would go to bed at dawn totally wired, praying I would not die in my sleep. I remember my routine: I would need to fold up a cold towel on my pillow and rest my head on it, because I was sweating so much. Fortunately, I always woke up the next morning, but feeling suicidally depressed.

Like I told you, these were the dark ages and I could hear it in the music, see it in the films and I wasn't the only one. People of my age, having experienced the highs of the sixties and seventies, were on a comedown of sorts and coke was the answer for many of us – but it wasn't the answer, it was making it worse. Those decades had been so high anyway that people wanted to stay high – or go higher – and they wanted it now. Cocaine gives you such a direct high that the brain decides it no longer needs natural serotonin, which normally gives a person that feeling of well-being and happiness and the 'nothing can hurt you' vibration. When the cocaine wears off, the brain is left without the serotonin and the depression hits. Bad depression hits. Those ten years were bad days for me. It's a miracle in fact that I managed to keep my working life together, but I had my father's blood in my veins – for entrepreneurs, not even the lowest of lows can stop them from putting in the work hours.

After I was breathalysed and lost my driving licence for a year, I had to find somewhere to hang out in walking distance of my Notting Hill flat. I used to score my coke from the Portobello Road, near a pub called the Portobello Gold. It was a lively place with that classic London mix of local free spirits and international travellers. The landlord Mike had lived in St. Lucia and because of it, the place had a tropical-themed feeling – the perfect spot to have a drink and a Sunday roast. You'd see all kinds in there, from the grubby through to the famous, like Ian McShane (*Lovejoy*), who I knew from the King's Road and Tramp, and who lived locally and would pop in from time to time. I'd like to mention Ian for one reason more than any: he's the only person I know who becomes more interesting to look at the older he gets. While others seem to disintegrate, he's just becoming better looking. One Sunday afternoon in the pub, some hippy was telling me how he had just got back from Goa and the hash he smuggled in was still rammed up his arse. Drugs: throughout history, humanity has done everything and anything to find them, transport them and use them. I shook Ian's hand, left the pub, picked up the drugs and went back to my cave.

During those ten years, I managed to keep an active social life, somehow, but with a difference. Without coke, I became asexual – a common characteristic of the drug. I had no interest in sex without Henrietta and the cocaine, but I had some wonderful platonic friendships during that decade, and Francesca (Chessy) Thyssen was one such good friend. Chessy's family owned the Thyssen steel company, which had been essential to the German rearmament between the two world wars. We went out a lot together and I would take her on occasion to dinner with the contemporary art collector Charles Saatchi, but Charles didn't like her much. It's hard to know why, but perhaps it was because her father, Baron Thyssen, was also one of the big art collectors of the world and she was an intelligent girl and wanted to talk about art, while Charles was always reclusive about his. She visited L'Hermitage in St. Petersburg while we were friends, on a private visit arranged by her father. She told me she went down to the basement on one occasion with a torch, where she found famous paintings like Matisse's 'Dancers' leaning against the walls in the dark. She was totally and utterly gorgeous and eventually married the heir to the Habsburgs.

I also hung out a lot with actress Maryam d'Abo. We met on a commercial for a chocolate and became good buddies. We went out a heap and she took me to a party at the Kensington Roof Gardens for the band Queen. Michael Jackson played, or was it Prince? We went together to the after-premiere party for the

James Bond film *The Living Daylights*, in which she played the Czechoslovakian cellist and sniper. Come to think of it, Maryam d'Abo and I went out a huge amount, but again, like with Chessy Thyssen, it was totally platonic. I took her to a roast for Eric Clapton, a roast being an American import, where having all their friends stand up and say rude or embarrassing things about them commemorates someone – a bit like a best man's speech at a wedding. We sat at a dinner table with Robin Gibb of the Bee Gees, who didn't say a word the entire night. Maybe, I thought, there were others who were on this downer. George Harrison stood up and announced to the room, "Eric used to be my best friend, but one day he came over to take my wife for a drive, and never brought her back."

★

Yeah, like I said, nothing happened with Maryam either, and she is married now, to Hugh Hudson, who directed *Chariots of Fire*. She brought Hugh and their friends Malcolm McDowell and his wife to my rented beach house in Santa Barbara. I had loved the film *A Clockwork Orange*, and Stanley Kubrick was to me nothing less than a unique genius, so I was pleased to meet Malcolm. I miss seeing Maryam; she really enriched my life, but of course... only to a certain degree. As always, after it got to a certain place, I'd make sure it was all over, and that's not to say I was always the one to end everything. A lot of the time, I was subconsciously making it easy for them to get bored – like with Maryam, like with all of them, but not Patti.

Another one of the era was Jane Birbeck and I was one of the first people in London to know her. I met her at the Belgrave Ball, which in those days was held once a year in Belgrave Square in Knightsbridge, working on one of the stands. Later, she had big romances with James Hunt, the Formula 1 racing champion, and Daley Thompson, the Olympic decathlon gold medalist. We hung out a lot together including going to Live Aid, and I was starting to realise how needy I was becoming, but not in an awful or typical way. What I needed was what I considered 'just the right amount' and it didn't need to come from a woman specifically. I adore women, so that was always better – I do have red blood, after all – but be it a man or a woman, it was human connection that I needed. I didn't need too much, though, and I'd freak if I was getting too little. I needed just the right amount, but for single girls who were looking for a man to provide, I wasn't a safe bet. History would repeat and repeat... and repeat.

I was also seeing a lot of my "first abortion", Siobhan Barron. She was now at her prime running Limelight, a very successful music video production company, and she always carried a big entourage of Limelight groupies with her. They would come down to Ridge Farmhouse, my home in Wiltshire, and she would cook Sunday lunch for up to twelve people. I would see much more of her in the nineties, when I was her neighbour in Malibu.

In Wiltshire I was seeing a lot of my friend Joanna Jacobs, who I had known since she was a fifteen-year-old model in Chelsea. Her father was the legendary disc jockey and radio personality David Jacobs. She did a wonderful garden for me at my new farmhouse, but still... nothing. Everything was platonic between us all, although we did discuss moving in together a couple of times... wow, big moves I know. The route of these confessions (as a terrible name-dropper) was beginning to crystallise: this, it, now... it's all been a product of my wanting to be alone. Wanting to be alone has caused me to spend most of my time alone. Spending most of my time alone has created a situation where I become a master observer and here I find myself telling a load of people I don't know nor will ever meet about what I have seen... namely a load of great gals who I didn't develop long-term relationships with.

★

I had to leave the country to get away from the psychological addictions to Henrietta and the cocaine, and that's what happened in '92. Paul Simon toured South Africa, Mike Tyson was found guilty of rape, the Freddie Mercury tribute concert was televised to over a billion and Clinton was elected forty-second president. I moved to LA. I've never seen Henrietta or touched cocaine again. Well, maybe once or twice.

CHAPTER 24

The East

"If you want to go east, don't go west."
– Ramakrishna

Throughout the seventies and eighties, I liked to take exotic holidays, travelling alone. I particularly liked the Far East because the people were so nice, the food so delicious, and the Asian girls... so many! I had already been a few times to Thailand before I started going for Christmas with the Saatchis, and I kept going back. I was really attracted to the nubile Thai girls. They were just so delicate and nice natured. They were not really prostitutes; most of them would never ask for money. They just wanted to stay with a Western man for the duration of his holiday and to be well-kept by him, if even for a weekend. Their ultimate dream was that someone would fall in love with them and take them back to live in Europe or America. Some men gave them cash presents when they left, but it was never demanded of them. Okay, I admit it: they were prostitutes, but they were very sweet.

Bangkok has got to be one of the great cities to go people watching, although in Bangkok it's more weirdo watching, with everything from the lady-boy to the lady-grandma, the sadist to the masochist, and the place where everyone gets their end away. Even for the healthy-living Muslim, Allah seems to turn a blind eye in Bangkok. People become pervs on a mass scale, from the moment feet touch the ground. With the concoction of bright lights, high heels, bums, beers, a heightened libido and Asian hot hot, Bangkok is, quite frankly, addictive, and unless you've the strength of a Thai Buddhist monk, it'll bring out the worst in you. Or was it just me?

I met a couple of pretty girls in a nightclub (not a girly bar) and within minutes of getting a drink in, I had them on my arms. Within hours, I had moved out of my hotel and in with them. What was I doing? We had a lot of fun together and I didn't pay them a dime. At their place, they both had photographs on their walls of their German boyfriends. They were hoping to marry them some day. They told me they'd add me to the list, though – as backup.

On one occasion, I went to a rather upmarket brothel called Boom-Boom in a very nice house that we had to take a taxi to get to. I went with two very well-known English people, both of whom are married and shall therefore remain anonymous! One of them had been there before and was friends with the Mama-San (the Madame), so he tipped us off that we should not just take two girls that we fancied, but rather choose one we liked and get her to bring along her choice as the second girl. That way, there would be a better 'atmosphere' and more 'cooperation' between them. There was no question: they really were prostitutes. But not like anything you're going to find around Soho, trust me. After I had made my selection, the occasion started with a bubble bath between the three of us, one at the front and one at the back, and went on from there – all afternoon (I'm smiling). All afternoon wasn't long enough. I think back now and damn it… I want more! Unlike Western hookers, these girls would kiss and make genuine passionate love. They were beautiful creatures from heaven and I adored them.

★

There is no girly scene in Bali; it is strictly Hindu. The people practise Balinese Hinduism and it is the only Hindu island in Indonesia; the rest is Muslim. It somehow, as a result, accounts for the more artistic culture of Bali, famous for traditional and modern dance, sculpture, painting and music. I first went there alone in the seventies and I returned again in 1980 with Donatella Moores. The first trip was particularly memorable. I think the first time you see the light bouncing across the rice terraces on the rolling hills is the most magical; the fresh and deep greens, broken with the occasional woman bent over and picking at the grain with her hands, dressed often in the brightest of colours, her skin the healthiest you've ever seen.

I like travelling alone because I believe that local people interact with a single person very differently to how they interact with a couple. It also leaves time to wonder, to daydream, to enter short periods of introspection that seem so necessary when you cross a border and walk through a village or over a hill. Or sit beside a stream. Or ride a bicycle alone, through the towns of

Gloucestershire as a child. As an orphan. Many a thing I have come to understand while travelling alone; a sense of empowerment, if nothing else. It teaches one to be confident to live and be in this world alone, to not need to be with another person all of the time. Mostly, I didn't have the patience to wait for anyone. It was as Henry David Thoreau had told us: "The man who goes alone can start today, but he who travels with another must wait till that other is ready." I can get quite impatient at times, so travelling alone, just me and the road – there's nothing better.

I hired a motorcycle and this required taking the Balinese motorcycle driving test, which consisted of negotiating sticks without your feet touching the ground. If you failed, you paid the fee again, *ad infinitum* until you passed.

I took the bike to the remote eastern part of Bali, an area where few tourists go. A young man who spoke some English adopted me and the reason he befriended me was obvious: he liked riding around on my motorbike and showing off to the villagers. I didn't get a single go on the blasted thing. It was always him riding it, with me on the back. He invited me to stay with his family and I lovingly accepted, and what a wonderful experience indeed to live with a Balinese family in a village. One thing to note: I couldn't believe how spicy the food was – even for breakfast. Goodness me, spicy food in England was something you'd get on at the end of a piss up, not on a weekday morning for brekky.

One evening, he (my friend who I'm going to have to continue referring to as 'he') took me to a remote village in the middle of God knows where, where there was a dance, accompanied by wonderful gamelan music. The girls were, of course, exquisite, and dressed in their traditional costumes with heavily made-up white faces. The men drew lots for the privilege of dancing with them and this was considered a great honour. I had never seen such effort by a man to dance; it was a form of courtship, in fact. From what I learnt, there had never been a foreigner at this village dance, and I attracted as much attention from the children as those extravagant and highly skilled dancers did. I didn't have my camera, but I didn't need it. I remember the colours and the smells and the heat and the sounds as if it were a moment ago. The senses intensify on foreign soil, "Travel is more than the seeing of sights; it is a change that goes on, deep and permanent, in the ideas of living."

I took the motorcycle to Ubud in the centre of the island. I love travelling by an open vehicle like a motorbike; you are in much closer contact with the environment and the people, too. On a bike, it is easier to stop and exchange greetings, take a photograph or turn around and have another look. The children in Bali are hysterical; when they see a foreigner, they run out and wave with both hands, running and waving. The light in their eyes – it was exactly as it should be. As Oscar Wilde wrote in one of my favourite books, when Dorian is being told of his youth: no frowns, just youth and passion, sunlight and springtime, youth. "Realise your youth while you have it… Be afraid of nothing… live… like this forever…"

Ubud is a beautiful town. It is the centre of the Balinese art movement and I bought lots of paintings to take back to England with me. I went to Mount Batur, Bali's most active volcano. There is a small guesthouse nearby, where at night you can watch the explosions of lava. In the morning, I climbed up to the rim in my sandals like tourists are meant to – in the wrong footwear and moving in the wrong direction. I didn't mind, though; at this stage, I had got used to sticking out like a sore thumb. I guess Africa really had toughened me up all those years ago. Usually in Bali, I stayed in a losman, which is a bed and breakfast with a local host family, at one dollar a night. I loved staying with the Balinese people because I knew I was always safe. I washed from a barrel of water with a small saucepan and listened each morning to the sounds of the birds, the wind and the wild. The cockerels would wake me up, and at night I would hear the wonderful gamelan music being played by the villagers. Bali is a magical place and the smiles on the faces of all the people are surely proof of that.

I had another interesting and rather frightening experience. I was staying in Kuta Beach, a surfer's paradise. I befriended a group of young Australians and they encouraged me to have a blue meanie omelette at the local café. These contain psilocybin mushrooms, which give a mild acid trip. I do have to say that the effect was very nice. The seashells on the shore seemed to sparkle like a million diamond chips and the sunset was extraordinary: an orange god in the sky, plunging into a deep purple and violet bed of paint. The night was magic, too. It was as if all the world was speaking to me with its wind and reshaping clouds, and I could understand the croaking frogs talking with each other in a nearby bed of trees. The wind that blew was like a voice. I felt that bliss, that connectedness that my friend Isaac used to talk about.

A couple of days later, I met a young American girl on the beach. She was staying in the hotel next to mine and I, now the professional, encouraged her to try the blue meanie. This took quite a lot of persuasion, as she had never taken any kind of drugs before, ever. I assured her they were very mild and a nice experience, that the ocean would seem more green and the feel of the wind would be like silk on her skin. She agreed. We went to the café and shared an omelette, so we only had half each. Then we went to sit on the sand, but after a while I started to feel a little strange, so I decided to go in the water – but the walk to the sea seemed to take an eternity, as if it was being pulled from me while I was walking to it. I got back to the girl, who told me she was feeling strange as well. At the same time, a beach hawker came by with wooden carvings of garudas. These mythical bird creatures are horrific at the best of times, but on my bad trip were terrifying, and I thought we were under attack from the beasts! It was the beginning of a bad trip.

I told the girl we should each go back to our rooms and I would fetch some Valium, which I carried for sleeping on the long-haul flights. I went to my room and she to hers. As I walked along the road heading back to her, I was behind a Balinese man, who I realised I could very easily kill with just my hands. The omelette, I knew then, was certainly a nasty. I got to the girl's cottage, but on approach, I sensed danger. I could hear her cries of anguish from yards away and on the bad trip the high-pitched cries were to me like a team of invading giant vampire bats, mixed with thunder, ringing church bells and the squawk of the garuda. I opened the door and I saw her standing in front of her mirror, tearing out her hair and looking at herself in the glass – the worst thing you can do when you are having a bad trip. Feeling responsible for her and being guilty of persuading her to take the drug made me get myself together. The tranquillising effect of the Valium I had taken kicked in and I was feeling cool again, thank God. I was able to calm her and reassure her with the help of the Valium. Thank Jesus for the Valium. I have never risked a hallucinatory drug since. If you have a bad dose, the trip is horrendous and very dangerous. Don't do it people (my message to the world).

★

I went to Cebu in the Philippines and booked into the only hotel I could find, the St. Moritz. As I was at the tiny Cebu airport waiting to collect my luggage from the Manila flight, I sat on a bench next to an American. His name was Nick and he asked me where I was staying, so I told him. He was staying on a boat, and informed me he and his crew would be at the St. Moritz the next day.

I didn't realise until I got there, but the St. Moritz was not only a hotel – it was a pole-dancing club and brothel. Nick came with his crew. I thought they looked a very rough, unsavoury bunch, but Nick was well educated and a WASP, he was rich and quite personable. Coincidentally, his family happened to own a film studio outside New York that my company used, so we were new best friends. He invited me to go for a sail with them the next day. I was expecting a forty-foot or fifty-foot sailing yacht, but instead a 115-foot, three-mast schooner appeared – the biggest in the ocean. It had film-editing equipment onboard and was used as a facility craft for underwater films, and had just returned from doing film work in the Truk Lagoon, where there was a sunken fleet of Japanese warships. The Americans sank twelve warships, thirty-two merchant ships, and 249 aircraft in 1944, in revenge for Pearl Harbour. Truk had been the main Japanese base in the South Pacific.

On the first trip on Nick's boat, we just went out for the day, but they were planning a longer voyage to look for diving locations and they invited me along. We met up at the St. Moritz before the trip and we all stocked up on girls for the journey. We each picked a girl we liked and they all came aboard wearing their dancing gear.

The trip was fantastic, one of the best experiences of my life. The crew taught me how to scuba dive and the coral in those islands is some of the best in the world. Even the snorkelling was fantastic, because there was an usually shallow shelf of coral and then a sudden drop-off into the darkness. It would make your stomach turn as you swam over the cliff, seeing that giant drop into the sea. We would sail at night and I did my share of night watching. Then, we would dive all day. Each day we would arrive at a tiny island, which was sometimes uninhabited, but I would swear, if there were people, they hadn't seen white men before. After a few days, we dropped all the girls off at an island where they could catch a ferry back to Cebu. I thought it was rather cruel, but also very funny, watching them get off our boat in their short tight dresses and stiletto heels on a remote island.

Nick visited me in London a couple of months later. I took him to dinner and to Tramp. He told me they had found a shrunken treasure ship containing Delft pottery, dating from the seventeenth century. He was in dispute with the Philippine government over the ownership of it. A couple of years later, I read, I think in *Time* magazine, that Nick was one of America's most wanted fugitives. He was a drug smuggler. That explained why his crew looked so tough and rough. The film work was probably a front, so now you know why I have only used his first name. Granny had warned me to be careful of "out of town folk". I guess the saying was right after all: Grandma knows best, Granny knows best, do as your grandmother would say, or something like that. I went back to Thailand on my own for more girls.

CHAPTER 25

Commercials

A very popular commercial is the *Yellow Pages*' 'J. R. Hartley', directed by Bob Brooks and produced by yours truly. In it, a nice old man goes around bookshops looking for a book called *Fly Fishing* by J. R. Hartley. He fails to find it, gives up and goes home. His daughter suggests he tries the *Yellow Pages*. He does and phones a listed company, finds the book and we discover that he is, in fact, J. R. Hartley. We filmed the home scenes in a house in Hampstead. It was a hot summer's day, and the house was pokey with no room for anyone other than the actor, Bob and the essential crew. The producer's job was done, so I sat in my car for most of the day. I didn't know that a journalist called Valerie Grove happened to own the house. A short while later an article appeared in the *London Evening Standard*, entitled something like, 'The day the film crew came to my house'. In the article, she wrote, "and then in came 'Mr Big', the producer John Cigarini. He came into my kitchen and put his feet on the table..." (I certainly did not), "... picked up the phone and started dictating, '1969 Mercedes convertible for sale...'" (I probably did that), "... then he went outside and fell asleep in his Mercedes..." (I definitely did that). It was all rather embarrassing. The day the article came out, someone had put 'Mr Big' on my office door nameplate. It was all very funny. Some enterprising person published a book called *Fly Fishing*, under the *nom de plume* of J. R. Hartley. It was a compendium of short stories on fishing. I don't believe it had anything to do with Abbott Mead Vickers, the advertising agency responsible for the *Yellow Pages* campaign, and apparently it did rather well in sales, from a character that had been made up.

A few years later, I ran into the journalist Valerie at Morton's bar. After we had both had quite a few drinks, I really believed I could have seduced her under the table. In my drunken state I thought she liked the idea of 'Mr Big'. I didn't do anything but I should have, so I'd like to take this opportunity to tell all the men of the world: when you get to my age, regrets start to creep in, so be bold while you're young, seduce women under the table and hit on the African maid when she's flirting with you. The worst than can happen is a slap in the face, which is worse than living with the truth – that you could have nailed the goddess on her kitchen floor. God, I wish I had banged her.

Another commercial Brooks and I did was for the VW Golf. It featured Burt Kwouk telling the camera that Japanese cars were the number one best-selling cars in Europe, but the VW Golf was the number one best-selling car in Japan. As he is talking, a car drops into the shot alongside him, he gets in it and drives it away. All in one shot. These days, computer graphics would be used, but in the eighties, things were shot for real.

We had to do tests to see how far you could drop a car and still drive it away. We destroyed quite a lot of cars finding out that the optimum height was exactly six feet seven and a half inches. This was a problem, because it is very difficult to shoot with something only six feet from the ground and not have the camera see it. It meant we had to use a long 200mm lens, and no studio was long enough for that. In the end, we got the longest studio we could find, opened the end door and built a tent outside. We had to build a white cove the whole length of the studio, because of the foreshortening effect of the long lens.

Burt Kwouk is a lovely man. He had also been in the *Pink Panther* films. He was Cato, Peter Sellers' manservant, who would kung-fu attack him when he got home each evening. He was incredibly plucky in this commercial. The claw holding the car would not always release it evenly, and sometimes the car would land on one side and bounce towards Burt. He was unconcerned, even when the car grazed against his leg. The spot won a Gold Lion at the Cannes Advertising Film Festival.

I produced another commercial for VW with Michael Seresin as the director. It involved a race between a VW and a falling chimney. Again, it had to be done for real and, for obvious reasons, with only one take. The car had to pull up in front of the camera for the product beauty shot, in the same take as the chimney bricks bouncing behind it. We had the car strengthened with a safety cage, but no amount of reinforcing would have been enough if the chimney had fallen on the car. First, we had to find the chimney. I spoke to Fred Dibnah, the famous steeplejack. He had become a TV celeb, not only for dropping chimneys, but also for his lovely Yorkshire accent and personality. He told me of a chimney he was about to drop in Accrington, Lancashire. The factory around the chimney had already been razed to the ground. In small industrial towns in the north of England, the houses for the factory workers had usually been built close around the factory. This presented a problem in the post-industrial age when you wanted to get rid of the chimney. Fred Dibnah could drop it straight down between two rows of houses, without touching them. I talked to him and persuaded him to hold off dropping the Accrington chimney. We first had to build a tarmac runway for the car.

This spot also won a Gold Lion at Cannes.

CHAPTER 26

Breathalysed

Like most drinkers of my generation, I didn't take much notice when they introduced the breathalyser; so, like most drinkers of my generation, I got caught.

The British cabinet minister George Brown was a well-known lush and I was listening to him on the car radio. It was a Wednesday and I was driving around at the time, aimlessly and in no direction. He said he always carried milk of magnesia with him in the car, as he claimed it oxidised the breath and eliminated the effects of the alcohol. From that day on, I kept a packet on me.

I was out on a bender with Dan Mindel on a Saturday in 1982. I had known Danny as a youngster working in the Hard Rock, when we hired him as a runner in our studio at BFCS. He worked his way up through the camera grades and is now a top Hollywood cinematographer, this year working on the new Star Wars movie. We started the piss-up with a lunch at Il Bersiglieri, opposite my old flat on the King's Road, and the bar crawl moved in zig-zags and circles until we finished it at Tramp in the early hours of the next day. We were driving home in separate cars; Danny was leading the way. He pulled over in St. James Street to ask for directions (no iPhones in '82). I pulled over behind him and a police car pulled in behind me. "Fuck." I saw the officer approaching in my rearview. I remember the song playing on my radio; it was 'Pretty Vacant' by the Sex Pistols. It's funny how everyone seems to have the anarchist in them, if only a small amount. We can go through our entire lives kissing arse and sucking up to the man, but I do believe that somewhere deep inside all of us, we have that trapped angry animal that wants to scream and break stuff. I guess that's all Lydon was doing at the time.

The officer was closer now. A smile came, I turned down the volume and quickly jammed the milk of magnesia in my mouth. The problem was, I hadn't done a test run and the effect took me by surprise. The magnesia instantly depleted my mouth of any saliva and I began to froth. Naturally, I was worried he would see the foam in my mouth, so when the policeman spoke I tried to reply to him with my lips closed. What came out was, "mmmm... mmmm... mmmm" and "mmmm". The Sex Pistols were still seeping through the stereo speakers. I was breathalysed and taken to the police station.

I was driving a Mercedes 6.3, which happened to be the fastest saloon car in the world, and the copper who drove it to the station told me it was the best car he had ever driven. Apparently, though, that wasn't enough to get me off the hook. I was left alone in the room and waiting for the doctor to arrive. I read the arresting officer's notes: "The suspect seemed to have extreme difficulty in speaking, so he was breathalysed."

When the doc came to take a blood sample, it was 3am and he found me running on the spot. He bent over with laughter. "That won't do any good, only glucose can help you now!"

A decade later, I was at Danny's wedding in New York. Us boys went out for the stag to a club called Pure Platinum. This time we decided to get less wamoed. Pure Platinum was the first in a new wave of upmarket lap-dancing clubs owned by Peter Stringfellow. Some of Danny's friends were male models – and I'm talking Calvin Klein models – so, of course, the girls in the lap-dancing club were all over them. One stunner was particularly friendly and came over to us whenever she wasn't dancing. I got talking to her – and, me being me, I couldn't resist asking how much money they make. It was about a thousand dollars a night in tips. Some clients put a hundred in the garter. They were open every night of the year. That's $365,000 a year, in cash, just in tips, and this girl was a student. Not a bad way to see yourself through college.

Oh, by the way, I was banned from driving for a year. Thanks a lot, George!

CHAPTER 27

Saatchi

Charles Saatchi is the biggest collector of contemporary art in the world. He has tremendous purchasing power in the art market and therefore huge influence. He can make an unknown artist famous merely by buying up an entire first show. My mate Sid Roberson introduced me to him in the eighties. Sid had been working at Benton & Bowles advertising agency where he met Charles, and where Charles met his future wife Doris Lockhart; Charles and Doris both worked as copywriters at the agency. When I first met Charles, he was well known for being a recluse, but he liked to play tennis and Sid was his partner, and that was how it all began.

I was in Italy, and Charles and Doris invited me to stay with them at a rented house in Ansedonia, near Porto Ercole, with Sid and Susie. Shortly after, Charles and Doris split and Charles met an American woman called Kay Hartenstein, who had a flat in Eaton Square. Sid and Susie were very fond of Doris and stayed friends with her. They just didn't take to Kay, and I think it showed, so the feeling was mutual. The long shot was that Sid and Susie Roberson's friendship with Charles didn't make the transition from Doris to Kay, but that didn't stop the lads playing tennis, and quite right too. I think Kay liked me, and I her, and Charles and I were now at the beginning of a long friendship.

Kay was a socialite, and had an A-list group of friends like Mick Jagger and Jean Pigozzi, the super-wealthy heir to the French Simca car family. Up until that time, Charles only seemed to have one or two friends, like Alan Yentob of the BBC. The Saatchi and Yentob Iraqi Jewish families had known each other since they had both come to England, when Charles was a baby. With Kay, Charles became much more sociable, mostly with her friends, and over the next four years we saw a lot of each other and he was about to be a big influence on me and on my views on the world. We would go out to dinner, sometimes just the three of us, a few times a week. For a few years, I think I was his closest mate. They would also have glamorous dinners at their home, with people like Mick Jagger, and I was reunited there with my old friend Malcolm McLaren. We wined, dined and we went to the theatre. Alan Yentob could get any tickets, but Charles would never last past the interval and everyone would have to leave – even Yentob.

On one occasion, I was with Charles in New York and we were walking the galleries. We were with the great Steve Martin, who is also a big art collector, and we went to Sotheby's. Charles was bidding for a Rauschenberg!

Charles and Kay Saatchi were incredibly generous with their holidays. They would rent big stinkpot yachts every year and motor around either the Caribbean or the Med. On one occasion, they had a 175ft motor yacht called the Havre de Grace. There were ten crew and eight guests. I was on my own, but not for long: I got lucky with a beautiful young blonde crew girl who took me to her cabin. Eric Idle and his wife Tania were there, too. He serenaded us on guitar with 'Always Look on the Bright Side of Life'.

The Havre de Grace was chased around Sardinia by the paparazzi. The other Charles – the prince – and Princess Diana were on a yacht in the same sea area, and as we were the largest boat in any harbour, they thought we were them. From a distance, Kay even looked like Diana. My nephew Luca and his friend Stefano jumped aboard in Sardinia – two handsome Roman hunks swallow-diving off the top of the ship. The Saatchis didn't always hire a motor yacht; it was often fantastic Italian villas, near Florence – the kind of palaces where the Italian State maintains the gardens. We had a few holidays like that and although it was all high-end, I was missing my alone time, roughing it in Africa or living in a remote village in Bali with locals. Charles would always have his Rolls Royce convertible and we would cruise around Tuscany in it. On these holidays, I was usually paired off with the charming Charlotte Barnes – an interior designer in Chelsea. She was attractive, very funny, and so, of course, nothing ever happened! I was still taking cocaine with Henrietta, and I was going through my asexual phase with anyone else (I could make exceptions for pretty young girls on the ship's crew, though). Disgraced yet?

Charles and Kay had their wedding at a palace lined with gardens, statues, fountains and topiary. We had been warned ahead of time to prepare for a talent contest, so I had rented a gold Elvis outfit. I was first up, but only knew one Elvis number, 'Heartbreak Hotel'. I would probably have won the contest, except David Puttnam, master of ceremonies, insisted I did another song because the first one was that good. Mostly, he was being a typical friend: he had caught me practising with the band in the afternoon and considered that cheating. By then, I had taken my Elvis wig off and I did a lame version of 'Be-Bop-a-Lula'. The band didn't know it and it ruined everything. I completely bombed.

Most Christmases, the Saatchis and I went to Phuket, Thailand. They stayed at the Amanpuri, but it was impossible to get a room over Christmas – and kind of out of my league anyway – so I stayed next door on the same beach. There was a regular crowd during Christmas and it was like a big reunion each year when we all arrived to meet friends like Richard and Joan Branson, David and Patsy Puttnam, Loyd Grossman, and Johan and Amanda Eliasch, and one year Björn Borg. He still played senior tennis with a wooden racquet. According to him, the modern racquets had ruined the professional game.

It was at Phuket that Charles, Richard Branson and I first went go-karting. Charles became smitten with the sport and went back to London and set up a team of professionals. He raced seriously, and I think became some sort of champion. Trouble was, he was racing against sixteen-year-olds who weighed half what he did. One cruise we went on, he only ate spinach the whole cruise trying to lose weight – for the go-kart racing.

As the years clicked away and I was back in London, I would go to see Charles and Kay at their own home, although sometimes they came to mine. When he first came to my flat, the first thing he did was take one look at my huge paintings, which had cost me a small fortune, and commented, "You want to get rid of all this stuff before you can't give it away." The fact that the paintings subsequently dropped in value so much gave me burnt fingers about buying art, from which I have never really recovered. I was my father's son after all, but I still have them – now in Italy – because I like them. On the other hand, when I told Charles I had got my Andrew Logan 'Cosmic Chandelier' because I couldn't afford an Alexander Calder mobile, he said, "But that's much better than a Calder." Win some, lose some, I guess.

I gave a small party for the Pink Floyd band members in my penthouse. Charles had been to his gallery for a private viewing with Mick Jagger and Jean Pigozzi, so he brought them along. Jerry Hall was heavily pregnant; in fact, I thought she was going to drop the baby in my flat. I didn't take any pictures of the rock superstars; I didn't think it would be cool. I wish I had now for this book.

On another occasion, Charles came to my penthouse for dinner. "You'll never guess what I bought today… a rotting cow's head covered in flies!" he told me. It was his first Damien Hirst. I went to the private opening of his Hirst exhibition – the one with the shark and the sheep – at the Saatchi Gallery on Boundary Road in '92. It was impressive, but no one could have imagined that Damien would become so huge and one of the richest men in Britain. Charles had the sheep in his house, next to Carl Andre's bricks and a large Picasso, but Charles had also once said to me, "You know all this British art I am buying, it won't be worth anything one day."

When the Saatchis discovered that Charles was going to curate the 1997 Royal Academy Sensation show, about three years beforehand, Kay told me, "This is really going to put Charles on the map." I couldn't understand that, because to me he was already famous as the biggest collector of contemporary art in the world. The effect the show had on the Britart scene took me by surprise. I wished that I had started collecting when I was hanging out with him, but he was always very secretive about his movements. He would never let on what he was buying or from where or why, and the truth was, I didn't understand conceptual art. I still struggle to know or feel the difference between a so-called masterpiece and a piece of crap. Actually… I don't think many collectors do! To me, they are all investing. In other words, trying to make a profit; or trying to appear to be knowledgeable, cool, sophisticated; or, in some cases, setting the standard for what is knowledgeable, cool, sophisticated – just by buying the stuff. Anyway, by the time of the Sensation show in '97, I wasn't seeing much of Charles and Kay, who later split. It was the beginning of the end of my time with Charles Saatchi.

I met Damien Hirst a few times in the nineties, when I used to stay at the Groucho Club, on my visits to London from LA. It was my London base and Damien was there every night. I told him about Charles and the cow's head. Damien was best friends with Keith Allen, who I had spent time with at the World Cup in Italy a few years before. Although I saw Damien in the Groucho, I didn't know he was doing the dot and spin paintings, otherwise I would have bought one of each – I like them… I think! It's irrelevant anyway; I can't afford them now he has gone stratospheric. Buggery buggery shit.

It's a phenomenal thing that's happened to Damien's spot paintings. When he had his retrospective at Tate Modern in 2012, Larry Gagosian, his dealer, filled all eleven of his galleries worldwide with over 300 spots, mostly borrowed back from the owners. There are apparently over 1400 spot paintings in existence, but there must be a big market for them, with one of them fetching a record price of £1.8 million. Just how many Russian oligarchs, Middle Eastern sheikhs, and hedge fund multi-millionaires can there be out there? Damien, of course, doesn't paint them himself, assistants do. He himself has said he "couldn't be fucking arsed" and with a net worth estimated at around £350 million, who can blame him? There's a funny story that one of his assistants who painted the spot paintings was leaving the factory and asked for a painting. Damien told her to paint one and take it. She said she didn't want one of hers, she wanted one of his. The only difference, of course, is the signature and the value. It all seems like a bit of a speculative bubble to me. I've seen it before, with classic cars, with property, and we all know what happened with tulips. I suppose real art will always survive the main test: time. I hope Damien's does, but only time will tell – and anyway, by then, we'll all be dead. It seems to me in my total ignorance, that the more shit there is, the more it becomes a magnet for the super elite. A woman walks into an art shop. The shop owner tells her "I've got something vile for you, darling." "Oh that's wonderful!" the woman replies. "No, you don't understand, it's really genuinely shit." "Wrap it up straightaway," she tells the shop owner.

    I went on four motor cruising holidays with the Saatchis. I behaved badly on the last one and didn't help Charles with his baggage at the airport! Charles can be difficult to be with sometimes and he was in a ferocious mood that day – the type of mood where everyone wants to steer clear. I was also in a bad mood. I was suffering with my Henrietta and cocaine withdrawals, and I was anxious to get back to London. It was the last holiday I went on with them. We parted like a pair of spoilt angry brats. Like Sid and Susie with Kay, I never did make the transition to a new wife and I didn't see Charles when he was married to Nigella. Nowadays, they invite my friends Trevor and Sharon Eve on their holidays and their children are all friends, but without a kid and because of our tantrum, I have been ousted. Now it's the Eves' turn to enjoy Charles's generosity. I certainly had plenty of it and I am very grateful to him. We had a lot of good times together. I have great memories and I miss him. A dinner was arranged quite recently with myself, the Eves and the Saatchis, but at the last minute, Sharon Eve got a call from Nigella. I thought enough time had passed, but I was wrong about that. Nigella told Sharon that "Charles doesn't want to go backwards."

I walk now along the Thames and watch the water turn, thinking of the past, the memories, the friends who have come and gone. Some are like the rain that now falls, disappearing into the river. Someone said that if you haven't learned the meaning of friendship, you haven't learned anything. That man's name was Muhammad Ali, and I was about to meet the great man.

*

In the end, I don't know what did happen between Charles and Nigella. There was much I didn't know about Charles – even when we were friends. Although I've never met Nigella, I was very sad when I heard of their break-up. That's all I want to say about that.

CHAPTER 28

Pink Floyd

I saw a lot of Pink Floyd in the eighties; it was mostly to do with cars. I had maintained my friendship with Steve O'Rourke, the manager, since the *Dark Side of the Moon* Hollywood Bowl concert in '73, and by the late eighties I was either earning too much money or all the cocaine was affecting my judgment, but I kept buying cars. As I told film director Alan Parker, when he asked me why I kept buying them, it was an obsessive need. It might have had something to do with my Tourette's, but I would obsess about a particular car, say an Aston Martin or an E-Type Jag – until I bought it, then I would immediately lose interest in that car and obsess about another. Gandhi said of greed that "There is a sufficiency in the world for man's need but not for man's greed", but I don't think he understood where I was coming from: I needed cars. Or had I missed something? If my obsessions were coming from my Tourette's and my Tourette's had been a product of my trauma as a child, then it is likely my obsession with cars is a result of the war. I'm buying Ferraris because of Adolf Hitler!

I finished up buying eighteen classic cars. I had four Ferraris, one Aston Martin, two E-Type Jags, an XK 120, three Alfas, a Maserati, two Corvettes, a Ford Mustang Shelby replica and... I can't even remember the others. Eighteen, all at the same time! Greed probably came into it. My friends were trying to warn me about it, but I didn't want to listen. Erich Fromm said that greed is "a bottomless pit which exhausts the person in an endless effort to satisfy the need without ever reaching satisfaction", but he was already dead and clearly didn't understand the rising market in classic cars. The trouble is, it was a bubble, and it caught me. "It is greed to do all the talking but not to want to listen" – Democritus!

Hanging around with the Floyd didn't help either; they were all car fanatics. Drummer Nick Mason had fifty-five cars and every one was worth all my cars put together. He even had a Ferrari 250 GTO, registration 250 GTO – the most valuable model in the world. One had recently sold for fifteen mil. I suppose we were all guilty of greed, although the irony was that I wasn't the one preaching the prophecies of love and consciousness that bands coming out of the psychedelic era seemed to.

I met with Nick when he and his wife Nettie were on the Mille Miglia historic rally in Italy, and we had dinner together on the overnight stopover in Rome. On another occasion, they were horrified when I drunkenly climbed into the bridal taxi taking them from their wedding reception in Holland Park, asking, "Can you give me a lift to Ladbroke Grove?" How embarrassing! I went with Steve O'Rourke and his wife Angie to the twenty-four-hour race at Le Mans, where his Emka Aston Martin came in seventh – the highest finish of a British car for years. He had a big trophy in his house, given to the highest British finisher at Le Mans, and it carried all the names of the famous pre-war Bentleys and post-war Jaguar C-Types and D-Types that had won the race. At Le Mans, Alain de Cadenet, a friend from London, told me a wing had come off his car at 200 mph down the Mulsanne Straight. Incredible! Pink Floyd and I went to many private track days at circuits such as Goodwood, and races at Brands Hatch. We went to the Goodwood Festival of Speed and I'd often watch Steve racing his Knobbly Lister-Jaguar.

Nick Mason and David Gilmour got the first two limited edition Ferrari F40s from the factory at Maranello, while they were touring Italy with the Floyd. Nick took me to Donington in his, where a magazine photographed it. He knew I was on the list of a thousand people to receive one. I got on the list thanks to my nephew Jimmy; his wife Laura's father was head of the Automobile Club of Italy. I had to wait five years before it arrived, and mine was the last one into the UK. By the time I got it, I was just about to leave to live in California, where it was not legal – so, can you believe it… I sold it! But before I did, I needed to take it for a spin, so I took it down to Wiltshire one Saturday. I was having fun on the A303, coming up behind motorists on the two-lane highway and putting my foot down when they pulled over, showing off the acceleration basically, and wadda-ya-know, I got busted for speeding.

It took the police ten miles to catch me (I was unaware they were chasing me) and when they pulled me over, I began to plead. I told them I was leaving the country, hoping they would let me off, but they weren't too sympathetic – and they took me down the station straightaway. Hysterically, the copper who needed to drive the thing couldn't do up the tricky seatbelt and was looking at the gear stick like it was some state of the art high-tech coffee machine. I told him "That's just the beginning, officer; you've really got to know how to drive these things well… otherwise you can cause accidents." I offered to drive it myself and follow them. His head turned to mine and I could see it in his eyes: he had no choice. "You aren't going to take off again, are you?" he asked.

I later appeared in court, with a solicitor. I was desperate not to be banned for my last month in England, when I had so much running around to do. Normally anything over 100 and you're a banned man. I had been clocked at 106, but this was fortunate; I was actually going up to 130. I had a plan. My solicitor didn't know what to do, so I had him step aside and spoke directly to the court: "My friends, the F40 has twin turbos!" I could see how silly they all felt not realising this crucial point. "This means they kick in when the car reaches 3500 revs…" (The three heads lifted, as if all in unison. I think my hook had caught them in one throw; I just needed to reel in.) "… which is around the legal limit of seventy miles an hour. Once the turbos come on, the acceleration from seventy to one hundred takes just one and a half seconds… so it is rather marginal whether you are doing seventy… or one hundred." They let me off with a fine and no ban. The solicitor said I should be an actor, as it was the best performance he had ever seen in court.

David Gilmour also collected classic cars… and planes! That is, until he nearly killed himself in an old one, and his new wife banned him from flying. I was trying to keep up with the Floyd, but the trouble was they were much richer, and for me it was a nightmare storing and repairing all my cars. Life was hard you see… I had to store and repair my expensive cars! The entire thing was ridiculous and I was going to live in LA anyhow, so I sold them all in one hit to a dealer at knockdown prices.

"There was a time in my life when I thought I had everything – millions of dollars, mansions, cars, nice clothes, beautiful women, and every other materialistic thing you can imagine. Now I struggle for peace." – Richard Pryor

★

In between the car stuff, there were some notable Pink Floyd musical memories. I went to lots of shows in London and Knebworth, where a real Spitfire flew over the crowd. I remember that show well: Steve O'Rourke threw someone who was illegally filming off the high stage. You have to be tough to work with a rock band, and Steve was. During a concert in America, I was standing with him near the sound engineers, and someone came up to him and handed him a document, accusing the band of stealing lyrics. Steve said it happened every night. I was with the band in New York. They were staying near the UN Plaza and we all took helicopters from the East 35th Street heliport to a show in the New York suburbs. It was wonderful, seeing Manhattan from a chopper. I went briefly 'on the road' too and we flew up to Cleveland. It was interesting seeing the musician's life on tour, and it was exactly as you read of it in mags and saw in the films: lots of sitting around the pool during the day between shows, with pretty girls floating on past, and lots and lots of parties. Lots.

These days, I was thinking much of my father and that life he had lived in London and Berlin. I heard he had an exotic 1930s Lancia Lambda and used to hang around with the Italian Ambassador. I wonder if what he went for was what I had gone for, the places I had gone to, the circles I had become part of. He didn't quite manage to get there from what I know of him, yet I had seemed to. Had I gone full steam for that 'unlived life of the parent'? Or was it all a coincidence, an uncontrollable chain of events, dominos, something that the reverend had begun? It was him, after all, who had the papers publish the orphan ad, and I certainly wouldn't have gone to Margate were it not for the war. So perhaps without it all, I wouldn't be flying in helicopters with Pink Floyd over Manhattan – perhaps I would speak Italian and be working in the fields, growing grapes, living a more peaceful life. Perhaps that was my alternative destiny, and perhaps sometime in the future I would move over there… to feel if that alternative reality was, in fact, something that should have been. Something that was predestined.

*

Becker won Wimbledon, *Born on the Fourth of July* won best picture, thousands passed through the Berlin wall, Madonna released 'Like a Prayer' and Pink Floyd played in Venice for free. It was 1989 and the band had towed an oil rig from the North Sea all the way to Venice, and positioned it off St. Mark's Square to be the stage. All afternoon, the square filled up with people and the lagoon with boats. I watched them from my room in the Gritti Palace Hotel. A special section was reserved in front of the stage for the gondolas. Steve O'Rourke told me later that just as it got dark and the band was due to start, the leader of the gondoliers decided it was perfect timing to threaten Steve that if he didn't give him $10,000, all the gondoliers would blow their whistles during the concert and ruin it. I told you Steve was a tough bugger; he laughed in the bloke's face. "First of all, the band's sound will be heard fifteen miles away, and secondly, blow your whistles, and we'll turn the rig's fire hoses on the gondolas and their paying clients." The concert went on as planned. I took all the wives of the band to dinner on the terrace of the Hotel Danieli overlooking the show, but got so coked up that I picked up the tab of $2000 – and they were all much richer than me! The next day, I took the band for lunch to a nice restaurant I knew on a quiet canal.

CHAPTER 29

Italia '90

"Football, it seemed to me, is not really played for the pleasure of kicking a ball about, but is a species of fighting. The lovers of football are large, boisterous, nobbly boys who are good at knocking down and trampling on slightly smaller boys. That was the pattern of school life – a continuous triumph of the strong over the weak."
– George Orwell.

We had become a nation of riot and robbery, anarchy and rampage. The late eighties saw a string of events that were to damage our sporting reputation and establish us as hooligans throughout the globe. English football hooligans were ruining Britain and we needed a team to get us out of it.

The Heysel Stadium disaster occurred on 29 May 1985. Rioting began, and it was started by the English. Escaping fans were pressed against a wall which collapsed at the stadium in Brussels, before the start of the European Cup Final between Juventus and Liverpool. Thirty-nine Juventus fans died. After it, Britain didn't think it could get any worse – but everywhere England played abroad, fans rioted. Only when it went local did the nation really have enough.

Even the words 'Hillsborough disaster' still make men shudder. It will surely forever be, in sport and British news, one of the truly sad things. It was an FA Cup semi-final and we have all seen the footage. The crush resulted in the deaths of ninety-six people and injuries to 766. It remains the worst stadium-related disaster in British history and one of the world's worst football events.

A horrendous thing now surrounded English footy. It was as if a carpet of disease had been placed over us and England were banned from entering any European tournaments. The press called it "the English disease". On the pitch, the players were not performing; off the pitch, coach Bobby Robson was the subject of a press hate campaign. So, the World Cup was set to be a disaster – there was even talk of a ban – and all were expecting English fans to riot and cause havoc. Instead, something else happened, something incredible happened, and Italia '90 is known today as a milestone in English football because of it. Italia '90 was a PR exercise. Everyone expected the worst, but instead of giving us riots, England gave us something else: Gazza.

★

During my hitchhiking days, I grew close with my three Roman nephews. They were sons of my sister Maria and one of them happened to know a production assistant on a Bruce Willis film. He knew that the producer had rented an apartment overlooking the Forum for a year, but that it would be vacant for the World Cup, because they didn't want to shoot the film during the tournament. I rented it for a month and it was the most fantastic flat. I had a party attended by my nephews and their well-to-do, well-connected Roman friends, but none had seen a view like it in Rome, across the Forum to the Colosseum. I simply wasn't to know how phenomenal a trip I was about to have as I sat drinking a cold beer, admiring that view. I didn't know how essential the events of the next few weeks were to be in the future of English football, or for England.

Against the hard battering on the team by an unrelenting press, everything was going great. Paul 'Gazza' Gascoigne had announced himself on the world stage and was appearing as something of a phenomenon; Lineker was banging in goals all over the place; and Robson was proving himself as an experimental, confident and capable manager. The boys' performance was having a knock-on effect across the country, and receiving word back from London, the pubs were filled with smiling, happy people. Everyone just loved Gazza, and Bobby Robson was no longer the country's enemy. Some people were even dancing on the streets.

Adam Whittaker, a friend from London, came to stay. He was managing director at Limelight, Siobhan and Steve Barron's company. Adam brought with him someone called Keith Allen and a girl called Helen who had a commercials production company. I didn't know Keith at that time, but he has since become well known as an actor, writer, singer and, of course, father of singer Lily Allen. Keith knew John Barnes, as he had written the lyrics to the England team World Cup song 'World in Motion' – a song that Barnsie rapped on – and this was how it all began…

★

The England team had done it the right way. Robson told them all to get it right on the field and all the problems would vanish. They did just that and football, not scandal, was grabbing our headlines. England had made it through to the semis to play West Germany in Turin. The four of us flew there and went to the stadium and John Barnes passed us tickets through the fence. The nation was on the edge of their seats. We needed out of this hooligan culture for good. Come on England!

Today, the game has gone down as one of the most important in English football. It was the game that saw Gazza receive his second yellow card. It was when Lineker turned to Bobby Robson (famously) and gestured for him to keep an eye on Gazza. You see, Gazza's second yellow meant he would not play in the final and Lineker was right – Gazza would burst into tears. But not yet; first they would need to lose to West Germany on penalties. One photographer captured the moment of Gazza lifting his shirt to his face and it was the image that came out of the World Cup for Britain. It was poignant, it was patriotic and it was England's first ever penalty shootout. For West Germany, it was their third. Shilton was in goal and was acting captain at the time, but he was not experienced at shootouts. Our kickers, Lineker, Beardsley and Platt, had scored, but Stuart Pearce hit it down the middle and Illgner blocked it with his legs. The country knew that the boys had taken us to a great place so far and the PR campaign had been a success; getting to the final would have been nothing but extra. Chris Waddle's shot left-footed over the bar to the left as Illgner guessed correctly. The question remains: if Waddle had scored and Berthold then missed, who would have taken England's sixth pen? My guess... Gazza, but it's academic now. The boys had lost to West Germany and they were out of the tournament. The thing was, they hadn't lost lost, they had done what the country needed of them: they had kept their dignity, they had remained gents, but... the celebrations had not yet begun.

The four of us drove our rental car, looking for the country hotel where the England team was staying. Eventually, we saw some carabinieri with submachine guns and we knew we had found it. We blagged our way past the police and were in the lobby of the hotel. Gazza was on the phone to his father back in Newcastle, in tears. Sometimes, there's nothing more heart-wrenching than seeing a man cry, especially over something so important in the world as football. I gave him a consoling hug and he cried on my shoulder. The rest of the team were in a small bar, dealing with the loss a different way. We were the only people there apart from the team. I sat next to Lineker and I still remember what he told me: "It's a scandal that important games end in penalties." The truth was, West Germany had a lot more experience in shootouts than England, and penalties were now to haunt England way into the future. Lineker told me that Pearcy (Stuart Pearce) was crying in his room because he had missed, but to understand this, non-football fans need to see it in context.

Football is something that is built into the English culture, like pubs or the weather. It is one of the essential ingredients that make England, England. The working class needed heroes, and for most of the country, those heroes weren't politicians, they weren't bankers, or any other upper echelon of society. No, they were football players. Representing the country in football at the World Cup is a lot of pressure, but Italia '90 was something else. There were political ramifications and we, the people, needed them to perform. It's worth noting as well that football was different then, and the likes of John Barnes, Gary Lineker and Gazza were heroes for British folk; they were men who kids could relate to. It was different to today, with all the money and the glamour. The players now are often seen as superheroes, but back then in Italia '90, they were human beings – Gazza, crying on my shoulder, was surely proof of that.

Bobby Robson kept coming around trying to get the players to go to bed. "You have an important game on Saturday, you can party after that," he said, but the boys were not convinced. Lineker said to me that no one cared about that game; it was the third-place play-off. Robson came back once more trying to get them to go to bed but he was struggling; these lads had the weight of an entire nation on their shoulders. Something happens during the World Cup and it is unique, much like the Olympics: but everyone on British soil comes together and manages to shelve any prejudice or forget any history of the empire, and instead support England. It's football that does it.

In the bar, Bobby Robson looked down at me and told me, "You are a very bad influence on my lads." Bobby Robson became a national hero for taking the England team to the World Cup semis, and he was knighted as a result. Sir Bobby Robson passed away in 2009 and will be remembered for a long time to come as a national treasure. I was proud to have met that man.

We were in the third-place play-offs, which was in Bari in the South. After the game, which England lost (because they couldn't give a damn), we went back to the hotel and arrived just as the team were finishing dinner and presenting commemorative medals to their coaches, trainers and physios. When the dinner and presentations were over, the players picked up Bobby Robson and threw him in the pool. I have some great shots of that. The boys were out of the World Cup and they had lost their play-off, but they had won the world's respect back and had done a great thing for the country. The job was done in a lot of ways and the pressure was off. As expected, they got drunk – and did they get drunk! We stayed up all night, boozing and singing anthems until it was dawn. I recall John Barnes even rapped out his famous ad and they all went skinny dipping in the pool. The players had their swimming costumes on, but we four from Rome did not! I've got great shots of that too, but I won't include those in the picture section of this book!

At 8am, all the wives and girlfriends (WAGs) arrived. They weren't allowed to travel with the team during the tournament, so they were shipped out for the last game and final party. After a month-long tournament, all the poor girls wanted was a night to celebrate with their men, but the players objected and didn't want any of their women at the final party. Our friend Helen was the only girl there, and I think she made the most of it with one of the better-looking players… who, of course, I will not mention. So, having flown from England especially, the WAGs were put up in a distant hotel and only saw their fellas when they collected the players on the way back to the airport. They had an open bus ceremonial ride when they got back to England. It was famous because Gazza was photographed for all the newspapers wearing a pair of fake female breasts. The beginning of Gazza's antics had just begun. I spoke to him on the phone later. He told me they were all completely hungover when they did that ride through London.

After the all-night party, the four of us from Rome drove back – also with hangovers. I dropped the others off at the flat and in great shock I realised I had a ticket to the final: West Germany and Argentina! I turned on my heels and ran for the car – but didn't arrive at the stadium until half time. I remember thinking as I walked into the stadium, I must be the only man in the world to get a ticket to the World Cup final and miss half the game! On that note, and after what I had experienced… my god, what a boring game! Or maybe I was just one of the ninety-nine percent of Brits who once again didn't give a damn about football now England were out? No, it wasn't true – and that game is now renowned as one of the most boring finals of all time. The England vs.

West Germany match, however, is renowned as being the most dramatic and intense in the entire tournament.

I went to another World Cup final in Los Angeles in '94, between Italy and Brazil. That was also a boring one: 0-0 and it went to a penalty shootout. The biggest tragedy was that Roberto Baggio, who pretty much single-handedly got Italy to the final, was the one who missed. He took the kick just below where I was sitting, and I have a photograph of him with his head lowered in shame and disappointment. My heart went out to him. He had been so brilliant throughout the tournament, and all I could do was think of the boys: Pearce, Lineker, John Barnes, Peter Shilton, Bryan Robson, Chris Waddle, Peter Beardsley, David Platt, Gazza. Football isn't the same today. It was different then; then it belonged to us. Like all of these things, it was a time. Even now, twenty-five years on, English football still rides the crest of the wave those men created on that field and the massive names that go with that squad – heroes to today's players. Everyone will remember the squad from Italia '90, especially me – I got pissed and naked with them! For Germany, it would be the last tournament to feature a German side representing a divided Germany. We were in the nineties now: Thatcher was out, Major was in, and Britain was changing. England were allowed back into European competitions. Change was coming, to us all.

CHAPTER 30

The New Heart Valve and the Farmhouse

I needed open-heart surgery again… the pig valve was falling out. It was possibly because of my cocaine habit through the eighties. In September of 1990, I went back in to have a carbon fibre valve fitted. I used the same hospital, the Princess Grace, and the same surgeon, Mr John Wright. By now, I guess he thought of me as an old chum. He came into my room the evening before the operation and sat on my bed. I think remembered my old sense of humour, so he thought he could confide in me. He put his head in his hands: "I've got to get out of this bloody game." Faced with the prospect of my surgeon having a nervous breakdown, I rushed to reassure him what fantastic work he did… for society, doing four operations a day; how impressed I had been eight years earlier that he was still doing his ward rounds at 11pm; how well the pig valve had been doing in me and how much younger he looked than the last time I… I was practically putting my arm around the man. "All I want to do is go to my vineyard in Hampshire," he said to me. "Now, come on old chap," I told him. "One more valve… for old times' sake."

These days, hospitals want to get rid of you soon after surgery, and after about a week in the case of open-heart surgery. They can't make much money off you when you're convalescing and just paying the daily room rate. The big money is in the surgery, so they want to free up the bed – but because I lived alone, I insisted on staying a few extra days – I was on insurance anyway. Mr Wright would put his head in the door on his rounds: "As far as I'm concerned, you are on holiday," he'd tell me.

After I left the Princess Grace Hospital, I still didn't want to go home alone. I'm not sure why, but it happened to me occasionally. Sometimes I guess it just got a bit… lonely. I went to the Champneys Health Club in Surrey and Jimmy

Page was in the next room, trying to lose some weight for the Led Zep comeback concert at Knebworth. We discussed cars – I had quite a collection by then – and he told me he had a Cord, which I knew was a very rare 1930s streamlined American car. "Hang on a minute…" I asked him, "I didn't think you could drive?"

"I can't!" he told me.

Also at Champneys were my friends Mike Rutherford from Genesis and his lovely wife Angie. It was quite funny, actually, seeing a load of mates in there; I had seen them very shortly before in New York at a Mike and the Mechanics concert. Hanging out in Champneys and clearing my head up after the surgery was the right move, and I took the rest of 1990 off work on convalescence.

By now, I had a beautiful seventeenth-century farmhouse in Wiltshire, on the 11,000-acre Fonthill Estate owned by Lord Margadale. I had bought it in 1985. I was in my office one Friday afternoon in June of that year. Our office on the North Wharf Road had big picture windows overlooking Paddington Station and I saw a train snaking out of the station. I said to my PA, Domenica Fraser, "Look at those lucky bastards, they're probably going down to Devon for the weekend."

Domenica is very posh (but gorgeous with it). Her uncle was Lord Lovat, Chief of the Scottish Clan Fraser. I went to her wedding later to Philip Dunne. He had apparently been an old boyfriend of Princess Diana, and she was at the wedding in the Brompton Oratory in Knightsbridge. After the service, I went outside and stood at the side by the columns to wait for Diana to come. I wanted to get a look at her, as it was surely a once-in-a-lifetime opportunity. I suddenly heard a rustling and saw Diana, standing behind me and a column. I turned to her. "Are you hiding behind me?" I asked.

"Yes, I'm trying to hide from them," she said and pointed across the road.

I hadn't noticed, but there was a battery of about a hundred cameramen over the road, all with their telephoto lenses pointing towards us. The next day, there was a photograph of her and me in the *News of the World*. The headline on the article read, 'Diana Sees Old Flame Wed'. The people in my office were very happy to put the clipping on the wall, having cut off the word 'wed', so it was just a picture of the Princess and me with the title 'Diana Sees Old Flame'. There was a similar photograph on the front cover of *The Observer*. This one was taken as I was talking to Diana and only showed the back of my head. I had a very short haircut at the time.

"I saw your photo in *The Observer*," a friend told me.

"Don't you mean the *News of the World*?" I asked.
"No, I don't read the *News of the World*."
"But you only saw the back of my head in *The Observer*."
"Yeah, that's how I recognised you." Remarkable!

★

Domenica told me about a friend who had just started videotaping properties for house buyers. This was new technology in '85 and search agencies were a new thing. In fact, only Pereds, owned by the pioneering Perry Press, existed at that time. I told Domenica to get her friend to come to my flat the following week. His name was Willie Gething and his new company was called Property Vision, later to become a huge organisation. I told Willie what I wanted, which was an isolated house needing restoration, with outbuildings for garaging. He told me he had the ideal house near to the cottage he rented on the Fonthill Estate. It was probably the easiest search job he ever had, and we went down to see it early on the Monday morning. I ran around it in ten minutes and knew it was perfect, although in a terrible condition. I was back in my office in Paddington by 11am and it was a ninety-minute drive each way. Willie told me it was coming up for auction on the following Friday, only five days away. I was going to the Cannes Advertising Film Festival on the Wednesday, but he said that that was no problem and that he could bid for me. I went home and added up what I could afford, including selling my two jukeboxes and a bunch of cars. My friend and solicitor Stephen Wegg-Prosser did all his normal rapid legal searches on the property, and Willie bid for me. I stayed on the beach of the Carlton all day on the Friday, and when I got back to my room and called London, I found out it was mine. I owned a country house within five days of starting to look for one.

The house needed renovating and Simon Elliot's Shelston Construction did the work. They look after the Earl of Shaftesbury's stately home near Blandford, and John Shaftesbury had recommended Simon. Simon's wife, Annabel, is the sister of the former Camilla Parker Bowles, now the Duchess of Cornwall. Their brother is a well-known man-about-town and author Mark Shand. Simon and Annabel's son, Ben Elliot, is the owner of the highly successful concierge agency Quintessentially. I had the interior of the farmhouse done by two married friends from Wales, Lesley Sunderland and Jonathan Heale. They were friends with

Julie Christie and had lived in a farmhouse owned by her. Through that connection, I saw Julie in Montgomery, and again later in Santa Barbara, California, where she lives. Jonathan designed all my furniture and had it made by Welsh carpenters. Together, they designed and hand printed all the curtains, bed covers and dining chair covers, and stencilled the walls. I had told them I wanted it to look like a famously decorated house called Charleston on the Sissinghurst Estate, but it didn't after they were done with it – it looked better.

During the remainder of the eighties, I went there each weekend. Being at Stocks House had taught me how nice it was being in the country. I told that to Willie Gething on the initial ride down to see the place, but unfortunately he misunderstood, and the rumour then went around the hamlet during the two-year reconstruction that a film producer was planning a hedonistic Playboy-like mansion.

Before I went to live in California, my best friend in Wiltshire was Nick Hoare – younger brother to well-known London rich man Tim Hoare. He had a weekend cottage, rented from the Fonthill Estate. I also saw a lot of him in London. He was part of an upper-class social set, of which I was on the fringes. You've probably got the vibe already, but I was always on the fringes and I guess I preferred it that way. The truth is, you are never really accepted by upper class circles if you are not upper class yourself, so it's all kept in the families.

One day, I was sitting outside the Prince of Wales pub in Notting Hill having a beer with Nick, when another friend of mine, Nigel Cooper, showed up. Nigel is a car restorer and he looked a mess in paint-covered overalls. I introduced Nick and Nigel.

"I think I've met you before," Nick said.

"Yeah, me too. Where did you go to school?" Nigel asked.

Nick is frightfully grand, and too much on occasion. He looked disdainfully at the dirty man, down his nose: "Actually, I went to Eton."

"Oh, so did I. That's where we must have met."

It brought Nick down a peg or two.

I went to Nick's wedding to Bella Heneage; in fact, I drove them. I had just done a shoot with comedian Mel Smith using an Erich von Stroheim-type uniform, so I wore that. I remember being shocked that it fitted me so well. I had deluded myself into imagining that Mel would be much bigger than me. I borrowed Isaac Tigrett's black Cadillac. On the morning when I was due to collect Nick and the best man, London was covered in thick snow. I managed to do my driving duties to the registry office, followed by the blessing in a church. Next stop was the Heneage home for the bridal lunch. The house was up a steep drive. As the Cadillac had front-wheel drive, my car with the bride and groom was the only car that could make it up the hill on the ice. All the other guests were walking in thick snow in their fine shoes and wedding outfits.

At the lunch, both families seemed to be having a competition to see which was the oldest. At the wedding reception that evening, I told Domenica Fraser's father, Sir Ian Fraser, about the Cadillac getting up the hill in the snow, and he said, "Should have used a Bentley." I didn't know that he had been the Chairman of Rolls Royce and Bentley. I took his advice in 2012 and bought one.

Before my convalescence at Ridge Farmhouse in the autumn of 1990, I had never spent more than a weekend in the house. That time off changed my life. I found that I loved being in the country, away from the frantic city and the stress of work, and that I enjoyed pottering around doing nothing. I found that I never got bored and was very sad when it was time to go back to work at the beginning of '91. That was the beginning of me wanting to give up work and live that so yearned-for life of the recluse.

★

Since I brought her up before and I'm writing my memoirs, let me have my sixpence worth on the death of Princess Diana, as this will probably be my only opportunity in print. I knew Dodi Fayed because he was always around Chelsea and in Tramp, and he was a very nice man. The last time I spoke to him was in Tramp in LA, when John Stephen was the manager there. I believe the main cause of their deaths in the Pont de l'Alma tunnel in Paris has been generally overlooked. The deaths occurred because the Mercedes had a head-on crash with one of the support columns in the tunnel. Had there been an Armco guardrail, the out-of-control car would have just slid down the tunnel until it lost momentum, without having an abrupt impact. I believe the city of Paris needs to take some responsibility for having a dangerous tunnel. I know the tunnel – I have driven through it many times – and it has a rapid drop-off going into it. Consequently, it would be very easy to lose control at the entrance, particularly if you are driving too fast. The fact that none of the deceased were wearing seat belts was also a factor in their deaths. The sole survivor, Trevor Rees-Jones, was the only person in the car wearing a restraint.

CHAPTER 31

Apocalypse LA

By 1991, BFCS Inc., the American company, was running full steam, now with an office in Los Angeles as well as New York. I had started it all. It felt like my own baby and first love. While BFCS Ltd., the London company, was pretty much on automatic pilot, America needed me, and I her. The LA office at that time was on 2nd Street in Santa Monica, one block from the Pacific Ocean. I remember having lunch in the Ivy-at-the-Shore restaurant. It was where executive producer Gary Feil said to me, "I can handle all the production work, I just can't handle the directors and the politics. I need one of the owners here." I was sitting in shirtsleeves, in the sunshine, in the middle of January. I was unhappy being back at work in London after my convalescence, and the British economy and advertising business were both in recession in '91. I could hear the ocean from where I sat. I thought of London, and getting away from my addiction to Henrietta and the cocaine. "I'll do it!" I told him.

I went back to London and told my three partners that I was going to run BFCS from LA. It didn't go down well, but it went down nonetheless. There was no reaction from the other partners for over a year, but after I settled in LA, the reaction came, and they forced me out of the UK company.

I was initially a bit apprehensive about living up a canyon on my own, so checked into the Sunset Marquis Hotel. By then, it was my hotel of choice whenever I was in the city of angels and where most English production companies stayed. I was there for three months, after which I was settled. I had become part of LA and it felt just right. I don't recall how Roger Waters and I met at the hotel, and he was the member of Pink Floyd I knew the least, but he was staying in one of the cottages at the back of the hotel while he recorded his solo album *Amused to Death*.

Roger had split from Pink Floyd in the late seventies. He once explained to me that after the success of *Dark Side of the Moon*, *Wish You Were Here* and

Animals, the band members wanted to record their own solo albums. David Gilmour released his first self-titled album in '78, but when Roger came up with his solo album, *The Wall*, the rest of the band said it was so good they should record and release it as a Pink Floyd album. It was a huge hit and gave the Floyd their first number one single with 'Another Brick in the Wall Part II'.

There was a lot of friction between Gilmour and Waters during the making of the album, particularly over the track 'Comfortably Numb', which had its origins in Gilmour's solo album. The argument stemmed from Gilmour's feeling that the material was becoming too lyric-orientated with not enough guitar contribution, and after *The Wall* was finished, Roger left the band, declaring it to be dead. Steve O'Rourke later told me that the other members of the band fought Waters over their rights to the name Pink Floyd, and after a few years of legal battling, won a landmark ruling that one person cannot prevent the others from earning their livelihood. Pink Floyd started recording again and touring without Waters, and Roger began his own solo tours.

Pink Floyd shocked the world when they reunited for the Hyde Park Live 8 concert in 2005. I remember what one of the fan's signs read: "Sometimes pigs do fly." It was the quartet's first performance together in over twenty-four years. Paul McCartney, The Who, Madonna, Robbie Williams, U2, Coldplay, Elton… the list of performers went on and on, but everyone knew the concert was only about one band. It was what Freddie Mercury was for Live Aid. Pink Floyd were the only band not to be verbally introduced and I remember the moment as if it were yesterday: the house and the stage lights were darkened while the introduction of 'Speak To Me' was played, accompanied on the video screens by an animated version of the heart monitor graphic from *Dark Side of the Moon*. They stepped onto the stage and the crowd erupted in applause.

It was a great moment in music history, many were crying and I had met many over the years whose lives had changed because of Pink Floyd. They were one of the few bands in music history that managed to speak on behalf of the people, to the rest of the world, capturing how and what they were thinking – not just with the words, but with the sounds. During the guitar introduction of 'Wish You Were Here', Waters said: "It's actually quite emotional standing up here with these three guys after all these years. Standing to be counted with the rest of you. Anyway, we're doing this for everyone who's not here, but particularly, of course, for Syd." After the last song had been played, Gilmour said, "Thank you very much, good night" and started to walk off the stage, but

Waters called him back, and the band shared a group hug. It became the most famous picture of Live 8. With multi-instrumentalist Richard Wright's subsequent death in September 2008, Live 8 was to be the final concert to feature all four bandmates.

I saw Roger for Sunday lunch at his country house the following weekend. He told me an amusing anecdote. They were rehearsing one of the songs, and Roger said that the ending should go up. David said it should go down. Roger said, "But I wrote the song", to which David replied, "Well, it's my band now."

In '94 when they finished the US tour for *The Division Bell*, David had to go to New York to supervise the soundtrack for a film of the last live show. After touring for months, he was exhausted. I knew how much they had negotiated for the film rights; Steve O'Rourke had told me. In the overall context, it wasn't all that much – just single figure millions! I had a telephone conversation with David and he told me how exhausted he was.

"Why are you bothering?" I asked. "You've just made a fortune touring the US. The band are only getting x amount for the film rights."

He replied, "Yes. But most of that is mine."

After the Live 8 reunion, word on the street was that Roger wanted to get the band back together, but he told Associated Press in 2010 that "Gilmour is completely disinterested." So Roger now plays *The Wall* and other Pink Floyd songs that he wrote, with his own band, on world tours to sold-out arenas, and he probably makes more money that way. Gilmour and Nick Mason are the only other surviving members of Pink Floyd, and they tour with other musicians under that name.

Back in the January of '92, Roger and I started hanging out together in the Sunset Marquis and for weeks we had dinner together – most nights, in fact.

We were getting closer as mates as the days went by. My room overlooked the garden and he would have to pass it to get to his cottage. He would bang on my door each night. "Honey, I'm home!" he would shout. I went to the studio a couple of times to see him recording *Amused to Death* and I think it's where our friendship was cemented; I recognised the voice of one of the singers, P. P. Arnold, and he seemed quite impressed by that. I realised I wasn't missing London one bit and it was here I had noticed how London and I were growing apart. It would soon become a place I would visit, but not live in again. Today, London has changed. It's busier than ever, everyone lives there now, and what with the globalisation of cities via the invasion of big chains and an increase in surveillance, the character of London that I loved so very much and was a part of on the King's Road was beginning to fade into a kind of memory. The signature of Britain was, to me, fading – or maybe it was me who was fading? I was out of love with London, perhaps.

I went with Roger to a benefit concert for Walden Woods where Roger, Neil Young, Don Henley and John Fogarty all played. Roger told me that Neil Young could only play acoustic guitar because he had damaged his ears. We went together to the Imax Theatre to see a film of a supposedly live Rolling Stones concert, but Roger deliberately ruined it for me by continually whispering 'studio' over every other shot.

Maryam d'Abo was also in LA around that time. I would take her to Matsuhisa, our favourite restaurant (the original one in the Nobu chain). "Do you mind if I bring Roger along? Otherwise he will be on his own," I asked her one night.

"Of course not," she said, "I'll invite a girlfriend," and brought along the beautiful Priscilla Phillips. Soon after, while still at the Sunset Marquis, Roger announced he had to go home to England. I thought it was strange he would leave the recording of his album, so I guessed something was up on the home front. When he got back, he told me he had gone home to tell his wife Carolyn he wanted a divorce. They divorced in '92. He married Priscilla in '93.

★

Eric Fellner was renting a house up in the hills and I used to go there for dinner. Eric, with his partner Tim Bevan, owned Working Title Films. Eric told me that Gary Oldman had rented a house for a year whilst starring in *Dracula* for Francis Ford Coppola, but he had left it with four months left paid for. I took over the lease, did a deal with the landlady and stayed there for five years. It was in Benedict Canyon and, my word, it really was beautiful. The view, in fact, could have been near St. Paul de Vence in the South of France, but was fifteen minutes from Sunset Boulevard. David and Bridget Hedison owned the house. He was the star of the original 1958 version of the horror classic *The Fly*, played Captain Lee Crane in *Voyage to the Bottom of the Sea* and Felix Leiter in two James Bond movies. Very Hollywood!

Siobhan Barron was also living in LA. It was the spring of '92 and she was working at the Limelight LA office. In fact, due to the recession back in the UK, there were many Brits I knew over here. I counted seventy working in film, advertising and music. Siobhan had just rented a beach house in Malibu, on Escondido – the last beach where the houses are on the sand. After that, the big swanky houses owned by Barbra Streisand, Richard Gere, Johnny Carson etc. were all up on the bluff and aren't visible from the beach. You could walk for about two miles from Escondido Beach to Point Dume and not see any houses on the beach, except one – it belonged to TV legend Dick Clark. I went to visit my friend Siobhan in April, the first weekend she was in her house. It was foggy, but I loved it. I remember the moment; everything was monochrome grey: the sky, the sea, the beach…I loved it so much I rented a weekend cottage on the same beach.

Living in Malibu was the beginning of one of the happiest periods of my life, even if I nearly died on many occasions, for it was the beginning of apocalypse LA! Fires, floods, earthquakes and riots – we had the lot. In fact, I had only been living in the house in the canyon for ten days when I was curfewed inside it. I couldn't go out at night and I watched on TV as Hollywood burned. It was the Rodney King riots, after the police officers that had been caught on videotape savagely beating Rodney King were acquitted. The black community rioted and every night for six nights the fires spread into the smarter areas of Hollywood. The National Guard was called out. Nigel and Jaki Carroll were living in Hollywood, and the fires were coming too close for comfort. Shortly after, they moved their family to Westlake Village – a quiet family neighbourhood in the San Fernando Valley. Eventually the fires died, but not before causing a billion dollars' worth of damage.

Next came the Malibu wildfires. I had the house in Malibu, but luckily I had a backup pad well away from the flames. The fires spread through the Malibu canyons and were fuelled by the strong Santa Ana winds that blow from the desert towards the sea. Arsonists usually deliberately set the fires when there is a strong Santa Ana wind, just for the fun of it. When you say the word 'arsonist', one often thinks of an anarchist, dressed in a hoodie and baggy jeans, someone with no education and a hate for the world, but that is not always the case – sometimes, the arsonists are the firefighters. Granted, firefighters are some of the bravest, most incredible people, but there are also the crazies who want to start fires and put them out – power maniacs. It's a weird world we live in… and I was watching it burn on TV.

Pepperdine University, just down the road from my Malibu house, was ravaged by the fire; all the trees were burnt down and the buildings were only saved because of the amount of lawn around them. All the Malibu canyons were burnt. I drove up some of them a few days later. The only things left standing were brick chimneys dotted around. It was very sad. Because of the earthquake threat, LA building codes stipulate that houses have to be made of wood. The only brick allowed was in the chimneys. Escondido Beach Road was only saved because the firefighters lined up their trucks on the Pacific Coast Highway and, with water hoses, stopped the flames jumping over it. Glyn Johns and a friend were caught in Glyn's home up a mountain off Topanga Canyon. They were trapped as sixty-foot-high flames travelling at forty miles an hour jumped over their house – while they were in it. They were only saved because Glyn had cut back his vegetation around the house. Danny Mindel came back to his house, intact in a burnt-out landscape, to find a note: "Your house was saved by fireman Bob."

January 1994, and a record cold hit the Eastern United States. The coldest temperature ever measured in Indiana state history was recorded at -36F. On the West Coast, something else was happening: the 6.8 magnitude Northridge earthquake at 4.31am on 17 January 1994. This was the single most terrifying moment of my life (and I have left a Ferrari on top of a wall in a car crash). The whole of Los Angeles, including all the mountains and all the skyscrapers, moved up… an entire foot and north a yard.

Lest we forget, this is how the mountains were created. I suppose we've become too domesticated in the modern age, with set buildings and roads and train tracks, when in reality, all land moves, all oceans move and nothing is stable. Only the weather dictates and we are nothing but victims of it. I think in modern times we have come to forget that. I certainly had, but I remembered it again when the jolt sent me flying out of bed. The bedroom TV went ten feet and I was thrown into the doorway. I hung on for dear life as the land shook to settle. I was being shaken like a rag doll. It was terrifying and I remember in my terror thinking, *Why have I moved to LA? Everyone knew the 'Big One' was coming.* The houses on Benedict Canyon sit on notches in the hillside and I was certain that either we would slide off our notch, or the house above us would come down on top of us. The shaking lasted thirty seconds. It doesn't seem long, but when you are in the middle of sheer terror, it's an eternity. The noise in the house was tremendous, as was the sound of the wooden frames creaking and glass crashing. The moment it died down, I rushed to have a shit and there was another 6.0 quake while I was sitting on the toilet. I was disappointed later to discover that this Northridge earthquake was not the 'Big One'. I can't imagine what that will be like. I just hope I'm not in LA that day.

I had to climb over broken glass to leave my house. All the mirrors, books and other crap was scattered on my floor. The coyotes that lived on the land next door were running around in circles, howling at the moon and the sky. It was apocalypse LA, like some sort of dystopian sci-fi movie. My drive was steep – I was lucky to be able to use it – and I went down the hill to see my friend Paul Weiland. He had rented a house near me while he was directing *City Slickers 2*. I went into his house, no more than 400 yards from mine, and all his family photos were still standing. I said, "You've tidied up fast." He didn't know what I was talking about, so I took him to see my house. "See," I told him.

"Jesus, Chiggars, I'd have shit myself."

"Well," I told him, "I kind of did!"

I went up to Maureen Tigrett, who also lived nearby, to see if she and her children were okay. I was worried about her as Isaac was away. All the residents of her gated community were sitting out on the lawns in the street. The aftershocks were freaking everybody out, and they did for days.

We also had floods and mudslides in Malibu, and an El Niño high tide in '95 that took away the sand from under people's houses and left the decks hanging in the air. For some reason, after all of that, it made more sense to me to be by the beach. Even though the mad weather nearly killed me, I did manage to have a good time too, and the beach had a lot to do with it. I fell in love with beach life and Siobhan and I grew closer. Due to her music video connections and her then boyfriend Howard Napper's modelling career, their house in Malibu was always full of young models, filmmakers and musicians. It was not unusual to have twenty people for lunch at the weekend.

Siobhan knew all about my Christmas trips to Thailand with the Saatchis and she wanted to go. In 1993, she sent a location scout to find a hotel we could take over on Koh Samui. As I have said, Siobhan and her Limelight company always had a large entourage, and we filled a hotel of about twenty bungalows with all kinds of rich and high-profile faces. Richard Branson included.

One night, a few of us went to a bar in the village where I met a Thai girl. I took her back to the hotel but walked into the lobby, and it was full of my English mates. "Err… uhhh. I ran into my niece…" I told them. They weren't buying it.

My prosthetic heart valve makes a ticking sound, the rhythm of which obviously depends on my pulse rate. Whilst doing the dirty deed with the young girl, I opened my eyes to look at her… it happened as I was about to come. She was lying there, oblivious to what I was doing, but holding her wristwatch to her ear and looking at it quizzically, wondering where the rapid ticking noise was coming from. I burst out laughing and it completely put me off the job at hand.

People can sometimes hear the ticking in a quiet room. I went to the ten-day silent Vipassana meditation retreat in Wales with my friend Howard Napper. The retreat was a long way from the nearest village, and en route in my jeep, we passed some New Agers walking with their rucksacks. After I found out how far it was, I decided to go back and give them a lift. Amazingly, they refused to get in the truck. They called it a terrible gas guzzler. On the one hand, I respected them for standing up for what they believed in, but on the other, weren't they all dressed in modern clothing and factory-made backpacks? Walking in hiking boots made from oil? Were they so committed to the prophecy of the hippy that they would never step onboard an aeroplane again, never sail on a boat?

Anyway, it was my introduction to Vipassana and I found the experience very interesting indeed – and fortunately didn't need to listen to any New Ager preaching like I had experienced in India, as nobody was allowed to speak. I enjoyed not talking for ten days, but mostly not listening to anyone's crap! It was difficult seeing Howard when we did the walking exercise, which was rather like a prison exercise-yard walk. Howard and I wouldn't be able to look each other in the eyes, otherwise we would get the giggles. We had to get up at 4am each morning to do the first meditation and that was particularly hard to get my head around: getting up out of bed… to go and sit down! I don't think I achieved enlightenment or perhaps I'm not one of the chosen few? But I did enjoy the silence and I enjoyed getting the giggles with Howard. It made me feel like a kid again, but the best thing was when someone complained about the "person with the loud watch". It was my heart valve, and they made me bind my body with clothing for sound insulation and sit right at the back like a naughty boy. Well, that wasn't exactly spreading love and harmony now, was it?

In 1994, I went to Antigua to join my friends Simon and Lorraine Kirke for Christmas. They were staying at the Copper and Lumber Store Hotel in Nelson's Dockyard and Keith Richards was there, on a family break from the Rolling Stones' US tour for the *Voodoo Lounge* album. Keith was a friend of Simon's, who is the drummer with Bad Company, and most days both families and I would go for a beach picnic. Keith would do the barbecuing. I'd had a previous run-in with Keith in the seventies. I had a new Swedish model girlfriend, who was the spitting image of Marlene Dietrich. I took her to Tramp, and we sat at a table with Keith and some other people. She was my beautiful date and he took her home.

One night Keith, Simon and I went on a bender in a spare room they had. Keith had received a Christmas present from the tour guitar roadie. It was a Dobro steel guitar, the same as the one Robert Johnson was holding on the cover of a biography that Keith had. He was very proud of it. Keith is a beautiful singer; in fact, his songs are always my favourites on the Rolling Stones albums. He sang songs all night; interspersed with anecdotes, interspersed with Jack Daniels, interspersed with cocaine. I hadn't done coke since leaving London, but I was weak that night. Gimme a break… I was partying with Keith Richards for fuck's sake.

At one point, I told them I had recently been to Graceland and had bought Priscilla Presley's autobiography to see what her life with Elvis was like. Keith told me he had been a close friend of Priscilla Presley. Mick had been a close friend of Priscilla Presley. In fact, the whole band had been close friends of hers. That was the difference between him and I: I was reading a book about her, while he had been there with Priscilla Presley! Keith was very dismissive about Elvis and his manager Colonel Parker. "Do you know what the Colonel's previous act to Elvis was? Dancing chickens! He had chickens in a cage on a bed of straw, and underneath the straw, he had live electrical wires, which he switched on and off. When the chickens got electrocuted, they danced!" It was one of the most memorable nights of my life and we all went to bed at dawn.

A few months later, the Rolling Stones were playing at the Coliseum in LA and I had tickets from the tour office through Ronnie Wood. They included backstage passes, but when I got there, I found there were about two thousand people backstage – none of whom were the band. There, I ran into Jo – Ronnie's wife. I had known her since she was a sixteen-year-old model and married to Peter Green, in the rag trade. He once told me, "You've got to get them young, so you can mould them," but then Jo left Peter and married Ronnie! I had known Ronnie when he was with Rod Stewart in The Faces through the super groupies on the King's Road, but in 1975 he joined the Rolling Stones. Jo had had a son Jamie from Peter Green, and Jamie, then a young man, was with her backstage at the Coliseum. She introduced me and told him, "This is my oldest,

oldest friend." She then took me into the inner-inner sanctum, where the band were and no one else. It was such a heartwarming thing she had said, and I shall remember it forever. It proved to me also how important it is to be nice and to be nice to your friends.

We went to the trailer that Ronnie and Keith Richards were sharing. Ronnie and Keith were in there alone and we all had a beer. It was just the two of them, the girl I was with and yours truly. Keith remembered me from Antigua a few months earlier. Eventually, a security man came and told them it was time for the show. We all walked together to the back of the stage, them carrying their guitars. They climbed onto the stage and my friend and I went to find our seats. She was very impressed. So was I. I felt very privileged.

CHAPTER 32

House of Blues

Isaac Tigrett was also in LA in the nineties. He had married Maureen Starkey, Ringo's 'secret' wife during The Beatles' heyday. I would see a lot of Richie, as she called Ringo, at her house, as his children still lived there. The Hard Rock Café was the world's biggest collector of rock 'n' roll memorabilia, and Isaac claimed with great affection that Maureen was the most authentic piece in the collection. I went to their wedding in the South of France. They were living in a large house on a year-long rental in Cap Ferrat, and held it there. I was one of the best men, along with Dan Aykroyd and his pal Larry Bilzarian. Before the wedding, we best men and Isaac stayed in the Château d'Eze, a fab hotel on a mountain peak that looked over the coastline. I remember the wedding well; it was a great party and Isaac spent $80,000 on caviar! I ruined a brand new Commes des Garçons linen jacket, jumping into the crowded pool to save a three-year-old girl from drowning. Afterwards, all her mother Carole could say to me was, "Oh, she's always doing that." Sometimes rich people really piss me off.

I also remember it because Isaac had a friend from Texas, Mike Powell, whose mother had been best friends since childhood with Princess Grace of Monaco. Consequently, Mike had known the Crown Prince Albert for years. We all went out on a motorboat to look around an American warship that was moored in the bay and Prince Albert told me the most disgusting joke: "Why do Tampax have a string? So you can floss after you have eaten." I thought, *I'll remember that when you are crowned Prince of Monaco* – which he is now. On that note, what is it with royalty and tampons? It reminds me of the time that Prince Charles had his phone hacked – wasn't he caught telling Camilla it would be his "luck" to "come back" as her Tampax? It just goes to show that royalty are normal human beings like the rest of us, and just as crude.

Isaac and Dan Aykroyd started the House of Blues in 1992, with the first being in Harvard Square, Boston. It was only a small club, but it got Harvard

University interested and they invested $15 million in the venture. I went to the opening of the next one in New Orleans, in January '94.

I was with Isaac and Maureen Tigrett, Dan and Donna Aykroyd, Ian and Doris La Frenais, and Jeff Lynne. Jeff, the La Frenais' and I regularly had dinner together in LA. Jeff was the former leader of ELO, for whom he wrote the great songs 'Evil Woman', 'Mr Blue Sky', 'Free Fallin'' and 'Sweet Talkin' Woman', and he is nothing short of a musical genius. He was previously with The Move, the pioneering British band from the sixties. He was also, with George Harrison, the instigator and founder of the Traveling Wilburys, featuring himself, George, Roy Orbison, Bob Dylan and Tom Petty. In 2008, *The Washington Times* named Jeff Lynne the fourth greatest record producer of all time. Ian La Frenais is best known for his creative partnership with Dick Clement; together they wrote many of the classics of British TV comedy, such as The Likely Lads, Porridge, Lovejoy, and Auf Wiedersehen, Pet.

We had a lot of fun in New Orleans; that place sure had some sleazy dives. I was sitting in an alcove in one club, with a lap dancer sitting astride my lap and my face buried in her naked breasts, when Doris La Frenais came in and started talking to me as if I was on my own. "Chig, where are we going for dinner tonight?"

"Doris, do we have to talk about it now?"

Doris is a great bird; I love her. She used to always embarrass me, though, and probably her husband Ian, by saying about me to friends, and in front of him: "This is who I am running off with, if anything ever happens to Ian."

Isaac had a House of Blues half-time show at the Super Bowl held in New Orleans, and he arranged for me to go on the private jet owned by Jean Paul DeJoria, owner of Paul Mitchell hair products. The problem was Chelsea were playing Liverpool that weekend, so there was no question – I had to stay in LA to watch it in the Cock and Bull. I soon regretted it, though, when Chelsea were six-nil down at half time. The Super Bowl would have been fun, I guess, but you can take the boy out of Britain… you know the rest.

Isaac is a character. He had a train car that he used to commute with from LA to New Orleans. The carriage had belonged to his mother's family for decades; her family built railways. Isaac tracked it down and restored it, but he restored it with a difference; the inside became an opulent Indian palace. He bought carved wooden panels, fabric and furniture from India, and it was absolutely splendid. Isaac would call up Amtrak and hook it onto the back of a regular scheduled train. The charge was $1.15 cents a mile.

The House of Blues on Sunset Boulevard is a wonderful building. The land drops off from Sunset very steeply, so all you see from the strip is a one-storey shack made of rusty corrugated iron. The rest of the huge building – containing the auditorium, bars and restaurants – is hidden down the slope. Isaac found the rusty shack at the Crossroads. The building itself is a piece of rock 'n' roll memorabilia, the Crossroads being the mythological crossroads in Mississippi where Robert Johnson was supposed to have sold his soul to the devil in return for the devil teaching him how to play the blues. It was on the route that all the blues musicians took to get from the Deep South to Chicago. Eric Clapton recorded an album called *Crossroads*, also the name of his rehab clinic in Antigua.

The House of Blues was said to cost $11 million to build and Isaac's attention to detail is wondrous, so you find in there walls filled with southern folk art and bar counters made of thousands of bottle caps. The large bar on the second level hydraulically splits in two and swings open to reveal the stage down below.

The opening parties lasted a week. Aerosmith, who were investors, were on the first night. I had never seen them and they really were that good. Top acts played throughout, including John Lee Hooker. A year later, I had a pee standing next to him at the Hollywood Center Studios where I worked, so I can justifiably claim to have hung out with John Lee Hooker... if you get what I'm saying. On the official opening night, James Brown and the Famous Flames played. It was, I think, the tenth time I had seen them, but not since the seventies. I once saw them three times in one month: twice in London and once in LA. They were the band that Mick Jagger regularly flew to New York to see at the Apollo, before he became a star – James Brown being Jagger's inspiration for his great dancing moves. I don't know how I did any work that week.

Isaac had also created an Indian room in the Hollywood House of Blues. It was the VIP area, called the Foundation Room, and you had to be a member to get in. Isaac, Dan and Donna Aykroyd, Ian and Doris La Frenais, Jeff Lynne and his girlfriend and I must have spent every evening there for at least two years. Maureen, unfortunately, didn't make a couple of years. She collapsed on the day of the opening party. She had been dieting to get into that 'special' dress, and everyone thought that was the cause. It turned out she had leukaemia. I went to see her in hospital in Seattle after she had a bone marrow transplant from her son Zac, but she didn't make it and she died in December '94. I cried on the shoulders of Fiona Copeland at Maureen's wake in the House of Blues, which was quite unusual for me. I had always dealt with death quite matter-offactly, but not when Maureen died; for some reason, it was different. I really loved her and I felt very sad for my young goddaughter, Augusta. I think that when my parents died and my granny died, it wasn't the end of the world. I always knew somehow I would be okay, but when Maureen died, I was sad for Augusta and I cried so damn hard.

Every night, we would have dinner in the Foundation Room and then go to see the show downstairs in a reserved seating area. I was a regular at the House of Blues and I saw some fantastic acts: Al Green, Ray Charles, Chuck Berry, Little Richard, Bobby 'Blue' Bland, the Neville Brothers, Willie Nelson, Johnny Cash, Leon Russell, Bo Diddley, Taj Mahal, John Lee Hooker, James Brown, Etta James (three times) and my mate Eric Clapton. Even Tom Jones played – the girls still throwing their knickers, which was quite amusing. Some of the bloomers flying through the air were just ginormous!

My neighbour from Escondido Beach and friend from the Playboy Stocks House, Stash de Rola, and I were at the club one night when we bumped into Tony Curtis. It was like a Stocks House reunion. Tony had another statuesque, buxom lady with him – his new wife, I think – and she also towered over him. He sure liked ladies with the big boobs.

I had my fiftieth birthday at the club on 8 June 1994, two months after it had opened. I booked all five tables along the bar that opened onto the stage, each containing ten people. Fifty special friends for my fiftieth. Junior Walker & the All Stars were due to play that night, one of the biggest acts on the Motown label. I remembered their big hits, 'Shotgun' and '(I'm a) Road Runner', from the 1960s, so I was looking forward to seeing the famous sax player. Unfortunately, Junior Walker had a heart attack that day, and the House of Blues house band took his place. Walker died eighteen months later, at the young age of sixty-four.

Having felt that I missed out on investing in the Hard Rock Café, I was keen to invest in the House of Blues. Initially, before the clubs had opened in New Orleans and LA, I had put in $20,000 and I hadn't even been in the clubs – but after I saw them, I was impressed. Planet Hollywood had gone public and made a fortune for Robert Earl and the shareholders. Robert Earl had been running Grand Met when they bought up Isaac's half of the Hard Rock Café. He had found that Isaac had built up a big collection of Hollywood memorabilia… and that was the beginning of Planet Hollywood. Isaac was talking about the House of Blues going public and I wanted in. I begged him to let me invest more, but he kept saying things like, "Those shares are reserved for John Goodman." In the end, he let me raise my shareholding to $300,000, but I lost it all. I thought you might all like to know – after all this bragging about cars and whatnot. If I'd invested that kind of money in 1995 in any tech stock, like Microsoft or Apple, I would be a very wealthy man, but I've stayed positive about it. I reckon I had my money's worth in fun.

Things started to go wrong for Isaac at the 1996 Atlanta Georgia Olympic Games. He always paid frequent visits to his guru, Sai Baba, in India and he was undecided whether to open a House of Blues at the Olympic Games. He asked Sai Baba, about a month before the Games, and the baba told him he should open a club, so Isaac had crews working double time through the night to get the club finished in time. It supposedly cost $9 million to build, for a club that was only going to stand for a month. Unfortunately, the thing that really did it for Isaac was the bomb that went off at the Atlanta games, killing one person. Whole areas where the House of Blues was planning to sell merchandise were closed off and the whole thing was a disaster. By then, the House of Blues had a number of large investors who had put in $10-15 million each. In addition to Harvard University, there was Disney and someone who had made a fortune selling Mexican salsa. After the Atlanta debacle, the public listing was cancelled and the figures no longer stacked up. Isaac fell out with the financial partners and left the company.

The whole House of Blues fun was over and eventually the clubs were sold to Live Nation concert promoters.

"Man learns through experience, and the spiritual path is full of different kinds of experiences. He will encounter many difficulties and obstacles, and they are the very experiences he needs to encourage and complete the cleansing process." – *Sai Baba*.

CHAPTER 33

Closing BFCS Inc.

"A man is born alone and dies alone; and he experiences the good and bad consequences of his karma alone and he goes alone to hell or the supreme abode."
– Chanakya

I had been in LA for one year but the US company wasn't showing a profit, so the other UK partners sold it to me. I was fine with that. I knew it would boom someday but they didn't believe in it. In fact, it was a job away from going bankrupt, but I knew a job would come. I don't know how or why I knew, I just did, and then it did – a $1.4 million production for the launch of the Lexus GS300. I worked hard, and within a couple of years, the US company was billing three times the UK company. I was the sole owner and by 1995 BFCS Inc. billed $25 million – its last full trading year. I paid myself a bonus of one million US dollars and I carried the cheque around for a week, showing it off to friends. Nothing cool about me!

In the US, BFCS made commercials for Ford, Toyota, Cadillac, BMW, Mazda and Chrysler. We also shot for Coca-Cola, Reebok, Nike, Cover Girl, Schweppes, Cadbury, Maybelline, Bank of America, the US Army, Texaco and many more, but our best-known hit that everyone remembers was the original ad for Grey Poupon, directed by Michael Seresin. In it, two English toffs (aristocrats!) draw alongside each other in their Rolls Royces, eating their lunches on the picnic tables of the cars. One says to the other, "Pardon me, would you have any Grey Poupon?" The other one says, "But, of course," and speeds off. Everybody loves that one.

My main director in the US was Allan van Rijn, who I had brought over from the London office. He would do huge car shoots, sometimes costing between three and four mil each. To begin with, he always went over budget, eating into the profit. It didn't bother him because he still got a big fat director's fee, and the more money he spent on the production, the better his film would be. It bothered me, because I needed the mark-up to cover my overheads. I gave him an offer he couldn't refuse: he could keep most of the underage, if he came in under budget. At least I would make my budgeted profit. Funny how he suddenly started to be profitable. He could make a fortune on big jobs. One car shoot, he made $500,000 in director's fees and share of the profit – for one month's work. Unfortunately, Allan was becoming really difficult to deal with. Rumour had it that he was mixing Prozac and Valium, something no doctor would ever prescribe together – the combination is just too dangerous. He was becoming erratic and, to this day, I'm sure he nearly caused me a nervous breakdown. He would also flirt with other production companies, give them false hopes, let the rumours fly around in circles and then never join them. On one occasion, he moved a snow shoot a hundred miles because he didn't like the snow in the first location. Eventually, he told me he didn't want to do any more car commercials, which was where the big money was. After I closed the company, Allan moved to RSA, Ridley Scott's company. I knew Bruce Martin, their executive producer, and he would call me at home: "Allan refuses to come out of the trailer" and "He won't talk to the agency."

"Was he always like this?" he'd ask.

"Yes, Bruce," I replied. "It's why I'm sitting on a beach in Malibu."

Running a production company in America was much more stressful than in London, especially with the added fear of the brewing 'Big One'. In the UK, agencies would pick who they wanted to do their commercial and wait for them to become available, even if it was two or three months. In my day, very rarely would we have to bid against another director. In the US, it was exactly the opposite. Agencies would always leave things until the last minute and they would bid a job between six or eight directors to shoot the following week. So, we could be bidding one small job for $50,000 and another one for $1 million, both for the same week. You wouldn't want to book the small job in case you got the big one. Then, when you got awarded the job, it was kick, bollock and scramble to get it produced in time.

I had overheads between the New York and LA offices of $175,000 a month, but that wasn't the end of the story. The directors and the sales reps between them took about fifty percent of the profit, so actually the company had to make $350,000 profit a month to break even – all with a black hole of no work two or three weeks ahead. It was incredibly stressful! Then, two of my principal directors went to do movies. I was used to Barry Sonnenfeld doing feature films. He was primarily a film director and he only did commercials to pay for the building of his Long Island Hamptons house, which he called the BFCS Palace. He would only ever do ten-day shoots and his daily rate was $25,000. He would get the art department to print up a giant cheque for $250,000, like a lottery winner, and it would be presented to him in front of the agency at the end of the shoot. To be honest, it was embarrassing, flaunting it like that in front of the clients and the crew, but they all found it amusing. In reality, they were just brown-nosing and I guessed he liked that a heap. On top of that director's fee, he got forty percent of the profit and went off to shoot *Get Shorty*. I went to see him on set and met Travolta and Gene Hackman, which was pretty cool. I always loved *Saturday Night Fever* from the seventies and I grew up watching Hackman on screen, plus we had some mutual friends: ex-Formula 1 racing driver Rupert Keegan and his brothers. Unfortunately, as soon as Sonnenfeld finished *Get Shorty*, he was persuaded to do another film. He kept calling in saying how much he hated doing it, but it was a big hit. You have heard of the film – it was *Men in Black*.

I went back to Ridge Farmhouse in Wiltshire for Christmas 1995. I was incredibly stressed out. Sid Roberson, who had owned his own production company, came to visit. I told him I was thinking of getting out of the rat race but something was keeping me in it, and he advised me not to walk away from it just yet.

After the Christmas holiday, I went back to LA. I was doing a lot of Kundalini yoga with a wonderful Sikh woman and Madonna's former teacher, Gurmukh Kaur Khalsa. The best I have ever felt in my life was on the day after a whole day of White Tantric Yoga. I mentioned it to my GP, the brilliant Dr Soram Khalsa, who is also a Sikh man. He told me that's why all the hippies started with Kundalini in the late sixties… to get high without taking drugs! Today, most of the Kundalini Sikhs are white Americans and you see them all over America. Their Master Guru, Yogi Bhajan, was an Indian, but very few of the practitioners are these days. It's an American thing, I guess. They wear white outfits with white turbans. During the White Tantric, which lasts a day, about 100 people are to sit cross-legged in yoga posture in lines, facing one another. The energy comes from the lines of meditation. People are alternated boy-girl and I was paired with a pretty French girl, with the day's activity consisting of doing yoga meditations for sixty-two and thirty-one minutes. One meditation

I will never forget involved staring into the other person's eyes for the sixty-two minutes. I think during that time I fell in love with the French girl, or infatuation took over. It's partially why I felt so good the next day. We saw each other a few times, but my love wasn't reciprocated... she had a girlfriend.

A band had come over from India and after a whole day of White Tantric Yoga, I'd lay on the floor exhausted, but feeling terrific, listening to that ancient and meditative Indian music. I think I felt that bliss that everyone was blabbering on about: enlightenment or something. By the end of the music, I can say I did feel blissful and I didn't want to leave it. I wanted it to be like it forever, so I made the decision to leave the Western world, to live a life apart and on the edge of all society, perpetual pilgrimage and the abandonment of all material and sexual attachments – to become like the sadhu and go live in a cave. Another thought popped into my head: a full English brekky and a pint of Guinness. The White Tantric was okay, but walking around outside, cold in a loincloth was a no-no. My mind was spinning and it was all to do with work.

I did White Tantric a second time a few months later. The experience was not so good, I think, as I didn't have the French girl. We were made to do one meditation that involved holding our arms in the air for sixty-two minutes. This is impossible to do without occasionally bringing them down, or so I thought. I've since seen a documentary on YouTube about the naga sadhus of India. Sadhus are mystics, monks who practise yoga with one life ambition: achieving moksha... liberation through meditation, contemplating Brahman and all teachings. They live in caves and temples, in cemeteries and with ghosts. Some are naked, some carry swords and some eat only fruit. Some stand up forever, but I had the most respect for the one on this documentary: he had kept one arm in the air for over twenty years. I couldn't do it for an hour and even got severe damage to my shoulder, which I exacerbated by playing tennis a few weeks later. I eventually had to have keyhole surgery on it back in England.

I got back to LA in the New Year of '96. Gurmukh knew that I was stressed out and thinking of giving up work, and she recommended I talk to a Kundalini psychiatric counsellor, Sat-Kaur Khalsa. I saw her every week for a few weeks, and after it I made the decision to finish my career and change my life. It had to be done. Six friends had died in '95 and I was living the same type of lifestyle. Peter Cook was the only one older than me. Johnny Chapulis, the friend of all the supermodels, had died of a brain tumour at the young age of thirty-three. Leslie Sunderland, who had done all the fabrics at Ridge Farmhouse, Gerlinde

Kostiff of Kinky Gerlinky and an artist friend, Luciana Martinez, had all died of aneurisms in their forties. I was constantly being reminded to enjoy every day, but at the same time… not too much. I had had open-heart surgery twice, my arteries were blocked, I was overweight and I was highly stressed. The truth was, I could have been next and I knew it.

I hired a personal trainer and saw him in the gym three times a week. In between, I was doing yoga and living on a fat-free vegetarian diet prepared for me by a different Kundalini Sikh. In the first six months of 1996, I lost 60lbs – going from 230lbs down to 170lbs. To put that in perspective, a twenty kilo suitcase that you take on holiday and heave up onto the belt for the check-in girl to weigh is 44lbs, so I lost almost one and a half suitcases of body fat in just six months, and I owe a lot of that to yoga. It works if you do it and I know there are a lot of sceptics out there, so think of it this way: in the words of John Lily, "Yoga is the science of the east while science is the yoga of the west."

★

I could not sell BFCS Inc. There is nothing to sell with a commercials production company. I was the glue holding it together. The only assets were the directors and they could walk away to another company at any time. I decided to close the company down and change my life. I paid all the bills, totalling nearly a million dollars. This was unheard of in the production business in America. Usually when companies close, they walk away from all their debts, but I had learnt about karma. I recall two English production companies going belly up and owing millions of dollars. The difference was, I hadn't gone bust, and after thirty years in the business, I wanted to go out with good karma. So, I paid all my bills. Some of the larger creditors, like the equipment houses and film suppliers, gave me a discount for old times' sake, but if people insisted on full payment, they got it.

The news of my retirement and closure of BFCS Inc. was announced as the front-page headline in *Shoot* magazine. The reaction was extraordinary. Jon Kamen, owner of bi-coastal @Radical Media, called his LA partner, Frank Scherma: "Frank, how old are you?"

"I'm forty-two," Frank said.

"So am I. Cigarini's fifty-two. We've got to work like FUCK for ten years so we can get out, like he has." I knew Jon personally, as he was the brother of my neighbour in Notting Hill, the brilliant film score composer Michael Kamen. I saw Jon in a restaurant a couple of years later, and he said a very sweet thing to me, "I've still got your photograph on my desk".

After the retirement announcement, I went to the Hollywood Center Studios, where the BFCS office had been. I ran into a casting director I knew. "You are everyone's hero," she told me. I think everyone wanted to get out secretly, but couldn't afford to. I'd had enough, but the difference was, I didn't give in to the fear of not working, which is often the thing that keeps people in the black hole. It is a black hole because then they die, forgetting to have lived. That's the key: to not give in to fear. It was just as Jim Morrison said it: "Expose yourself to your deepest fear; after that, fear has no power… you are free."

I retired at fifty-two.

*

I had some great staff working at BFCS Inc. I think it's true to say everybody loved working there and, looking back, that's something I can be proud of. It had a family ambience. The grovelling staff would often tell me it was the best company, or that I was the best boss they ever had. I still keep in touch with some of them. Patricia Judice and Cathy Dunn were outstanding in the production department. Tim Sullivan now has a cult following as a director of horror films. Katy Tipton was my absolute fave. She was a production coordinator who had come over to the LA office from London. Goodness me, I remember when she first came in for her interview as a receptionist. She was, and still is thirty years later, very pretty, but also very shy. My heart went out to her. "How many interviews have you been to?" I remember asking her.

"This is my first," she told me. I couldn't resist, and I immediately jumped in. "You've got the job," I told her, and I never regretted my impulsiveness.

After my initial years in LA, I wondered why everybody in England didn't move to California, but the grass was always greener and the New World soon wore thin. I yearned for the Old World. Steve, Siobhan Barron's brother, wed in Italy, in Bellagio on Lake Como, to a beautiful girl called Andrea Brenninkmeijer, from the Anglo-Dutch family who own C&A. Como epitomised everything I missed in LA. The lake is beautiful and the old villas on the lake are a dream. I remember, oh so clearly, being on a boat on that lake and taking it all in: the history, the sounds. It was everything that America was missing… age. People came from all over the world to be at the wedding. I had just shed 60lbs and was able to buy smart new suits for the occasion. The main base was the wonderful Grand Hotel Villa Serbelloni, dating from 1872. It was on the peninsula where the two branches of the lake meet. Most of the wedding party stayed there, including me. One outstanding day was when Andrea's parents hosted a lunch in a restaurant called Locanda dell'Isola Comacina, which stands on its own little island of Comacina. There was a fleet of launches to ferry the guests down the lake to the island. It was an unforgettable day. During the festivities, I was hanging out with Siobhan and Jamie Morgan. A friend of Andrea, Stella, made the dresses for the two teenage bridesmaids. She was an up-and-coming dress designer from Notting Hill. It was only months later that I found out her surname was McCartney. The Bransons were there, too, and we reminisced about Thailand. Most of all, I was back with my closest friends and I was back in my Europe. I was back, but I'm sure you're getting the vibe now, I get itchy feet. It doesn't take me long to pack a bag and hit the road because, like Kerouac said, the road is life.

CHAPTER 34

Travelling

"The world is a book and those who do not travel read only one page."
– St. Augustine

1997 was the year after I retired. For tax reasons, I was only allowed to stay in the States for fifty days and the UK for ninety, so I had to travel. I started with Cuba and, wadda'ya know, my old company BFCS were doing a shoot! Out of the 196 countries to start my travels, I picked the one where my company was working. The first I knew of it was when I walked into the lobby of the Hotel Nacional and saw all my old chums from the camera department lining up to check in. They looked at me nonplussed, thinking I was part of the production team. It was very nice for me, as for the first time ever I didn't need to look after the clients. I could just eat with the crew after they'd been out slaving, while I had been walking the streets and chatting up the locals.

BFCS had hired a Cuban lady to be the local fixer. She was paid $40 a day – a considerable sum for her, because her husband, the top reconstructive surgeon in Cuba, was only on $16 a month. I became very friendly with both of them and saw them even after the BFCS crew had gone. I loved having them over for dinner at the Hotel Nacional (the only place in Havana that served meat) and enjoyed watching how much they lathered in the fine dining. They were uncomplaining about his small salary. Their point of view was simple: everything was provided for them – the house, the car and food stamps. As the story tends to often go, it wasn't a perfect socialist system, and the food stamps were of no use when the shops ran out of provisions – often after only a few days each month. I didn't realise the world was such a small place, but then in Havana, I ran into more old chums from London and LA. It was getting ridiculous.

Ex-Formula 1 driver Rupert Keegan and his elder brother Jeremy had been invited out to Cuba for a sponsored go-kart race. In LA, they lived down the road from me in Benedict Canyon and they had cocaine-fuelled orgies every weekend. I didn't want to get back into that Henrietta stuff, so I always gave them a miss – but we saw a lot of each other, as they had a very popular bar that was always full of girls. Unbeknownst to most of us, it turned out later that one of the girls, Heidi Fleiss, was running a high-class call girl racket, with most of the other girls (aspiring actresses) I knew from the place. She became known around town and the media as the Hollywood Madam.

The Keegan boys were dangerous people to be hanging around with if you were trying to get off cocaine. One night, we went to a stag party in Hollywood. I got so stoned that night that the lesbian hookers who had been hired in for us to all goggle over were, to me, the most beautiful things in the world. I didn't think it could get better… but one of the girls left, and Rupert's Brazilian girlfriend Mimi took over the show. That was Hollywood. With Rupert and Jeremy in Havana was another friend we knew from LA, Kevin Cogan. He had been an Indy car driver until he had his accident at the '91 Indy 500. He only just survived. Jeremy Keegan, unfortunately, did not and was killed a couple of years ago in a car accident in Malindi, Kenya.

"Cigarini!" Next, I found myself on Harbour Island in the Bahamas, but I wasn't the only one who had found myself! I had arrived at Pip's, a hotel of private bungalows, by golf buggy, the only transportation on the island… "Cigarini! What are you doing here?" It was Ann Jones, wife of Mick Jones, the leader and owner of the band Foreigner, and previously of that great sixties band Spooky Tooth. I had known Ann since she was Ann Dexter-Jones, even before she had married Laurence Ronson – brother of the rich and famous English businessman Gerald Ronson. Ann and Laurence's son Mark Ronson is the successful English DJ, musician and producer of Amy Winehouse's albums. Ann was not staying at Pip's (the bungalows), she was staying down the road with Jane Wenner, founder of *Rolling Stone* magazine and ex-wife of the publisher Jann Wenner. Ann Jones is a big-time socialite, which I am allowed to say, as these are my terrible name-dropping memoirs.

There was an illustrious crowd staying at Pip's: Anna Wintour, editor of American *Vogue*, Elle McPherson and her husband, French financier Arpad Busson. I had met Elle previously when she was going out with my friend Tim Jeffries, so I hung out a lot with her at Pip's. We had dinner together most nights and that makes me a legend, right? Charles Finch was there, too. I knew him from LA and he was part of a rather cliquey British set that revolved around the offspring of famous British actors, like Charles's father, Peter Finch, John

Huston, and Irish hell raiser Richard Harris. Harris married the beautiful American model and actress Ann Turkel. I worked with her once before they got together, and she said a very flattering thing to me: "You, Cigarini, are the best looking man in London", but I would never mention that in my autobiography. Hey… she said it… not me. Charles Finch was at Pip's with Julian Metcalfe, the owner of Pret a Manger. Charles's girlfriend was a very nice Australian girl who was a jewellery designer in Notting Hill. She told me she had just sold a necklace for £1 million to my old flame Donatella Moores. Donatella had obviously come into some of that family money. After I heard the story of the necklace, I couldn't help but feel quite jaded. When I broke up with Donatella in '82, love was then dead to me, but now I found myself surrounded by couples in love and I was still alone – happy, though, just slightly jaded.

Rifat Ozbek was there, too – a well-known English fashion designer who I had previously met in London through mutual friends. He was with the gay actor Rupert Everett, which is now worth a short story as I had an amusing first encounter with Rupert. You know how you only ever get one chance to make a first impression? He had only just arrived and I hadn't yet met him. (Everybody at Pip's got to know each other; it was like an English country house party.) I was walking down the steps to the beach and looking down at the ground to watch my footing, when a large lizard ran across my path. Thinking I was alone, I said out loud to the lizard, in my best impersonation of Kenneth Williams, "Oooh, you're a big boy!" I looked up and there was Rupert Everett, taking in the sun with his shirt off. He heard me and he saw me; he did not, however, see the lizard. He obviously didn't fancy me, because he ignored me all week. Shite, that was embarrassing.

I also had two interesting encounters in the sea at Pip's. I was swimming one day and out of the water popped David Jacobs, like I had just entered the territory of a predatory sea mammal. David is a legend in British broadcasting and is the father of one of my best friends, Joanna. He was staying on another island and had come over to Pip's for a spot of lunch. He was with a nice man called David Profumo, who was the son of John Profumo – the man who had resigned from government over the Profumo Affair with Christine Keeler.

My other encounter in the sea was with an actual predatory sea mammal. I was swimming in the sea while the others were running along the beach and pointing to the water. The water was not deep, only waist high in fact, but there was glare from the sun on the water and I couldn't see what they were pointing at. I only saw the big shark after it had swum right past me, inches away. Apparently, it was only a nursing shark, which is harmless, but a shark's a shark as far as I'm concerned. I could now add great white to my baboon list of killer mammals that I've come face to face with. I know, it wasn't actually a great white, but when you're almost seventy, you'll learn how to make yourself sound better than you actually are.

The sand on Harbour Island is pink from the coral. Down the beach from Pip's was a hotel called the Pink Sands, owned by Chris Blackwell – former owner of Island Records. Chris came from the Crosse & Blackwell family and had been brought up in Jamaica. Through that connection, he had introduced reggae to the Western world. He had particular success with Bob Marley. Island Records was also the record label for the huge Irish band U2. Chris sold the company for something like £400 million and passed a great deal of his fortune around his mates. When I heard of that, I thought of Lord Beaumont and how half of this life of mine is owed to a man who I'll never meet or get to thank.

Chris had a beautiful black Jamaican girl called Esther Anderson living with him. Apart from being very pretty, Esther is a talented filmmaker, photographer and actress. I had known her for years. She too went out with Peter Biziou, my friend who had shared the pretty French girl. I bumped into Esther once on the King's Road when she was with Bob Marley, one of her best friends. She introduced us, but when I went to give her the normal kiss on the cheek, she recoiled. I saw her again, alone, a few days later, and commented on how she had been rather 'cool' the last time we met. She explained it all to me, in that unique and wonderful Jamaican accent of hers, "Bob don't like me kiss white boys anymore."

It was the summer of 1997, Paul McCartney was knighted and Madonna starred in the great *Evita*. I went to see a fabulous film called *Kama Sutra* in my local cinema in Salisbury, and that made me go east... again. This time to India, which had been a long time calling.

I first came to India for a short holiday in the eighties, and like anyone that goes, you promise yourself you'll return. Even if you stay for six months, you still only scratch the surface... India is diverse.

My first stop was Kerala, South India, to check in with my friend Davina Phillips at her hotel the Lagoona Davina. When you hit India, it hits you: the heat, the culture, the cocktail of exhaust fumes and essential oils. I'm sure she would agree that my time there was a bit disorganised, but like Davina pointed out, you're meant to be a mess when you go to India... so you can find yourself!

I worked my way through Kerala and her backwaters – the thatched huts, the tropical wild of the deep South India where trillions of snakes and creepers lived – and I entered into the tea-growing foothills of a game park. While I was there, elephants trashed the lodge's garden and I learnt how to eat classic thali from a banana leaf with my hands. I stayed in a fine hotel in the centre of the Kerala canals and would wake to the sounds of pelicans, parrots and the great hornbill. I shared the hotel with very large and affluent Indians visiting from Bombay (Mumbai), which was a first for me as many of the Indians are very thin but for a potbelly of rice and roti – especially the women breaking stones into gravel by the side of the road, or wet cloth onto large rocks. Strangely, many looked like models, with undernourished yet beautiful brown faces. I took a boat trip on the canals and sat in a low chair as my guide with shining deep brown skin steered the boat, in his white lungi, bandaged head and black sandals.

Throughout India, I mostly travelled on the cheap and that was the key there; you don't need to spend much money, especially if you want to soak up the real India. Hide in private resorts for honeymooners and you'll miss it all. My hotel was on a point in the harbour and I had a room with a wonderful view of the bay to watch the Keralan fisherman call to one another while tugging at long nets and being circled high by the great birds. The area of town across the bay, known as Old Cochin, plays host to the merchants selling spices, oils and dry fish. You definitely feel transported, and you know you have been when the sight of something Western like a brand or a chain immediately feels wrong, and as if it is something you don't wish to look at. The smells of Cochin must have changed little from the old days, when it was the centre of the spice trade to England. In India, they say that "anything is possible", like the synagogue I stumbled upon, dating from the sixteenth century when some pioneering Jewish families had travelled down the west coast of India from the Middle East to settle. With no consideration whatsoever, the Queen of England decided to visit the synagogue while I was there, and some MI5 security officers woke me up at 5am to grill me about why I was in Cochin. I told them I was here to find myself... but I had been looking everywhere and couldn't find a damn thing. They weren't amused.

I travelled through India all the way to Nepal. I took trains, planes and buses. They say you haven't travelled in India until you take a train, so I took an overnight one. There is something about travelling, about actually physically moving, that seems to clean the mind. I guess something happens when you cross borders. I was beginning to feel lighter, life was beginning to feel easier, and as I looked around at all the beaming smiles of all the locals, I felt happier – the happiest I had felt in a long time, in fact. My train took me through different states and each state played host to a different culture, a different language and different foods. I watched it all change out of my window: the miles of virgin farmland, the rice fields, the men on bicycles carrying goods in baskets. I woke up and I was in the Rajasthan. Women picked their way through fields in their saris, the emerald greens and sunshine yellows so vibrant in the landscape – so real, so India. It was morning and children on the train were giggling and playful. One wanted to know my name, but when I tried to tell him, he just laughed and ran away. I couldn't help but burst into a great long smile. Everyone here just seemed so happy.

I found myself in Pushkar, a Rajasthani commune for hippies, backpackers and tourists. As I was getting down at the station, I quickly learnt from an Indian man why there were so many tourists here in Pushkar.

"Now is camel fair," he told me. "Beautiful and best time for desert peoples. We loving camel." He helped me flag a cab and welcomed me to 'his' Pushkar. En route to my hotel, it became apparent why it was the "best time for desert peoples": Pushkar now played host to half a million horses and camels, all in town to celebrate and rejoice in the power of the desert sands. Rajasthani folk music was played on drums with hands, and again, apart from the odd backpacker, I had been transported. At the time, there was not a cloud in the sky, just blue, the deep red of the sun, the yellow of the sand dune. I was led into the desert where tribal warriors were dressed in white, tight shirts, billowing trousers, red and black turbans and fantastic moustaches, each of the man warriors being followed by many wives, all wearing their most colourful and vibrant of saris.

All the hotels in Pushkar were booked out, but one hotel had tents on its roof, and as I had tackled the night train, I was ready for more adventure. I hit the tents and fell asleep under the trillions of stars that covered the black desert sky like white powder clusters. All night, I could hear the deep beating rhythm of the Rajasthani drums being played out of the town and into the navy night sky of North India.

Jaipur: the pink city, population of three million, the desert lands of the

Rajasthan. Famous for its ceramics, marble statues, gems and jewellers, forts and monuments, temples and gardens, magic and a kite festival. It had big roads, hardly any cows and was home to some of the world's finest Indian restaurants. I went to Shekawati, where all the havelis (palaces) are painted with murals. It is located north of Jaipur, and visitors can stay in hill fort hotels, run by the descendants of the former rulers. They were tall, proud and magnificently built men, and you could see their ancestors' warrior blood still lived inside them. The prosperous early merchants on the spice route across the Rajasthani desert built the painted havelis of Shekawati. Their descendants now control most of the large conglomerates in India, and are based in Bombay and Delhi, but they retain the painted havelis as a family heritage. I suppose nothing changes and it happens all over the world: the rulers, the royal bloodlines, it all stays in the family.

The pink city: where street kids line railway tracks and old women sell onions on the side of the road. It is also home to the greatest opulence I have ever experienced, even in England. Some of the palaces, like the Wind Palace, are extraordinarily ornate. It is where the Maharaja kept his harem. The windows are designed so the concubines could see out, but not be seen by the people in the street below. I bought and shipped a container full of Jaipur pink sandstone, cut into 60cm slabs, to put around my pool back in Wiltshire. It looked wonderful, alongside the 10,000 four-inch cobalt blue tiles that I had bought in Thailand, for the inside of the pool. When I swam in it, I thought only of Asia.

In Jodhpur, all the buildings are painted blue. From the magnificent Mehrangarh Fort, there is a wonderful view over the whole blue town. Like each and every place in India, it is uniquely different from anywhere else. India was becoming intricately more diverse, the more I saw of it. All the languages and all of the idols and all of the sights. I was beginning to consider it one of God's truly great countries – jungles, deserts, lakes, mountains, cities, beaches – and it was changing, being mowed down by industry and software companies. On the train, I thought about the miles of virgin farmland and I became sad. It was to be replaced with motorways and business, and I didn't want it to. I wanted it to stay like it was, like real India.

There was no opulence like in Udaipur. I booked a room in the Lake Palace, but when I got there they had no record of my reservation, so they put me in the Maharaja's Suite. All the walls were painted, mainly with portraits of old warriors and the ancestors. Whilst sitting in the bath, I could practically put my fingers in the water of the lake. It was not bad at all.

Jaisalmer was what they call The Golden City, and my favourite part of Rajasthan. It was built out of dry stone with no cement on a ridge of yellow sandstone that rises out of the desert, like a lost city that archaeologists have found after centuries of digging. Its havelis have great stone windows that are carved like lace, and there is the most wonderful Jain temple, lined with fine works of stone carvings. The Jain nuns are a particular sect of spiritual devotees. They wander the streets of India carefully avoiding any acts of violence from town to town, arriving in villages barefoot without even a rupee and still treading lightly, so as not to kill any plant or bug life. Some people consider that life quite harsh, like the tearing out of their own hair, but they see it as the route to the almighty and a beautiful thing – not a painful thing. The temple is near the Pakistan border and the military airport had only been opened up to commercial flights the week I went there. Prior to air travel, it was a three-day journey by bus and I may not have bothered. I would have missed something special, like learning about the Jain people.

I went with a photographer friend, Robyn Beeche, and a Hindu lady friend of hers on a pilgrimage to the source of the sacred Yamuna River, high in the Himalayas. There was nothing quite like the Himalayas – totally and utterly silent. So still and quiet, in fact, that even whispers can be heard around town. It was a powerful place, with bent-over Buddhist monks hobbling up hills and through little lanes. I knew I had been transported once again, to a special place: the Himalayas, the crown shakra. The trip required driving for days up a precipitous mountain road, then climbing on foot for three days up a stony path on a cliff edge. Many other pilgrims were making the journey, from all colours and all religions, just to find the source of the river – the lifeblood of mother earth.

For Hindus, going to the source of India's holy rivers – the Ganges and the Yamuna – is a sacred journey. One day, when darkness fell, we hadn't reached the lodge where we were going to sleep that night and I had to climb onto a mule. I had never ridden an animal before and I didn't know that you should put your weight on the stirrups. It was terrifying. The damn thing was clambering over the rocky path, getting too close and almost throwing me down it. I was swaying and hanging on for dear life in the dark, with a drop of 2000 feet and nothing but the sweating and the panting of the mule to keep me company. I remember calling to my companions, "I'm not even a Hindu!" My goodness, was I relieved when I got there. The next day, we arrived at the river's source, and all the men, including yours truly, stepped fully clothed into the hot thermal pool.

Before the pilgrimage, I spent a month on the ashram where Robyn Beeche lives in Vrindavan, near Mathura. Vrindavan is the centre for Krishna followers and this doesn't just mean members of the Hare Krishna movement – who are usually Westerners – but Indian Krishna devotees. I was there for Diwali, the festival of lights, where lamps and candles are lit to signify good over evil. In Vrindavan, the town became full of sadhus during Diwali – the Indian monks who could be seen walking around playing their musical instruments. The real sadhus have chosen to live on the edges of society, have renounced all material possessions and are often painted in white powder, wear long beards and have dreadlocked hair. They are an extraordinary sight, like everything in India.

It is, of course, difficult to talk of India without mentioning cows. They are as common in India as dogs or cats in England, and they are members of society – sacred and holy. But I wasn't convinced they were being looked after as well as they perhaps could. On one occasion, I happened to watch one eat its way through an entire plastic bag in a skip full to the brim with garbage and shit. Considering how a cow has four stomachs, that really did prove how biodegradable plastic bags aren't! In Vrindavan, the temple floors were patterned with elaborate displays, all made of cow dung, and I had heard that in certain parts of the country, they even drink their 'holy' urine. Cows in India are everywhere and all of the time, like in the middle of motorways or at your hotel reception – quite different to England and the occasional squirrel or robin. I thought the cows were quite scary at first, but then I saw the monkeys – the monkeys of Varanasi.

Varanasi is the oldest city in India, and the spiritual capital. Mark Twain once wrote that Varanasi was "older than history, older than tradition, older even than legend, and looked twice as old as all of them put together", and he said that over a hundred years ago. Varanasi crawls with tourists who have travelled the world to come and watch. I was one of them and this place was certainly old India, and there was a real atmosphere of death.

In Hinduism, death at Varanasi brings salvation. As it is located on the riverbank or 'ghat', many people go there to die or make provisions – sometimes years prior – to be in Varanasi for the moment of death. Some come too early, and they will remain there until they die. When they die, they are cremated on the banks of the holy river (or Ganga) and along the river there are funeral pyres. Babies, though, are not cremated; they are tied to stones and dropped in the river. This is because they need not be burnt, as they are 'already holy', like the sadhus, who are already dead, and have no connection with this world (they're not even listed as citizens when alive). The unburnt corpses often release themselves from the binding and bob to the surface. When I took a boat trip, I saw a bloated infant corpse floating down the river. There are also many dead cows in the Ganges; they too are sacred, having saved Indian society.

It was all becoming quite claustrophobic and I walked downhill towards the river through the mist to find some peace, but there was no escaping it. I passed some French brothers down a side road eating street food, practising their Hindi and their head bobs, when suddenly – a great crash – a woman had collapsed down some steps and into some baskets and a crowd of men quickly came to her rescue. As I mentioned, people have made provisions to arrive here for their deaths and it's the ultimate wish of a Hindu to die and be cremated on a riverbank. She must have just died. The holier the river, the better for the soul, but put more accurately, it's not dying, it's 'leaving bodies'. Hindus believe in reincarnation because stuff or matter has never been made or destroyed, just transferred from one thing to another. Most Hindus will be burnt where they part with their physical selves and are released from the never-ending cycle of transformation, samsara, and suffering through reincarnation. A rumbling had begun and suddenly the people in the street began to part. I looked uphill and saw a line of men carrying a body that lay dead on bamboo. They carried it toward the river while chanting ancient mantras. I got swept into the traffic and ended up back at the burning ghat, Manikarnika Ghat, which is the main attraction (so to speak) where the dead come to be weighed – so the men in charge know exactly how much wood to spare for the burning. The bodies are then burnt and sunk.

I left Manikarnika and walked up river. Kids played their beloved cricket on the bank and one boy tried to force a pack of dogs to eat a cow. A group of tourists played kites with some children and a sadhu sat on a step around a group of ten smoking charas – a common practice among the holy or babas to destroy all sexual desire and help contemplate 'the mysteries of the cosmic'. He had a tin pot for spare rupees and I gave him some, but not enough. It was never enough in this country; too many people are incredibly poor. India is highly overcrowded. It has over a billion people and unless you leave the cities, you will rarely see a tree. They have all been cut down for firewood, so in much of India, the people dry and then burn cow dung for heating and cooking.

In India, the traditions and customs run to infinity. Hindu religion is unimaginably diverse, with more lineages and philosophical schools than any other, and over 320 million gods. I was still walking along the riverbank and I decided that I wanted to come back again one day. The sun's rays leaked through clouds and I could see a mother standing with her daughter beside the river with lips chanting light mantras. An elderly man was in the lotus position praying before wetting his head in the holy water, and there were Buddhists and Muslims too. A group of tourists clambered into a boat to record it all on camera and in journals. They will return to the West reporting to their loved ones what they have seen or what they think they have seen. Astonished, astounded, we are fascinated.

Beautiful India, I have seen merely the surface of you.

*

I went to Nepal and stayed at my friend Mary Heale's Lakshmi Lodge, on the trail toward Machapuchare mountain – a fish tail, as it is known, angling its spike into the ocean blue sky of upper Nepal. It is in the Annapurna Himalaya of north central Nepal, revered by the local population as sacred to the god Shiva, and hence is off limits to climbing. Her village Birethanti is a Gurkha village, where there were many distinguished-looking elderly military gentlemen with very smart houses. There are no roads to the village. You have to walk for about half an hour from the nearest road, crossing a small bridge – normal for the guides who begin hiking at age four, carrying the luggage as porters for the tourists on one dollar a day. I went for a hike in the magical foothills, with a guide from Mary's lodge, where we stumbled across a sloth bear that was sleeping on the path in front. It woke up with a start and a loud roar, but fortunately ran off and hid behind a tree. They can be dangerous, but this one seemed more frightened of us – or maybe it was me? The air here was clean, the sounds of the birds as sharp as a knife blade, and the food – dal bhat – was fresh and ripe mountain food; the same Sherpa diet my guide's ancestors ate.

I stayed a few days at Tiger Tops. I didn't see any tigers, but lots of elephants and rhinoceroses. It was where my guide told me: "Two things tourist people never getting bored of, Mr Johnny… elephants and rhinoceroses." I certainly agreed with that.

Kathmandu is a great city, and as the main city in Nepal, it is a cross-section of cultures and nationalities – including the Tibetan people, who are so very peaceful and light when they speak, Indians, Chinese and visitors from Israel, Germany, Argentina and England. It is a place people come to from all the world's far corners. Something has called to them all, and here, it was something you could feel – in the Himalayas. There truly is nothing quite like this powerful mountain world, one I saw on a dawn flight over Mount Everest.

I love India, but after three months I was nearly screaming to leave. With the vast population and intense cultural change, it is quite unadoptable and unadaptable! If another young boy had asked me where I was from, and what my name was, and if I would like to visit his brother's store, I swear I would have throttled the bugger. My hat goes off to any Westerner who has managed to settle there, or for that matter worked out how to use the squat loo and hose. On that note, "Happiness is having a hard shit", I remember one traveller telling me when she had just finished her second stint of Delhi belly. That pretty much summed it up for me in the end – it was exhausting, it was exhilarating. It was time to get out!

*

Laos was the perfect antidote: peaceful and calm and untouched for centuries, apart from a hideous amount of illegal American bombing during the Vietnam War. Flying across the country is a depressing experience. Seen from the sky, the ground is pockmarked with craters, where the Americans tried to destroy the Viet Cong supply routes. It is estimated that Laos received one B52 bombload every eight minutes, twenty-four hours a day, for ten years between 1964 and 1973. I read it was the equivalent of thirty tons of bombs for every man, woman and child in Laos. US bombers dropped more ordnance on Laos during this period than was dropped in the entire Second World War. Appalling behaviour. It is now very peaceful, and the people are so gentle and friendly that my heart went out to them for the suffering and pain the older people must have endured during the bombing. I went to the capital, Vientiane, a nice town with French influences in its architecture, and also in the café life. My favourite town was Luang Praband, a sleepy little town on the banks of the Mekong River.

Vietnam was beautiful and it rained the whole time I was there. Experiencing Asia in the rain is something everyone should do, because when it rains, it pours, and when it pours, it can do it for days, and another world emerges. It is a very different world to ours. Not better or worse, just different – the sounds, the smells, the thoughts people have. I got depressed in Hue, which was the scene of the Tet Offensive of '68. Hue was actually in South Vietnam, just south of the border with the North, but it had been infiltrated by the Viet Cong and was therefore bombed by the Americans in the Battle of Hue. The whole city was practically razed to the ground. I went to visit the Forbidden City and it had truly been lost; there was only a perimeter wall remaining. After being in India with all the wonderful temples, it was very sad to see this. Very sad indeed.

I went to Cambodia and visited the fabulous Angkor Wat temples, seat of the Khmer Empire, dating from the ninth to the fifteenth centuries. I was practically the only tourist there due to the civil war and Cambodia was still on the Foreign Office list of places not to visit, but I ignored their advice. The Angkor Wat temple complex is the largest religious monument in the world and dates from the twelfth century, and it takes at least three or four days to look around it. I particularly liked the Prasat Bayon, about thirty tall towers with large faces carved on the four sides of each one. The main Angkor Wat temple itself is staggering. The apsaras and other bas-relief carvings are still in mint condition. My favourite temple was Ta Prohm, which has been left almost untouched since the temples were discovered in the middle of the nineteenth century. Thick roots of fig, banyan and kapok trees grow in and around the temples. It was like a real version of an Indiana Jones movie. That day, my guide and I were the only people there. I felt like the French explorer who discovered them. I needed a guide because these temples were dangerous. If one strayed away from the paths, there was danger of landmines.

I went to Thailand and stayed with Jamie Morgan in Bangkok. He was one of Siobhan Barron's Malibu gang. At that time, he was living full time in Bangkok in a cheaper hotel. So I stayed there with him, but it was something of a junkie hangout. One night, a young American lad, presumably tripping on acid, rushed down the third-floor corridor, shedding his clothes in a trail on the floor, and tried to dive into the pool from the upstairs window. The pool was a long way away and he went straight down. He hit a porch, which broke his fall, and that saved his life. It's a story we've all heard too many times. I think acid helps you realise how free you are, but because of the amount of suppressed freedom there is in the modern mind, people who trip can experience a massive unbalancing, so they often think they are so free they can fly.

Jamie and I also went to Phuket for Christmas. Jamie is a fashion photographer, and friends with supermodel Helena Christensen, who was staying in the Amanpuri with her boyfriend Michael Hutchence – the lead singer from the great Australian band INXS. Jamie and I were staying in the Pansea next door, but we spent every day at Michael's villa at the Amanpuri. We all stayed together the whole week, and went into Patong town to see the sleazy bars and lady-boy pick-up joints. Michael was a really nice guy and Helena was just gorgeous. She was always wearing open-fronted Versace silk dresses, which left nothing to the imagination. Naomi Campbell was also there and hanging out with us. She was staying in the Amanpuri with her boyfriend Nellee Hooper, a great record producer of Massive Attack, Björk and Madonna. It was all a bit different to slumming it through India and Laos, but it was still part of my travels. Celebrities are still people, after all.

When we got back to LA, I arranged for Michael Hutchence to have his birthday dinner in the Foundation Room at the House of Blues. There were other members of INXS present. Johnny Depp was also there with his then girlfriend Kate Moss. I chatted to them. They both seemed nice, unassuming people.

Michael died a few years later, of strangulation. By then, he was going out with Paula Yates – former wife of Bob Geldof and mother of his children. Paula had one child from Michael and she sadly became a junkie after his death, and would later die from an overdose. The coroner ruled Michael's death was suicide, but I believe he was stoned, and he was fooling around with autoeroticism. I think a lot of people knew that was the case, but for some reason, it was more convenient for the media to demonise Michael this way and just say he was mentally unstable. In reality, he was a great man, a creative soul and a gent. Ironic, then, how he described the English press: "So nosy… and the English seem to love that eavesdropping."

I knew Paula from the Roebuck pub on the King's Road from '76, when she was a young girl. I met her again when the film *Four Weddings and a Funeral* had a launch party in the House of Blues Foundation Room. The public relations king Matthew Freud was with Paula. His connection to the House of Blues was Isaac Tigrett. I believe the Hard Rock Café had been Matthew's first ever client when he set up his PR consultancy. I had known Matthew for years, because he'd sometimes visit Stocks House late at night when he was a young man. There had just recently been a big spread on Paula and Michael Hutchence in the *News of the World* because they had just started dating, and had been caught by the paparazzi at a country motel. There were photographs of Michael fighting with the paparazzi. I was talking to Matthew and Paula, and I said to them, "You know, you could never buy the first five pages of the *News of the World*, that's fantastic publicity". Paula pointed to Matthew and said, "Yes, and Matthew wrote all of it." He is a brilliant PR man, and the whole incident was a publicity stunt. He is now married to Rupert Murdoch's daughter. And that was Matthew Freud.

*

These days, I still have big travel plans. There are still so many countries I'd like to visit, cultures I would like to learn about, quiet towns I want to walk through. Some people say the grass is always greener, but that thing inside me that has kept me quite restless has kept me adventurous – I thank God that I have that. It's helped me travel and yearn for even more adventures. John Steinbeck said that: "A journey is like marriage. The certain way to be wrong is to think you control it." I guess I feel that way about my life sometimes: the great journey of life. I think it was the thing he was talking about. Sometimes I got lost on the road, sometimes I was lost in my head, but I kept going, somewhere, and I always ended up in the right place eventually. I guess that's the key – to just keep going. "For my part, I travel not to go anywhere, but to go. I travel for travel's sake. The great affair is to move."

CHAPTER 35

Terrible Name-Dropping

Twiggy

In LA, I always see my old friend Mary Lindes. I first met her when I was doing a shoot with Twiggy, her closest friend. Mary accompanied Twigs to the shoot. A short while later, I went to a party at her flat in Chelsea, where she lived with her husband Hal Lindes. Hal was a guitarist in Dire Straits. Mary had been previously married to superstar Peter Frampton. I know Twiggy through her marriage to my friend, actor Leigh Lawson. Both of them are super duper and they'd often visit me at Ridge Farmhouse. I went to Twiggy's fiftieth in the private room at San Lorenzo in Beauchamp Place, Knightsbridge. I remember talking with Jeremy Irons and Bob Hoskins. Actually, Bob chatted to me. I was sitting next to his wife and he seemed to think I wasn't talking to her enough, so he asked me to change places with a lady. Same old complaint!

I always have dinner in LA with my lovely friend Fiona, wife of composer and Police drummer Stewart Copeland, and with Liz Dalling and her ex-husband, now boyfriend again, Michael Dalling. Lizzie works too hard, with her very successful management agency Special Artists, handling stars like Pierce Brosnan. She took me to lunch with Pierce at his Malibu house. It's funny living in Malibu; you run into many famous Hollywood stars, just out doing their shopping. I used to see Pierce at the supermarket. Another time, I was in Blockbuster and they had a big display of *Saving Private Ryan* videos, which had just been released, and Tom Hanks was wandering through the store. I used to go to the Malibu Gym – where my trainer was Angie Best, former wife of footballer George Best – and Mike Myers was often in there. He would like to practise his English accent on me, as he was playing an Englishman in an upcoming film. The film turned out to be *Austin Powers: International Man of Mystery*. I often saw famous stars in restaurants in Malibu: Clint, Robert Redford, Warren Beatty and Demi Moore. Doctors' waiting rooms in Beverly

Hills are also good places for star spotting. I've sat waiting with Lauren Bacall, Julie Andrews and Little Richard. I suppose it's a universal law, 'cause even they have sod all to say in those bloody places.

Freud

I had a previous connection with the Freud family. I produced many of the Pedigree Chum commercials starring Matthew's father Clement Freud, and a bloodhound called Henry. There was not just one Henry; the part was played by a number of different identical dogs, due to the difficulty of getting one dog to sit still all day in front of the camera. I remember going to the apartment of the dog trainers in North London. They lived in a small basement apartment with six huge bloodhounds, and the stench of dogs in the flat was something horrendous. Clement Freud was an anti-smoking pioneer. Years before the reports of passive smoking were released, and before the subsequent ban on smoking in offices, bars and restaurants, he insisted no one smoked in the film studios – an inconsiderate demand at the time as far as the crews were concerned. I also met Clement's daughter Emma Freud, now married to Richard Curtis. I met them at Paul Weiland's Italianate country house in Bradford-on-Avon. Paul and his wife Caroline have star-studded house parties in the country every weekend, and Rowan Atkinson regularly flies in in his own helicopter.

Senna

Ayrton Senna was a Brazilian racing car diver. He was a hero to millions and a three-times Formula 1 world champion. He was different from everyone else, and everyone knew it. I guess in life, sometimes people are just good, and everyone knew it about Senna. But only the good die young; I just never would have dreamt he was going to be one of them. Senna fought relentlessly to improve the safety of Formula 1, and during his fight he had to watch the tragic death of fellow driver Roland Ratzenberger – it happened just one day before his own.

Allan van Rijn directed many commercials for Marlboro cigarettes, featuring the Marlboro McLaren Formula 1 team and its driver Ayrton Senna. Over a period of years, Allan filmed him at Silverstone in England, at Jerez in Spain, and in the studio. One shoot took place live at the San Marino Grand Prix at Imola, and although I wasn't producing the spot, I went as a fan of motor racing. The complexity of the technology alone is staggering, and once you get your head around the skill necessary to drive one of these cars, then you are beginning to understand. Formula 1 racing is to me the most thrilling but terrifying experience, and it's because I know and understand what it is I am watching. The more you know about it, the more you understand its dangers; the more you understand its dangers, the more thrilling it becomes. Every square inch of design is at the cutting edge of our human ingenuity; the machinery leads the way in mechanics; the science behind rubber on concrete; the different aerodynamic forces, 'wings', ground effect, pressure, double-wishbone suspension, disc brakes, springs and dampers; the oiling, the revs and the speed; the fact that the whole car, including engine, fluids and driver, only weighs 640kg, the minimum weight set by the regulations – then you begin to understand. But then you get into the race and the circuits, the politics, the money and the big big big big business, and the event becomes more than just a spectacle. It becomes something to marvel at. Anyone who steps into the cockpit has my attention, but anyone who can drive the things – they have my respect.

Our access was incredible; I had passes to all the pits and track areas. You should have seen me; I was out-of-control excited. I was able to sit in the press stand with the photographers to watch the start, but I couldn't sit still – the whole thing was electric. During the race, I could wander around on the grass verge bordering the track, with the cars screaming past me feet away. I had access to all the pits, even Ferrari, and I met the man: the one and only Ayrton Senna. We bought him a remote controlled helicopter. It was his hobby, and he loved our gift. I was with Allan when we learnt of his death, and he was in tears. Ayrton, like for many people, was Allan's hero. I wanted to cry, but I couldn't. I'm not sure why. The world was shocked when he left us. I guess it hit home how quickly it can get taken from you. It was just as he once said of it: "because in a split second, it's gone."

Muhammad Ali

BFCS had a commercial to shoot with Ali, for Birds Eye hamburgers of all things. Michael Seresin was the director and I produced. Ali's voice was beginning to fail, so we had to get him into our office in North Wharf Road to see if the commercial was feasible, as he needed to talk to the camera. We decided it was doable and we celebrated with a nice photo of Ali with Michael Seresin and yours truly outside our studio. He later signed it, "To John, best wishes from Muhammad Ali", and it is a great and proud possession of mine. We shipped an English film crew to Los Angeles, where we were to shoot in his house. Ali lived in a gated community of mansions in Hancock Park. It had been a very upmarket area in the 1930s Hollywood heyday, but was now bordering rough areas of Hollywood. Still, I could understand why anyone would want to live there: the houses are wonderful. We filmed in the house for three days and Ali's family were all there; he had a beautiful wife called Veronica and two young daughters, Hana and Laila. Laila herself would later become a female boxing champion. As the producer, I spent a lot of time with Ali and I enjoyed every minute. One thing that I'll never forget: he told me he couldn't forgive himself for accidentally taking a double dose of his thyroid medication on the day of his last big fight with Larry Holmes. It had made him tired and short of breath, and he lost the fight.

Ali was fun to be with during the shoot. In between filming set-ups, he would do magic tricks and boy did he love an audience – more, I think, than any of the actors I had worked with.

A couple of years later, he was diagnosed with Parkinson's disease.

Trevor Eve

When they returned my driving licence, I got another Mercedes; this time a 280 SE 3.5 Cabriolet – a little gift to myself, because I really needed a car! It was a very desirable and rare convertible. For the car geeks reading, there were only thirty-six imported into the UK in right-hand drive form.

It was 1983 and I was living in Notting Hill. One day, I pulled up outside the Prince of Wales pub on the Portland Road to find a matching car outside. "Buggery buggery shit," I recall was my first reaction, considering its rarity, but then I thought it was meant to be. As I said about my introduction to Nigel Carroll, people with similar cars often talk to one another. I went into the pub, stood in the middle of it and cried out to anyone who would listen: "Whose is that Mercedes 280 SE 3.5 Cabriolet?" Someone replied, "It's my bloody

Mercedes 280 SE 3.5 Cabriolet", and that was my first meeting, and the start of a great friendship, with English actors Trevor Eve and his wife Sharon Maughan, who lived just over the road from the pub.

People always thought Trevor and I looked similar… and we have been mistaken for brothers on more than one occasion. I saw plenty of the Eves for the next few years, and again in LA in the nineties, when they would travel back and forth from London. Trevor even moved in with me at my Notting Hill penthouse on one occasion, when he had been a naughty boy and Sharon kicked him out of their family home. They had had their first child, Alice, in '82 before I met them. Alice is now a Hollywood star and has just finished the *Star Trek* movie. Jack followed and he's now an actor, producer and director, and I am very proud to be godfather to their third child, Gorgeous George. He has just left Bedales School and is going to be a rock star – there is no question about it. He already has fan clubs at girls' schools as far away as Cheltenham Ladies' College. I asked him recently if there was room in his band as a piano accordionist, but apparently there was not.

Michael Gambon

For a couple of years, I had a very illustrious neighbour at Ridge – the great British actor Michael Gambon. He is now infamous for having Gambon Corner named after him on the worldwide television phenomenon *Top Gear*. He was renting a cottage in the hamlet and he came with his girlfriend over to my house for lunch by the pool, and said I had created paradise. He is a very funny man and told me he had once tried to be gay, but had to give it up because it made his eyes water.

CHAPTER 36

Curing Tourette's

In 1998, I was home in Wiltshire for the summer. I read an article in the *Sunday Times* colour magazine about a family who all had compulsive tics. They had all started twitching at around seven years old. I remember thinking, *That's me!* It turned out they had something called Tourette's syndrome. I had heard of that, but I thought it only applied to people who shouted profanities in the street.

A short while later, I was back in LA. I had a heart scan and the doctor who was checking my computer imaging had a very bad head tic. I told him I had the same thing and mentioned the magazine article. I asked him if he knew it was called Tourette's syndrome. He said he knew, and that the world's leading authority was nearby. I went to see this so-called 'leading authority', Dr Comings, at the City of Hope Hospital at Duarte, a few miles away. First he tried me on various medicines and patches, none of which had any effect beyond making me feel drowsy. Eventually he tried me on a tiny pill called Orap, and this miracle drug has changed my life. I immediately stopped twitching – although even just writing or talking about it, I feel I could get back into it. Thanks to Orap, I don't. I am like an evangelist for the thing these days. If I see someone twitching in the street, I stop him and tell him about it.

I have emailed two Tourette's associations to tell them about Orap, but didn't get a reply from either of them. Weird.

PART 3

CHAPTER 37

Italy, the Return

Faced with the certainty of internment, my family packed up and moved to Rome. It was there where my mother took supplies from the Allies, the Americans, and because of it, I survived. Maybe I wouldn't have been born if Giusseppe had lived. Life: what a strange and incredible thing, and I don't try to make sense of it. There are still things I don't know, even after writing this book, like why my mother really did leave my father, but I think it's okay not to have all the answers. I just try to enjoy it and I encourage you to do the same, 'cause it'll go pretty fast. I returned to Italy to live, and live I do.

★

My life is completely different now, and I like it that way. I live a quiet life in beautiful, peaceful places. I don't like cities and traffic anymore, so consequently I don't often see all of the trendy people and celebrities in London and LA; instead my friends are normal people, like me. I'm in a different phase of my life, and I think when you are retired and nearing your seventies, good friends and good wine are the keys to a happy time.

I spend the summers in Tuscany, on the Umbrian border, in an 1840s farmhouse. I bought it for £20,000 for my sister Luisa in 1984, and I never thought for one second that I would one day live in it myself – but something happened and, like I've mentioned, a journey is like a marriage. The certain way to be wrong is to think you control it. The house was a favour that came back around to repay me. Luisa had been destitute. She was living in a squat in the Umbrian hills, with someone I presumed was a junkie. He wore shorts, which showed open sores all over his legs. I don't think Luisa took heroin; wine and pot were her things. "Why are you living with this guy?" I asked. The story is often the same: "I had nowhere else to go." That upset me tremendously and I had been fortunate with money, so I told her I'd buy her a house if she didn't live with him. She agreed and I sent her a million lire every month, for twenty years. It sounds impressive, but that was only £500 a month – almost enough for her to live off, excluding her drinks bill. I would visit Luisa regularly because I was always filming in Italy and she would take me to both bars in the village of San Leo Bastia, where she always had a huge tab of another £500 in each. I would, of course, pay them off. Luisa was very socialistic in ideology; she thought rich people's money belonged to the poor, or more precisely, that my money was hers. Her favourite expression was, "Don't worry, my brother is rich. He will pay." And that's two of the reasons they now like me in the village. They know that I looked after my family and that's important to the Italians, but they also know that I honoured her debts, and they respect me for that too.

Things were getting worse and Luisa was living with a woman, Stefania, who was supposed to be looking after her, driving her around, doing her errands. Instead, Stefania would go to the bank with Luisa each month and snatch the money from my sister's hand. I had to get Luisa away from her, so I bought her a small house in the village, hoping she could live alone. Unfortunately, it was over the road from one of the bars, and she would get hopelessly drunk and lie comatose in the middle of the road. She was soiling herself and leaving pans on the stove in the house. I was in LA so I suggested putting her in a home, but things like that don't really exist in Italy. In Italy, old people live with the family. Friends of mine tried to help and put her in a home of sorts, but it was more like a loony bin and she was molested. When that news came in, it seemed to open old wounds and I reached out to my other sisters for help, because it was so difficult for me to do anything from LA. Christina went to live with her in the little house in the village. The thief Stefania refused to leave, and I had to sue her to get her out. By this time, Luisa kept having strokes and could no longer talk. Eventually she got too bad and came to Cornwall, where she was looked after by Christina and the social services. She died about five years ago. By then I was retired, so moved to Italy.

★

My house is actually in Tuscany, but more often than not I call it Umbria. I am the second house in Tuscany, one mile from the border with Umbria. I rarely go into Tuscany. If I do, it's for the thirty-minute winding drive over the mountain to Cortona, which is a lovely town. I think of Luisa when I'm there, too much sometimes, but I guess that's normal. Could I have done more to help? It's hard to know, I suppose. Questions like this come to you in old age. It's normal they tell me, and not to dwell on it too much. It – the past – is something I think a lot of these days, here in Italy.

Instead, I head for the local village, San Leo Bastia, which is five minutes away in Umbria. As Cecilia from my local bar says, I sleep in Tuscany, but I live in Umbria. I spend more time in Citta di Castello and Umbertide, two mediaeval towns in Umbria, than I do in Tuscany. Since the great American success of Frances Mayes' book, and subsequent film *Under the Tuscan Sun*, Cortona has become crowded with American tourists. I don't blame them coming here; it is a beautiful city, but it's now a bit too touristy for my tastes – now that I'm officially retired.

One of the reasons I like Italy so much is the circle of friends that I have found. The life I have is like a commercial for an Italian pasta sauce. We have lunches on long tables of eight to fifteen, sometimes twenty-five in the summer. We meet three times a week, eat two courses and all the wine you can drink for €20 a head – €10 if it's pizza.

I am not embarrassed that most of my friends here are expats, even if it is a bit of a cliché, but we live a different lifestyle to the locals; we're Brits, after all. The Italians work mostly in agriculture or in logging, and their lives don't fit with ours. I suppose it's always the case when communities try to integrate in foreign countries; they usually always try really hard, but regroup in the end. Umbria is covered in trees and is known as the Green Heart of Italy, not only for its colour but its oxygen too. The villagers either cut down the trees or transport them to the lumber merchants, or chop them into firewood. They live in big family houses with four generations living under the same roof. The old people often make it past 100, so who says wine and pasta aren't good for the heart? Their lifestyle is quite commendable to me – it is slower, more focused on the important things. I like that, and in the modern hectic world of mobile phones, computers, and high stress, we can learn from them.

I hesitate to say one friend is my best, as I love them all. But I am closest to Jim and Jill Powrie. They live in Umbria, but have their holiday home in Croatia, in an unspoilt fishing village called Supetar on the island of Brac, just off Split. I spent a month there last summer. It, too, is like going back in time, like San Tropez must have been before Brigitte Bardot discovered it: a harbour full of traditional fishing boats, and no luxury motor yachts.

David Monico and Neil Brown are in a civil partnership, having been together for forty years. David was an actor and Neil worked at the BBC. We have lunch on Saturdays, at Fez in Citta di Castello. Sometimes it's just the three of us, or with Ian McDonald, but in the summer it tends to get a bit more crowded. I'm not homophobic, but I do feel a bit outnumbered sometimes! Robbie Duff-Scott is a wonderful painter and gets up at 5am to a rising sun to begin his art. It certainly is a quieter life, but occasionally there is a drama. Robbie's mother Barbara also lives in Umbertide, with her partner Lenny. Lenny recently got arrested at his home and was taken to the post office, which had been evacuated of its entire staff and cordoned off by police holding submachine guns. Inside, there were forensic experts in white protective suits, tentatively poking at a package addressed to Lenny. It had burst open and a suspicious yellow powder was all over the post office. Lenny confirmed the package was his, and that it contained Bird's custard powder!

Dick Pountain and Marion Hills summer here. Dick worked at *Oz* magazine, with Felix Dennis, Richard Neville and Jim Anderson – the editors. They were put on trial for obscenity after publishing an edition created by schoolchildren. They were found guilty and given long jail sentences, but were acquitted on appeal. There was popular support for them, led by John Lennon and Yoko Ono.

Tim and Anna Maltby pick olives and bottle the oil, and host wonderful lunches; Rob and Amanda House have a fabulous home and also love entertaining; and Ken Stott and his artist girlfriend Nina Gehl live here too, when he isn't filming *The Hobbit* or appearing on the West End stage. Ian McDonald is a summer visitor. He is known as the Chairman, by virtue of being the Chairman of the Umbria Lunch Club. He had his moment in the spotlight during the Falklands War, when he was the Ministry of Defence spokesman on television.

One swell couple are John Fraser and his long-time companion Rod Pienaar. John was a fine actor and had many starring roles, playing the king alongside Charlton Heston in *El Cid*, Lord Alfred Douglas in *The Trials of Oscar Wilde*, and Colin in Roman Polanski's *Repulsion*. However, his big passion was for Shakespeare, and John ran a touring company, which toured Africa amongst many other places. He is still a fine looking man in his eighties and a good author, too.

David and Jenny Nichols are overrun with seven dogs and cats, and sometimes a goose. Jenny is another great cook and is hostess for residential cooking holidays. David is a film producer; his last two big productions have been *The Tourist* and *To Rome with Love*. I also have to thank him for telling me I should write my autobiography. A month later and it's almost finished, David!

The only people I know in Cortona deserve a mention, not only because they are nice people, but mostly to keep in the spirit of the subtitle of the book. My friend Lisabette Brinkman is the daughter of Jeanne Crain, the former Hollywood star. I met Lisabette through a Baja connection. During the peak of her fame in the late 1940s, when only Betty Grable bettered Jeanne Crain's fan mail, she was nicknamed 'Hollywood's Number One Party Girl', and would attend over 200 parties a year. She was nominated for an Academy Award for Best Actress for her starring role in the 1949 film *Pinky*.

There are many other friends, as expat crowds all seem to know each other, and there is no one I don't like. We all have a great time and I am grateful to them all for enriching my wonderful Italian world. In addition to all my expat mates here, there are all the lovely Italians from my local village, San Leo Bastia. They are the best people in the world: friendly, kind and generous, in spite of the fact I find it difficult to understand what they are saying. Many of them, like my builder Luciano Muffi and his wife Camilla, invite me to dinner or lunch, where huge tables are laid with sometimes three or four generations of family, and tons of food. One amazing thing about the villagers is how much they loved my sister Luisa, despite what happened.

The village Pro Loco will organise my seventieth birthday party next year and it will be a dinner for 300 expat friends and all the locals. I just wish it could be more. There are so many who have helped me in this little life and I want them all to be with me, but sadly I know too many of them will not be able to come and will be sadly missed, like Alba…

The Pierini are a typical San Leo family. Nine siblings all in their sixties and seventies: five women and four men. One of them, Giobbe, is the village plumber with his son Diego, Rosato cuts down the trees, his handsome son Francesco cuts them into logs, and another brother Menco drives the lumber truck. I am particularly friendly with Menco and his three sons Emmanuelle, Enrico and the younger one Lorenzo, who is at Rome University. The family had a terrible tragedy. Their mother Alba suddenly collapsed and died; she was in her early fifties. She was the classically strong Italian woman who ran the household of four men. It was touching watching the men make do without her, but they coped fine. They often invite me to Sunday lunch and they cook up a terrific meal, but it's still sad not having Alba, the wife and mother, there. It made me think of my mother who died young – but like I've mentioned, it can't all be happy times, can it?

I am very fortunate to have a wonderful family in Italy. They are the husband and sons of my sister Maria. As I spent so much time with them when I was a teenager, we are all very close. I love my brother-in-law Peter, or Pietro, Rebecchini. In many ways he was like a father substitute for me in those early years, when I hitched to Rome as an orphan. He is now eighty-eight and still married to Maria, although they haven't lived together for over forty years. He still sends her half his pension every month and that is the Italian way. They have three lovely sons, now in their fifties, and I remember them all being born. Jimmy, Marco and Luca are the three brothers, all covering the whole gamut of hair colouring. They are all very lucky to have the Cigarini hair genes; the Rebecchinis on their father's side were all as bald as an egg by the age of twenty.

When I first met my brother-in-law Peter, he must have only been in his mid-twenties, but he looked very old with a bald pate and hair around the fringe. He doesn't look a lot different now, and he's eighty-eight. He tells me that God only gave hair to the people who don't have good-looking heads. All my nephews' wives and children are just a delight. I love them all very much and I am very lucky to have such a great Italian family, thanks to my sister Maria. She still lives in England, in Bournemouth, but I think she would like to move to Italy to be nearer her sons. She should, as she is nearly eighty. Maria… come.

My other sister, Christina, seems content living alone in Cornwall. Her ex-husband Gordon died a few years ago, but they had already separated. She has a very active social life, partially through the church, and has many friends.

In November of 2012, I treated Maria and Christina to a cruise to commemorate Maria's eightieth, Christina's seventy-fifth and my seventieth. We went to China, Japan, Taiwan, Hong Kong, Vietnam and Singapore. The destinations were wonderful, but I won't pretend it was always easy between us all. There are deep-rooted issues between the sisters, stretching back to their childhoods. I doubt it's different in any other family, it's just that our history is a bit more complicated than most. It was the first time we had spent so much time together for sixty-three years, since Maria and I left Rome in 1949. In spite of that, I hope they enjoyed themselves – I certainly did. We toasted the beloved missing sister, Luisa. It was sad, but life is sometimes.

Italy, the Return

★

In 2012, I bought myself a Bentley Continental. I decided to buy one when I read Keith Richards' autobiography *Life*. That was the car he had in the 1960s, and I love them. The scene when Anita Pallenberg gave him a blow job in the back of it may have influenced me. Bentley was one of the few makes of cars I had never owned. I was offered an R-Type Continental by Peter Frankel, my dentist, in the early eighties, for £40,000. He used it as an everyday car in Knightsbridge. I have always regretted not buying it, as they are worth twenty times that now. I bought the modern-day version of the Continental, having decided I would like to spend my seventies swanning around Umbria in a Bentley (like a flash git), but my ownership had an ignominious beginning. I bought the second-hand car in England and was waiting for the Portsmouth-Le Havre ferry, to drive it to Italy. I bought a fire extinguisher and reflective jackets, as required in France, at the ferry terminal shop, and put the bag in the front passenger footwell. A short while later, I opened the glove compartment and the lid lightly touched the bag. With a pop, the extinguisher went off, filling the car with white powder. I had to quickly throw the bag out of the car. It was all very embarrassing, as there were other cars waiting for the ferry. I could even hear them laughing and calling to me, "Flash bastard!" They weren't wrong and it got me thinking that because Anita Pallenberg gave Keith Richards a blow job, a fire extinguisher had gone off in my Bentley. Work that one out… 'cause I can't.

CHAPTER 38

Baja, Master of Two Worlds

"... and so becomes ripe, at last, for the great at-one-ment. His personal ambitions being totally dissolved, he no longer tries to live but willingly relaxes to whatever may come to pass in him; he becomes, that is to say, an anonymity."
– Joseph Campbell

It can be brutally cold in Umbria, and it is now twenty years since I spent a winter in Europe... so I seek the sun! I'm sure if I had been born in 'the olden days', I would have been one of those people who worshipped it religiously. I absolutely adore the sunshine. I spend the winters on the East Cape of Los Cabos in Baja (pronounced Baha), California. My great friend since 1970, Roberta Booth, discovered it. She told me there were these gringos spreading up an unspoiled coastline, "Where the desert meets the ocean." It sounded idyllic. I went down there, and it was. I am only allowed three months' residency in America, so Mexico happened, where the water is warm enough to swim in, eighty degrees every day, and I am allowed in for six months. The property values are also much cheaper. So, I bought a beachfront house, and I am now in my twelfth winter there. I am there now as I am writing this, listening to the ocean, thinking of London. I don't miss it these days, and here is why.

The house is art deco in style or 'Streamline Moderne', according to Alex Matijas, the Argentinian architect who built it for himself. As you walk in, all you see is the ocean through four huge windows and sliding doors, a curved staircase, walls and ceilings. You can't see the beach or any land when entering, as it is on a point, and from the front deck the sea horizon is so wide it is curved. Here, you really feel that the planet is round. The house has a lighthouse tower, like a minaret – the Casa Divina. Alex told me that after he built the house, he had a visit from the narcotics police. They thought the lighthouse was for signalling to drug smugglers.

On one side of the house, I just have the beach, sand dunes and cactus trees. The nearest house is a quarter of a mile away, but cannot be seen. On the other side, I have a neighbour, Renate. Her house is also set back from mine, so I don't see it. They have dogs, and I always know when I have a visitor. They have a caretaker, Fano, and his Mexican family watching over their home, and they look over mine too. I think people realise I have no family here, no wife or children, so they help me in all the little ways – like people have always done, ever since I was five.

★

The East Cape is a wilderness with miles and miles of empty beaches that run as far as the eye can see. Behind, there are desert forests that run for over a thousand miles to America. There are huge cardon cactus, terrote (elephant trees), pitaya and palo blanco trees. In front, we have the real Baja celebs, the whales. The grey and humpback ones come to Baja to give birth. They live here in the sea for just two or three months from January through to April, until the calves are strong enough for the journey back north. The mothers are forty feet long, and the calves sixteen feet at birth. From my house, I can see them breaching (leaping out of the water), or slapping their tails and flippers, causing huge splashes like something from an Attenborough documentary. The mothers seem to be teaching the calves how to do it. I hear them slapping their tails at night and sometimes I hear them groaning, or is it singing? The annual migration of the grey whales is the longest of any mammal on earth – over 7000 miles from Baja California to the Bering Sea. The whales only feed themselves when they get to the Bering. They gorge on krill all summer and then sustain themselves all winter on their blubber, including milking the calves. We hear that the great ships create too much noise pollution for the whales and it hurts them. It interferes with their navigation and makes it harder for them to speak to one another. Sometimes, they get lost on their journey. Don't we all?

One great trip we can take is to Bahia Magdalena, or Mag Bay as we call it. It is where the whales mate and give birth. It is a 50km-long bay, protected from the Pacific Ocean by the barrier islands of Isla Magdalena and Isla Margarita. It is more like a lagoon than a bay. On approach, the small plane circles the bay and the pilot points out the male grey whales guarding the narrow entrances, keeping out the killer whales – who will kill the baby grey ones merely in order to eat their tongues. Two open panga boats, each containing fifteen people, go out to the whales in the bay. They are accustomed to humans and will allow people to touch them, but only in the bay – they would never allow it on the open sea. In the bay, even the calves can be petted. Being so close to these huge mammals is a wonderful experience. It really is humbling to know there are such great beasts living with us here on earth. It helps one remember that we share the planet with everyone, even sea monsters. Their size is impressive, and their blowing of air from close up is a giant and terrific sound. When I was there, I saw one breach from the water, right near a panga. The whales stay in the bay for a few weeks with their calves before going around the Cape in front of my house, where they are plentiful in January, February and March. They start to leave for the migration by April. When that happens, I wave them goodbye.

The other highlight from my house is the full moon rising out of the water. For three or four evenings each month, it comes up golden and reflects in the sea. I call it a moon river. The dawn needs to be mentioned also, as my bed faces toward the sun rising through a thirty-foot curving window. If I am awake in time, then I see a red sky every day. I often open my eyes at 6am and say, "That's nice" and then go back to sleep. Because there is no air or light pollution in Baja, the stars are very clear and run down to the horizon. I can lie in bed at night and see the stars all the way down to the sea. Living in a city doesn't allow us to experience the stars, or the sunrise, or moon rivers, but here I get it all and I wish I wasn't the only one. Sometimes it even makes me sad that all the world cannot see it, as it was meant to be.

For me, some of the best things in Baja are the birds. On Saturdays, not only do I get a choice of all the Premier League games on Mexican Sky, but while I am watching them I often see four whales through the large windows either side of my telly, while the pelicans dive into the deep blue, the magnificent frigatebirds soaring on high thermals, and the large turkey vultures flying past my window. Sometimes I see dolphins. Sometimes.

My favourite bird of the sky is the osprey, which comes to visit me each morning at the same time, as regular as clockwork. It is especially exciting for me as an Englishman, because they were extinct in Britain and only reintroduced to Rutland Water in 1996. It hovers in front of my house, and sometimes I get the thrill of seeing it dive and catch a fish in its claws. My house is raised from the beach on a dune, so it hovers almost at my level. The osprey loves to sit on my lighthouse tower, chirping out to sea. I have a fine pair of Zeiss binoculars for whale watching, which I use for the osprey too. I hear they are known as the sea hawk or fish eagle, and they can grow a wingspan of six feet. I like to watch it because it seems wise, and it is also alone. Sometimes I watch it for a long time, wondering what it will do next. I often wonder what I will do next, but I cannot know, so I just keep watching the birds. That's fine for me, for now.

More common large birds are the turkey vultures, which the gringos call buzzards – an American name. However, in the Old World, the name buzzard is reserved for a buteo, which is called a hawk in America. The turkey vultures will always give way to the Caracara birds at a meal. These are magnificent falcons, usually in pairs. They have red heads with a white stripe around the neck, and another white stripe on the wings. The male has a crown on his head. They are only a once-a-week sighting, usually sitting on a large cardon cactus. They are not fast flying aerial hunters, but are usually scavengers.

The pelicans are the most plentiful bird. I see half a dozen of them diving into the water for fish right in front of my house, all day, every day. I think the rocks in front of me are a good source of small fish; the panga fishermen also go there to collect their baitfish in the early mornings. The pelicans are lovely to watch while they are flying in formation. The gringos call it the Mexican Air Force. They either fly in a V formation of up to thirty birds, or in one long line, and ride the waves. They skim the front of a breaking wave, inches from the water, riding the air thermal caused by the wave. The birds take it in turn to flap their wings, those behind riding the slipstream of the bird that's flapping. Pelicans apparently dive into the water with their eyes open to catch fish. Consequently they get cataracts and can go blind, and then starve to death because they can no longer fish. You sometimes see an elderly pelican sitting forlornly on the beach, waiting for its time to become a meal for the turkey vultures.

One bird I see each day is the magnificent frigatebird, and I can usually see a dozen. They have beautiful Z-shaped wings and use them to fly very high, sometimes up to 2500 metres, and soar in the thermals and then descend to near sea surface. They spend days and nights on the wing and never enter the water to catch fish; they catch jumping fish or scraps left by larger fish. They sometimes attack other seabirds and make them disgorge their meal in flight. They were sometimes previously known as the man-o-war or man-of-war, due to their rakish lines and aerial piracy of other birds. They rarely seem to land; I have never seen one on the ground, but I wish to. I hear the males have a scarlet throat pouch that inflates like a balloon in the breeding season.

I have two ravens that seem to have adopted my house. They love to sit on the lighthouse tower. They come each morning and sometimes wake me with their clucking and calling. They are larger than a crow, with long beaks, and they are always in a pair. Ravens have coexisted with humans for thousands of years, and due to their ability to solve problems, they have always been considered highly intelligent. In some cultures, including those of ancient Ireland and Wales, they have been revered as a spiritual figure or god. They can live up to twenty-one years, which is much longer than most birds. I don't think the number twenty-one is coincidence – in numerology, it is a power number and the number of the great spiritual masters of humanity. In Greek mythology, ravens are associated with Apollo and are considered good luck, and were God's messengers in the mortal world. In Middle Earth, the ravens of Erebor brought secret news to the people of Thrór. Tolkien had them capable of speech in Ravenhill. I wouldn't rule anything out; they are secretive, and wise ones of the skies.

In addition to the large birds, there are also wonderful small and mid-sized birds. I have a cactus wren, which visits me a few times every day. It sits on a tree in my patio, singing away. I think it must have a nest in my garden. Then there is the woodpecker, which also likes to sit on the cacti. The yellow and black orioles are daily visitors, and the wonderful bright red cardinal birds are more rare, maybe only a once-a-month sighting. Only the male bird is bright red, and he has a crest. Because of the red crest, which is reminiscent of a Catholic cardinal's mitre, the colonialists named them cardinals. I had a real thrill one day when I had five red male cardinal visitors eating the berries off one of my bushes, all at once – as you're in luck to see just one. The people who live in the back get more of these colourful smaller birds; there is more vegetation than on the coast where I live. I get more of the big birds such as the turkey vultures and pelicans. There are many other varieties of birds on the beach, like gulls, sandpipers, terns, cormorants, egrets, and the occasional grey heron. In the garden, I also have quail, doves and hummingbirds. We have beautiful butterflies and moths, too – including a plentiful one about six inches long, which we call the bat moth.

★

The sea in front of the house is the Sea of Cortez. That is the Mexican name, but the Americans call it the Gulf of California. The ancient Spanish name was the Vermilion Sea, as it is called on the old sixteenth-century maps. The reason is we sometimes get wonderful reflected sunsets over the Sea of Cortez, which in turn makes the sea turn red. Hence, the name Vermilion Sea.

Although my view of the sea faces east, I am on the Cape, so I also face south into the Pacific. I have a 200-degree view of the sea from my house. There is no land between me and Antarctica and New Zealand, none at all. That's why there are occasional big waves that the surfers love. It is mainly a summer thing, when I am not here, but when there is a southern hemisphere winter storm in the Pacific, the surf here is huge. Shipwrecks Bay, just a mile from my house, is an internationally well-known surf break. The waves have travelled an enormous distance when they reach us. Fortunately, during the northern hemisphere winter, when I am in Baja, the water is calm and I can swim in front of my house on most days. But I have to be careful; the big waves can catch one unawares. On the Pacific side of the peninsula, you cannot swim unless you are a surfer. People drown over there. A few years ago, and again recently, an elderly couple were taken by a rogue wave while walking down the beach. If people drown in the Pacific, due to the currents, their bodies are rarely recovered. Chances are they end up in Hawaii. Not a bad place to rest, I guess.

The Tropic of Cancer runs near to La Paz, a three-hour drive north. John Steinbeck, in his *The Log from the Sea of Cortez*, says that California was named after the arch and beach at Cabo San Lucas. The United States bought US California, along with Arizona, New Mexico, Nevada and Utah, an area known as the Mexican Cession, for $15 million in the Treaty of Guadeloupe Hidalgo in 1848 (just after the Mexican-American war over the Alamo) – not really that long ago if you think about it, in the lifetime of my paternal grandfather.

The Mexican Cession area had been called Alta (Higher) California, to distinguish itself from Baja (Lower) California. After the Treaty, the US took the name California for its Western State, and Mexico retained the name Baja California. When the transfer of the Mexican Cession took place, the few residents of Baja appealed to be allowed to become part of the British Empire, but they were refused and Mexico retained control of the remote region. In those days, the whole area, including Alta California, was desert. It's still like that down in the East Cape; it is like Santa Monica and Malibu were 100 years ago. Just a few houses dotted along the coast, with nothing but desert forest behind.

There is British history in Los Cabos. There are still old Mexican Baja families with British names, like Green. Trade with Ming China through Manila was a major source of income for the Spanish Empire. The Spanish Manila Galleons, carrying treasure from the Spanish Philippines back to Spain, would head east from the Philippines, because passage around the Cape of Good Hope in Africa was reserved by Treaty for the Portuguese. The galleons would cross the Pacific on the trade winds until they reached Alta California, the present day California. They would then navigate down the Pacific coast of North America until they got to the arch at Cabo San Lucas, and then go around the arch to get to mainland Mexico. The arch was an important marker for the galleons. It really is the southern tip of North America. The galleons would stop off in San José del Cabo, to get fresh water from the San José River. They would eventually offload the treasure at Acapulco, and mules would carry it across Mexico to Veracruz, on the Gulf of Mexico, from where it could be shipped across the Atlantic Ocean to Spain. That's if they made it to Acapulco. British privateers and pirates, such as Thomas Cavendish, Captain Morgan and Sir Francis Drake, would lie in wait for them around the capes of Baja California – the area now called Los Cabos, meaning the Capes. Drake was a hero in England, but in Spain was considered little more than a pirate. The only difference between a pirate and a privateer was that the privateers were sanctioned by the Queen and shared their booty with her; the pirates, however, were outside the law and looted it all for themselves.

La Fortuna is one mile from where I live. It is an arroyo, which means river valley, and is about fifty metres wide. Arroyos are usually dry, the water only running when it rains, which is once or twice a year. Where this arroyo meets the beach, there are three ranches containing Mexican families, who have lived on the land for generations with ancient rights. The rancheros are the only Mexicans living out on the coast of the East Cape. Some of the ranchers have cattle and goats, but many of them now live doing construction work or other jobs for the gringos.

When Thomas Cavendish, the English privateer, captured his richest prize, the 600-ton sailing ship and Manila Galleon Santa Ana, in Cabo San Lucas, for which Queen Elizabeth I knighted him, he was said to have buried some of the treasure at La Fortuna – hence the name. My neighbour Mark Faulconer and I will go out there one day with metal detectors to look for it. I suppose that will be the final and ultimate test of my golden bollocks. I had a Cavendish connection while living at Ridge. Sophie Cavendish, daughter of the late Duke of Devonshire and sister of the present duke, whose family goes back to Thomas Cavendish's ancestor Roger Cavendish, was my neighbour. She was the first wife of Alastair Morrison, later to become Lord Margadale, the owner of the Fonthill Estate, where I lived. Sophie's cousin, *Bridget Jones* film producer Jonathan Cavendish, was also my neighbour.

★

In Baja, I live fifteen miles from the small Spanish colonial town of San José del Cabo. We have no hotels on the East Cape and only one road, and that is just what we want. The people who winter here love the tranquility and the undeveloped nature of the East Cape, but some visitors can't handle it. I do believe it takes some adapting to. Perhaps we are so used to busy lives that when we're hit with tranquility and the sounds of the natural world, we freak out. The first time I came here, I found the place by accident. I was staying in Cabo San Lucas and I drove out to the East Cape looking for my friend Roberta Booth and her dome home. I missed my turn and drove another five miles up the coast to the La Fortuna ranch, one mile past the house I would end up moving to. I remember thinking that only a madman would live out here. Now, I do.

★

The people of Baja are the *crème de la crème*. True beauts and I am proud to know them and call them my dear friends, of course… in no particular order, like my agnostic Jewish guru Percy Hendler and his wonderful wife Estela. Percy and I go on our quad bikes up the beach to visit the fishermen two miles away and buy huachenango, the red snapper. We are eating it within three hours of it coming ashore. There is my old chum Roberta Booth, the wonderful Dennis and Gun Bush, the Phillips family, Jenny Armit from the beautiful Hotelito in Todos Santos, my neighbours Pete and Donna, and Dan and Erika Byrne, Rick and Brenda Johnson, Mark Faulconer, Peter Mock, Jeff (the best fisherman on the coast), Pier and Norma Azcona, Diana and Studie (the Vietnam War vet and wild man of the East Cape), Howard and Maciek – or DJ Magic, as he is known, the organiser of the full moon parties. They take place deep in a dry arroyo (river bed) and you've just got to see these arroyos to appreciate how beautiful nature can be: fig trees, palo blanco and cardon cactuses growing out of the rock walls, usually with their roots showing. When I go, it's only with friends... and it's perfect.

A few years ago, Maciek, the organiser of the full moon parties, was stoned and got hit by a car as he was walking across the slip road to the main highway. He was unconscious in hospital in San José with a broken pelvis. His friend Kirby Brown was called, because her number was on his cell phone. She moved him from the public hospital to a private clinic, called me up and I went down. Maciek had no medical insurance, but had lived in Calgary, Canada fifteen years earlier. I had to act fast and act I did. I went into producer mode and it was as if all my training had been about this very moment. Funny how life works; it was just like being back at the office, setting up a production. For two days solid, I was on the phone, negotiating to get Maciek treatment. I spoke many times with the hospital in Calgary and with the surgeon, pleading with them to take him, and with the Canadian Consulate in Cabo San Lucas. In the end, I got the hospital in Calgary to agree to take him, at which point the air ambulance agreed and came. We did it, thank God, but Kirby Brown was not so lucky. She was one of the people killed in the New Age sweat lodge tragedy in Sedona, Arizona, organised by the self-help guru James Arthur Ray. He was jailed for two years.

Mose Mosley likes to call himself the executive producer of the East Cape. He arranges the Shipwrecks Film Society's Cinema in the Sand. Mose has built a giant wooden screen where he shows up-to-date films. He told me about his plans before he started Cinema in the Sand. Being a typically cynical Brit, I told him it was a terrible idea and no one would show up, but about eighty people now attend, drink margaritas and eat popcorn. Ah well, I guess in the words of the great Hollywood scriptwriter William Goldman, "Nobody knows anything." In between, Mose makes short films about the East Cape, which get a few hits on YouTube, including a funny one you can find under the title 'Cinema in the Sand'. I am featured with my sexy inflatable bonking sheep, Baaarbara.

*

We have no shops or amenities out on the East Cape, and had no restaurants or bars until Zacs opened up in Zacatitos – thanks to Angel and Paul. Another has arrived, by Fano, Maria and Pedro at La Fortuna. We all hope they will do well, as it is much nearer than Zacs, and when you are nearing seventy… yards count! Pedro's usual job is to drive along the beach on a quad bike in the middle of the night, looking for turtle tracks. He retrieves the eggs and puts them somewhere fenced off from dogs, as they will dig them up if they are left on the beach. Sometimes, we see baby turtles hatching. The magic never stops.

*

I used to visit my friend from London, Kellyann Page, in Oaxaca, which is in the south of Mexico. She used to winter there in my favourite Mexican town. I stayed in a wonderful sixteenth-century former monastery, the Camino Real Hotel, and one night I counted six different types of music being played around the town. There are fantastic Mayan ruins nearby at Monte Albán. Kellyann and I also went together to the silver town of Taxco, and to Mexico City to see all the Diego Rivera murals. I wrote to tell her I was doing an autobiography and she replied:

> *Oh… that's good. Hope you will write the truth… that I ws the best shag you ever had not to mention the perfect tour guide*
> *besos,*
> *kellita*
>
> *if you write that I will confirm that you have the largest most perfect penus i ever experienced*
>
> *xxxxxxxxx*

It seems like a good trade-off and a nice way to begin ending this book.

CHAPTER 39

What's in a Name?

There is only one John Cigarini. Cigarini is a very rare name, even in Italy. Many years ago, my eldest sister Maria did a cheap genealogical search and traced the family name back to patriarchs from Venice in the 1400s. There has always been talk in my family that a title, Conte di Nuova Modena, was sold by one of my father's brothers to a French family in the 1940s or '50s.

I go by many names. John Cigarini was my working name, although John is my least favourite. Many people just call me by my surname, Cigarini. Chigalini was practically the first word ever spoken by one toddler I knew.

Johnny is my family name and is used by my sisters, all the villagers in San Leo Bastia, many of my friends in Baja California, Glynis Johns, and older friends such as Maryam d'Abo and Roger Waters. Johnny Chig is a common variation.

Isaac Tigrett, the adorable Susie Roberson, Siobhan Barron and my nephew Luca Rebecchini all call me Johnny-Boy! But for Joanna Jacobs, it's Johnny Baby.

Caro Ritchie calls me Baja Johnny, or Johnny Baja. In Baja, a few people call me Lighthouse John. Or English John. It differentiates me from Goat Hill John.

Chiggers is my preferred nickname, in spite of meaning a flea in the USA. Jim Powrie, Neil and David, in fact most of the Umbrian expat crowd and Eric Clapton use it.

Victor Lownes and lots of friends like Carol Adler, Mary Heale and Jill Powrie keep it to just Chig. Liz and Mike Dalling call me Chigs. Other people such as Josh Ritchie call me Chiggy, but Ross Cramer used to call me Chiggy-Poo.

Steve O'Rourke, Dany Holbrook, John 'Butch' Stephen, Johnny Gaydon, Legh 'Leapie' Davies and the others of the 1970s King's Road crowd all called me Cigar – which is funny, because I have never had a cigar, or even a single cigarette, in my life.

What's in a name?

Rupert Keegan used to call me Pigarini, when I had the pig valve, and even when I no longer had it.

Ronnie Holbrook used to call me Shangri-Lani, and Golden Bollocks Cigarini – both with the same message, lucky bastard. He also called me JC, as does Roberta Booth.

Nike Williams, former fashion editor of *Honey* magazine, who I still see in the Chelsea Arts Club, calls me Fingerelli, or Fingers for short. My fingers have never been near her – it just sounds Italian.

The lovely Emerald Armit calls me Uncle Pete.

Gorgeous Georgina Powrie calls me Dirty Uncle Johnny.

At Durham University, they didn't have much to go on with Davies, so I was sometimes called Smiley.

I still like Johnny Margate; my friend Corinna Liddell-Gordon calls me that.

My nephews in Italy call me Zio Grande Stronzo. Aka, Uncle Big Shit.

I once had a collection of misspelled envelopes; I must have had about 20 or 30. I was going to make a montage of them, but I never got around to it and eventually threw them away. There were lots of names beginning with Sh. I remember some in particular: John Shaggerini, Johnie Jiggerini and Mr G. Karini.

I have to thank Dave Trott, who is featured elsewhere in this book, for giving me the inspiration for the title. Dave is a legendary advertising creative director, responsible for 'Lip-Smackin', Thirst-Quenchin', Ace-Tastin', Motivatin', Pepsi' and 'Hello Tosh, Got a Toshiba?' Bob Brooks shot the Pepsi ad in the 1970s and when Dave was our client, he amiably called me a 'King's Road Cowboy'. The name stuck.

Epilogue

Two years after retiring, I was wintering in Santa Barbara when I got a call from Nick Hippersley-Cox, Allan van Rijn's producer. I immediately thought the worst about Allan, but it was not his turn yet. Nick was to give me different bad news: that my great friend and ex-director Larry Williams, a lovely, lovely guy, had dropped dead of a heart attack whilst walking the dog, at the age of forty-nine, leaving a beautiful wife, Lesley (his co-director), and two young children. A year later, Nick called me again. This time it was Allan. Dead in his sleep at the age of fifty-two. I'm sure the combined Prozac and Valium gave him a heart attack, but I never did find out the cause of death.

I'm very cold about death; I've had it all my life. I felt extremely sad about both of them, but a little bit of me felt vindicated for retiring early and getting out of the rat race.

Bob Brooks, Jim Baker and Len Fulford, the original partners in Brooks Baker Fulford, all recently died within a year of each other; they were all in their mid-eighties.

In Baja, we get constant reminders to enjoy every day and take care of our livers. My dear friend and house caretaker, Richard Bembenek, died a year ago of liver cancer, a mere month after being diagnosed. This year, we had the same problem with another leading member of the gang, Doug Green. I try to avoid alcohol for two consecutive days every week, but, along with the other expats, I drink too much – both in Baja and Umbria. I think it's been one of the main reasons for writing this spiel… to get it out of me, just in case I cop it. It's been a wonderful experience, thanks to you, the reader. But one question, how have you managed to get this far? Get a life, for God's sake.

★

Yep, that's all folks, the end of the story (almost). I guess the very end is still pending and I guess I don't mind where that happens. I think I have had an interesting life. I hope you agree and have enjoyed the book. If you disagree, I couldn't give a damn – write your own bloody memoirs.

★

I am enjoying my life now as much as I ever have. I feel very fortunate. The bad luck I had at the beginning made me into the person that I am, and turned itself into good luck later in my life. By this stage, I'm sure you're wondering whatever happened to the Revd Ken Senior. Well, I can tell you about that. He came back to England and he worked in a private chapel, but couldn't kick the old habit. He got caught fooling around with the choirboys – one, I believe, he was even paying money, to let him molest him. As the story goes, the boy's mother found out via a note the boy had left, so the reverend got arrested and went to court (before the whole paedo thing went mainstream), but he got off… somehow. He wasn't put in jail but got one of those deferred sentence things, so he retired in Salcombe. He was one of the first people to get one of the hospital superbugs and he died from it. He wasn't even sixty.

I visited him many times over the years in Germany and in England. I even attended their kids' weddings. I was like one of the family and even grew close to Nora, the reverend's wife. I'm still in touch with one of the children; she is in my will now and I see her as a foster sister, perhaps. It was different back then, but pervs weren't like they are seen today and it's hard to explain to the young readers of this book. Despite the reverend molesting me, and his habits with other boys, I was grateful to him for the other help he gave; he was a father figure. I would have preferred for that person to have been my own dad, but in life you've got to work with the cards you're given. My message is not to complain, get on with it, make a bit of money if you can, and make a whole load of people happy, 'cause when the end comes, and come it will, there will only be one question you'll ever ask: Have I had a good life? Well, that's for you to decide. And I shall end with this: I'm not afraid of death. I won't be there… I'll be dead.

Thank you, goodbye and goodnight.

Appendix

I am very fortunate to have a great capacity for friendship, and I would like to thank many people for enriching my wonderful life. Here is a name-drop for them all.

UK:
My sisters Christina Miller and Maria Rebecchini, the Ritchie family, the Eve family, Glyn and Glynis Johns, Sid Roberson, Susie Roberson, Jose and Dickie Kries, Pattie Boyd, Joanna Jacobs, Mal and Lal Poynter, Robert Tilleard, Mike and Sue Roberts, Alastair and Amanda (Lord and Lady Margadale), Penny and Paul Brewer, Leigh and Twiggy Lawson, Victor and Marilyn Lownes, John Stephen, Mike King, Jonathan and Mary Heale, Ruth and Kenny Hague, the Holbrook family, Trevor Myles, John Fraser and Rod Pienaar, and Kellyann Page.

Los Angeles:
The Carroll family, Nigel, Jaki, Charlie, and William, Mike and Liz Dalling, Stewart and Fiona Copeland, Mary Lindes, Ian and Doris La Frenais, Dan and Donna Aykroyd, Augusta Tigrett, Wendy Asher, Stash de Rola, and Siobhan Barron.

India:
Isaac Tigrett.

Italy:
The Rebecchini family, Jim and Jill Powrie, David Monico and Neil Brown, David, Jenny and Daisy Nichols, Rob and Amanda House, Ian McDonald, Tim and Anna Maltby, Tim and Louise Hudson, Dick Pountain and Marion Hills, Marianne and Andrew Newell, Andrew and Goska Lloyd, Robbie Duff-Scott, Barbara Scott and Lennie Edwards, Terry and Michele Gross, Ken Stott and Nina Gehl, Miles and Tessa Emley, Mark and Dorothy Freeman, Colin and

Gerry Pritcher Howarth, Al and Betty Stuart, Pat and Andy Hale, Jed Smith and Simone Bugini, Pam and Graham Stroud, Ken and Stef Coombes, Alastair and Juliet (Viscount and Viscountess Chilston), Chris O'Donoghue and Kate Percival, Terri and Keith Wrightson, Peter and Silvana, the Muffi family, the Caracchini family, the Bucci family, and the Pierini family.

Baja California, Mexico:
Roberta Booth, the Hendler family, Dennis and Gun Bush, the Phillips family, Renate Schiff and Don Suttles, Peter Mock, Studie and Diana, Howard, Jeff, Gus and Jill, Ben and Ruby, Tom and Jan, Colorado Al, Jordan, Goat Hill John, and the rest of the horseshoes crowd, Gail Scarlett and Nick, Mark and Pam, Dan and Erika Byrne, Pete and Donna, Bruce and Debbie, Bryce and Cheryl, Doyle, Amber Thorpe, Penny Payne, Jenny and Emerald Armit, Rick and Brenda Johnson, Mark Faulconer, Pier and Norma Azcona, Bruce and Cody Oreck, Peter and Brenda McGonagle, Ian and Suzy McGonagle, Neil Glover, Raven, Maciek Bielecki, Mose Mosley, and Angel and Paul Rini at Zacs.

I love you all, and sorry if I have left anyone out.